The
Perfect Ride

The *Perfect Ride*

by GARY STEVENS
with MERVYN KAUFMAN

—————— ◇ ——————

FOREWORD BY BILL SHOEMAKER

CITADEL PRESS
KENSINGTON PUBLISHING CORP.
www.kensingtonbooks.com

Please note that every effort was made to track down the photographers of the pictures used in this book. If we have failed to properly credit your photo, please contact us at agents@ventureliterary.com

CITADEL PRESS BOOKS are published by

Kensington Publishing Corp.
850 Third Avenue
New York, NY 10022

All Kensington titles, imprints, and distributed lines are available at special quantity discounts for bulk purchases for sales promotion, premiums, fund-raising, educational, or institutional use. Special book excerpts or customized printings can also be created to fit specific needs. For details, write or phone the office of the Kensington special sales manager: Kensington Publishing Corp., 850 Third Avenue, New York, NY 10022, attn: Special Sales Department, phone 1-800-221-2647.

Citadel Press and the Citadel Logo are trademarks of Kensington Publishing Corp.

Unless otherwise noted, all photographs are courtesy of Gary Stevens's personal collection.

First printing: May 2002

10   9   8   7   6   5   4   3   2   1

Printed in the United States of America

Library of Congress Control Number: 2001099777

ISBN 0-8065-2361-1

For my children: Ashley,
Tory, Riley, and Carlie

Contents

——— ◇ ———

Foreword

— ◇ —

I have known Gary Stevens since he first came to Southern California to ride. He was a kid then with a bad temper and an even worse case of homesickness. He was a good rider then, but he was a better rider when he came back, five years later. He had grown up a little, mentally as well as physically. I always liked riding races with him. He was fair. Riding with experienced jockeys helped make him a better rider himself. He was certainly better than when I first became aware of him.

When you're riding, you take advantage of every situation you can in a race, if you can do so legally. Gary learned to do that better and better, and he eventually learned to control his anger—and not let his temper get the best of him. As a kid, the only way he knew how to handle a difficult situation was to fight somebody, especially if he felt he'd been bothered in a race. He mellowed, over the years.

For any rider starting out now, Gary would be a good role model—because of the way he handles himself and his mounts on the track, and also because of his stature as a rider. He has developed into a first-class professional in every sense of the word. He knows his horses—when to move them, when not to move them. He can switch his whip from right hand to left; he can sense whether a horse likes to be hit or not; and he knows the pace of a race. All of that comes with time; it's something a rider learns. I would say that it takes five or ten years for anyone to become a top rider, and many of those who make it early don't last very long.

When Gary had to stop riding, he was very unhappy. "I can't stand it out here at the races," he told me. "I gotta get back to riding." But a lot of people gave him other advice. He was talking to so many people at the time that he didn't know *what* he should do. He often turned to me, but all I could say was, "If you really feel like that's what you want to do and that's what makes you happy, *do it*. Don't try to be something somebody else is telling you to be."

Today, I think he's got it all. He's a champion rider, he's become an articulate speaker—which he wasn't, when he first came to California—and he's a gentleman. I think a lot of him today—as a person, as a rider and as a human being. There's nobody better.

—Bill Shoemaker
San Marino, California

Acknowledgments

———◇———

This book was written mostly from memory; I have kept no journals. Although I have been as accurate as possible, I may have unintentionally omitted or distorted some fact or incident, and I apologize for any inaccuracies. I could not have produced this book without the unyielding patience of my wife, Nikki, and the patience and support of my coauthor, Merv Kaufman, and his wife, Nancy, whose beloved Uncle Harry first brought horse racing into her life.

I owe a debt of gratitude to my mom and dad, Barbara and Ron Stevens, for the way they brought me up, and to my brothers, Craig and Scott, who have been there for me, all my life. I wouldn't have the career I've enjoyed without Ray Kravagna, for it was he who introduced me to Southern California and the top rung of Thoroughbred racing. This book would not have been written without the faith and friendship of Ron Anderson—he's truly its godfather.

Ed Goldstone, Asher Jason, Julie Barer, and Pete Fornatale each nudged the project along the bumpy road that finally led to its publication, but it was Frank Scatoni and Greg Dinkin of Venture Literary who located a welcome home for the book. They also provided invaluable assistance in selecting and describing the photographs. I am also indebted to Dean Keppler and Charlie Hayward of the *Daily Racing Form* for providing past-performance records of the most significant Thoroughbreds. Finally, no book comes into existence without the energy and enthusiasm of its editor and publisher: Ann LaFarge and Bruce Bender must be saluted for the sure, sensitive hands they applied to see my efforts through, from rough idea to finished book.

For my coauthor and me, this project has created an amazing long-distance partnership and resulted in a labor of love that has made us both very proud.

Introduction

——— ◇ ———

Pain and joy. These have been the hallmarks of Gary Stevens's life and career. A stellar jockey for more than two decades, he stunned the Thoroughbred racing world just before the millennium when he announced he was ending his riding years—after racking up 4,512 victories and $187 million in winning purses. Then, nine months later, he was back, determined to ride again. Hopefully, without pain.

Pain first struck him as a six-year-old when a potentially crippling hip ailment confined him to a leg brace and clumsy built-up shoe for eighteen agonizing months. Later, as a high school student wrestler, he suffered a dislocated shoulder, experiencing pain that jabbed him like a coal-hot sword, which ultimately ended his involvement in a sport he had become devoted to.

At age twelve, while toiling in his father's Boise, Idaho, training barn, Stevens climbed aboard his first Thoroughbred and immediately fell in love. He realized that he loved the power, the responsiveness, and the trembling excitement of being on the back of a race-trained animal. Eventually, he would lust after the joyful sense of fulfillment *he* would experience by being able to harness, control, and focus that power. As the third son in a sports-minded family, his need to compete—and win—had finally found its true outlet.

"Gary is great," he once burned into the headboard of his boyhood bed—not in arrogance but as a way to psych himself up. "Gary is an athlete, but he was a horseman long before he became a jockey," his former agent and long-time friend Ron Anderson once declared, and that may be a clue to his success. According to Anderson, "Where horses are concerned, Gary has a sixth sense. His intelligence and determination help place him among the very best and most dependable of any jockeys in the sport."

An injury had forced him to withdraw from competitive wrestling. His diminutive size had dimmed his passion for football. His impatience had halted his formal education—he never finished high school. At sixteen, he left his home and family to ride. In Southern California, a teenager away from his family for the first time, he lived in a Motel 6 and fought his way through the pain of separation.

"It was hard, really hard, for him to pack his stuff and go," his mother, Barbara Stevens, told me. "And then it was equally hard on him after he left. He was so homesick." But, true to his nature, Stevens persevered and eventually adjusted to the demands of travel, of living out of suitcases, of being on his own. These were parts of the price he would have to pay to further a career that would take him to every major racetrack in North America and to Hong Kong, Tokyo, Dubai, and the racing landmarks of England, France, and Ireland.

I first became aware of Gary Stevens in the 1980s. Listening to the trackside banter at Belmont Park in Elmont, Long Island, I heard from more than one opinionated rail-sitter, "*Listen,* they didn't send Gary Stevens back here to *lose.* Know what I mean?"

"They" were the West Coast trainers, like D. Wayne Lukas, who had begun bringing Stevens to Belmont Park, Saratoga Springs, Churchill Downs, and other headline tracks to ride the horses he had won on in California. And, as I was to learn, if Stevens had flown to New York to ride a mount, that was a horse to put money on, no matter what the posted odds.

I watched him in the walking ring: intense, totally focused, sitting tall in the saddle, chin up, his eyes narrowed beneath his helmet. He cut an elegant figure, a profile that was easy to distinguish among hunkered-down jockeys he habitually rode with. He was a fierce competitor, a sore loser whose outbursts of temper—in his early racing years—earned him notoriety in the jockeys' room. But on a horse's back, he more than passed the test of character; he was a gentleman. I never saw him savage a fellow rider or brutally whip a horse in a desperate attempt to cross the finish line first.

Gary won his first Kentucky Derby in 1988 aboard the Lukas-trained filly Winning Colors. It was a wire-to-wire win, a triumph for that stunning three-year-old and her twenty-five-year-old rider. Seven years later, he won the Derby again, aboard Thunder Gulch, a colt that five weeks later would bring Stevens his first Belmont Stakes win. But that 1995 Derby victory was an emotional one for the young jockey. A mentor of his, from his racing days in the Pacific Northwest, died shortly before the event.

Stevens crossed the finish line with tears on his cheeks. He raised his whip above his head as a silent signal that he was dedicating the win to his departed friend. That's when my own awareness of Stevens came into focus, for I realized he was not just a driven athlete with burnished skills; he was also a human being with powerful feelings.

When he and I met to talk about collaborating on a book about his life and racing career, it was clear to me that because he was so astute—so earnest and forthcoming—it would not be difficult to capture his recollections as well as the actual tone of his recall. But first: "Why do you want to do this book?" I asked him. The answer was simple, offered without pause or hesitation: "I want my kids to know what their dad does; I want them to know who their dad *is*." His first marriage had failed, and in 1994 he and his wife separated. He had left four youngsters behind.

That was pain of a different sort. As he once told me. "I don't feel I really started to know my children until after their mother and I were apart." Only then, I remember him saying, could he begin to share with his children the passion that had been his driving interest since he himself had been a child.

Recalling his career right after his abrupt retirement, Stevens told a reporter that if he couldn't ride as he had been riding—at the peak of his form—he wouldn't ride at all. "I knew when I walked onto a racetrack there was no one better than me and no one who could finish with me and nobody who could ride with me," he said.

When he thought his racing years were behind him, he sought new challenges. Ultimately, he decided to work toward becoming a trainer—a job that would keep him out of the jocks' room but bring him to all the world's great racetracks as the knowledgeable, career-honed professional he had become.

He passed the trainer's test and was awarded his license. He had always loved being with horses; the pulsating life around the racetrack was something he would never abandon. But being on the sidelines could never be as challenging, or rewarding, as being *up there* on a Thoroughbred's back. Stevens had always been a proud competitor, always strategizing, always psyched up to win. He had also learned to be humble, conceding graciously in defeat.

Defeat was always painful, a different kind of pain from what his body had come to experience. "I've got very mature knees," he said, describing the damaged tissue and degenerative arthritis that plagued them. Although his knees failed him, he fought back—rested, trained religiously, and took his medications. He listened to his doctors and to his own inner voice—and he came back. His is a spirit that will never be crushed. He knows his body and has learned how to handle pain. He is also a sensitive, sensible man with a compelling story to tell.

—*Mervyn Kaufman*
New York City, New York

1 Point Proven

*I*t was Belmont Stakes Day, June 9, 2001, and I felt more confident than I ever had going into a horse race. I was riding Point Given, a horse that had built up such a following that 73,857 racing fans crowded the grandstands. It was mayhem. As I walked my horse out of the paddock toward the tunnel leading to the track, I could see that Point Given's ears were pricked forward. He was moving with authority, unfazed by the crowd, even though the roar those people made when we reached the track seemed to echo off the front of the stands. The horse warmed up well, too. The aggressiveness I sensed underneath me gave me the feeling that I could do whatever I wanted during the race.

As we had drawn the extreme outside-post position in a field of nine, I thought it important that the horse be focused while standing in the gate and that we get a good break at the start. I tried voicing my concern, but the noise of the crowd had reached such a level that the assistant starter who was assigned to us couldn't hear a word I said, even though he stood only two feet away. I wanted the guy to stay on the ground until Point Given was standing still—to make sure he was balanced on all four legs—before climbing up beside me in the starting gate. It's not that my words were being ignored, they were just unnoticed.

As it turned out, Point Given was standing calmly as the gate opened, and he got an alert start. We broke fast and came alongside AP Valentine, the only other horse I was concerned about. I wanted to make sure I knew where he was at all times. Going into the first turn, I was able to maneuver

Point Given right next to AP Valentine and then slightly ahead. We were running fourth, three horses wide and just behind the three pacesetters. I had Point Given under a strong hold. He was aggressive but seemed very relaxed, waiting for me to signal him. As we turned into the backstretch, with a mile more to go in this mile-and-a-half race, I knew it was all over; it was just a question of my telling the horse when it was time to make his move. The run down the backside was uneventful. I believed that with the strength and power Point Given was showing me, no other horse would be able to come from behind and beat us. At that point, the horses in front were of no consequence.

As we ran toward the far turn, Victor Espinoza on AP Valentine tried to make an early run at us, and as he did, I let out my reins a notch to get Point Given to lengthen his stride a little. I peeked under my right arm; AP Valentine was behind and outside of us, and Espinoza had already put him into a pretty stiff drive. I, on the other hand, was just galloping along with tons of horse underneath me.

Three-eighths of a mile from the finish line, I let Point Given lengthen his stride again. He did it on his own, with no encouragement from me. I still kept a snug hold of him but gave him his head a little bit. I hadn't planned to be in front yet, but Point Given was going so easily I couldn't keep him off of the lead. He was there because of his ability; he was so much better than the rest of the horses on that particular day. I took a shorter hold of him just before entering the stretch, which was his cue— *okay, it's time to get it on.* I wanted him focused totally on me as we moved ahead. When I cued him to go—by shortening my reins and tightening the bit in his mouth—he really accelerated coming off the turn.

As the track straightened out, I switched the stick to my left hand and gave my horse two hard raps on his left rear. He responded by accelerating again. I had no idea how far in front I was at that point and didn't care. I was having a flashback to the 1997 Belmont Stakes aboard Silver Charm. I was certain I was going to win that race—and the Triple Crown—until Touch Gold came flying and whipped by us in the last fifty yards. The memory of that defeat flashed through my head as Point Given and I were entering the last furlong, so I stayed really, really busy on the horse. When I felt him starting to idle with me, I tapped him five or six times. He wasn't

slowing down, but with no target in front of us he was becoming unfo-
cused. He was looking for challengers to reclaim his attention, but in response to my actions, he accelerated again. I still didn't know how far in
front we were.

Certain that Point Given would be given a long rest after the Belmont
Stakes, I felt no need to conserve his energy. Fifty yards from the finish, I
felt secure that no one was coming and that we had won. The noise from
the grandstands was unbelievable, but as usual I blocked out that sound
until the race was over. As we crossed under the finish line, I stood up in
my stirrups and craned my neck around to see how far behind the other
horses were. I assumed at least one of them would be three or four lengths
behind us, but they were much farther back than that. It was an incredible
moment—my third Belmont Stakes win. A very special feeling.

It had felt similarly special, some months earlier, when Bob Baffert
phoned to ask me to ride Point Given. The colt was just a promising two-
year-old then, and Bob wanted me to ride him in the Breeders' Cup
Juvenile at Churchill Downs in Kentucky. I had ridden so many of the
horses he trained, including Silverbulletday, Real Quiet, and Silver
Charm, that I was the logical rider of choice. However, I hadn't had a
mount in nine months; I had been retired. My arthritic knees, injured too
often and surgically repaired too many times, had told me to find a new
focus. For most of 2000, I had been a trainer-in-training, reporting daily to
the California barns of The Thoroughbred Corporation owned by Prince
Ahmed bin Salman of Saudi Arabia.

I had been working hard as an assistant trainer. The hours I kept were
totally different from those I had been accustomed to over the previous
twenty years. I was up at 4 A.M. and at the track by 5. I would take a break
in late morning but be back at the barns to check on the horses by 3 P.M.
The schedule was exhausting; it wasn't the work that eventually got to me,
but the structured demands on my time. I didn't like feeling that I *had* to be
at work at a certain hour. Although nobody told me I did, I knew that my
not being there, for whatever reason, would raise questions. Actually, I
would have been there anyway, no matter what, but I realized that I preferred knowing that I could make my own hours. All my life I have worked
as hard as I've wanted to work, which is very, very hard, but I've done so

because I *wanted* to do it. The months of my retirement represented the first time in my life that I actually held down a job.

As time passed, my knees improved, but that was only one reason why I started riding again. The other reason was that I wanted to be my own person. As November 4, the Breeders' Cup racing day, came nearer, trainers began calling me. Among those I heard myself say yes to was Bob Baffert. He had a lot of promising juveniles in his barns at that time, but he thought that Point Given was sure to be one of his Triple Crown hopefuls, a horse whose ability was great enough to win the million-dollar Kentucky Derby, Preakness, and Belmont Stakes races the following spring. Bob and the owner—who happened to be Prince Ahmed—wanted a rider who would stay with their colt through the coming racing season and also help train him, reinforcing the lessons he had already been taught. That invitation to me, coming off a nine-month sabbatical, was welcome, of course, but in the back of my mind there was a bit of the fear I always feel going into a big race. For no matter what I have accomplished, I always feel I must prove myself again, and prove *to* myself that I am still all right and will be as good as I was before.

The Breeders' Cup Juvenile was not my first race after coming out of retirement, but it was a significant one because it carried with it the promise of a relationship with a specific mount during the next racing year. Thus, I was less than pleased when I learned that we had been assigned the number-one slot, right at the rail. That starting position wouldn't give me any choices. I knew that Bob didn't want the horse rushed early, as he had been when he lost his previous race, and I also knew the risk of being buried at the rail, trapped behind other horses unwilling to let us push through. When I met with Bob, the prince, and Richard Mulhall, president of The Thoroughbred Corporation and the stable's racing manager, it was decided that I would take Point Given back early in the race and make one big run with him at the end.

The annual Breeders' Cup championship races bring together the finest Thoroughbreds from all over the racing world. If, indeed, Point Given deserved to be among that rank, I thought, it would not be easy to break an established pattern with him. Horses that are top bred and well trained are creatures of habit. They remember everything that was done to them during a previous outing. You show them something one time and they think they are going to do the same thing the next time they run.

I knew Point Given had been schooled to break quickly when the starting gate sprang open, but my plan was to get him to relax out of the gate, as soon as I could. I needed to take him back, away from the front-runners, and communicate my intentions to him. Thoroughbreds are bred and trained to run, and to win; that's what they try to do when they get on a racetrack. Considering that the Breeders' Cup Juvenile was a million-dollar race, it would be a difficult time to try to teach a horse something different. That race is not supposed to be a schooling ground, but for me that's exactly what it turned out to be.

When changing tactics, you have to be prepared for a horse to over-react. When I signaled with a slight tug of the reins that I wanted to take Point Given back, he fell farther back than I had anticipated. I remember, as I turned down the backstretch, being some fourteen or fifteen lengths off the pace. I knew I had to make up some ground, but it was too early to make a significant move. I thought to myself, *Just stay relaxed, stay where you are, wait till you're three-eighths of a mile from the finish and see if the colt makes some kind of move around the far turn. Maybe we'll get lucky and pick up a piece of the prize money.*

I sat quietly, patiently, taking no action until we hit the far turn. At the three-eighths pole, I gave Point Given a little pop on the shoulder with my whip, and he picked up his pace immediately, passing horses with no added encouragement from me. Up in front of us at that point was a whole wall of horses. There was no opening, and no way for us to get through on the rail. I had to swing ten horses wide coming into the homestretch. At that point, I thought, *Well, maybe we'll end up fifth.* I reached back and tapped my horse one more time.

Suddenly, we were running by horses as though they were standing still. Point Given had put on a burst of speed that was mind-boggling. An eighth of a mile from the wire, I thought to myself that, with any luck, we might be third. About five strides later, I found myself thinking, *I'm going to win this race!* About fifty yards from the finish, the front-runner, Macho

Uno, began running erratically. A mile and one-sixteenth race is taxing for a two-year-old; he began to duck and dive. At the end, I thought we had won by a nose; instead, when the photo was flashed on the screen, it seemed we had lost by a nose. But it was probably the happiest I have ever been in defeat.

That may have been one of Point Given's most impressive races. I had never experienced the kind of acceleration he showed me through the stretch. Afterward, I stated publicly that I wouldn't have to look any further for my next Kentucky Derby mount, and I meant it. I wanted it known, by both the owner and the trainer, that this horse had my confidence. A rider's confidence in a horse can make the difference between winning big races and getting beaten. In my first ride on him, Point Given had given me that confidence. I knew I was riding a very, very special horse.

He proved his specialness again in another mile and one-sixteenth race, the Hollywood Futurity at Hollywood Park in December. It was his last race as a two-year-old, and he won it in what had now become his characteristic style. He dropped way back in the early stages and just ambled up to the leaders in the backstretch. He ran down Millennium Wind, another promising colt, and bounded to the finish. I remember, at the time, feeling that he was in high canter during the last sixteenth of a mile. He was running—and winning—on maybe 65 or 70 percent of his capability. The challenge for me was to keep him focused, because of his tendency to play around when he was out front by himself. He reminded me a lot of his sire, Thunder Gulch, except that at seventeen hands, he was bigger. As good as he was then, I was certain he was going to get better.

He won at the same distance in his debut as a three-year-old, the San Felipe Stakes at Santa Anita in March 2001. He had been rested for three months, but it was no rest period for his trainer and me. Bob and I felt the pressure from fellow horsemen and the press—and from a host of naysayers who insisted Point Given was not quite the superhorse he was said to be. But the critics had to step back when he won the mile and one-eighth Santa Anita Derby in April, a $750,000 race for the West Coast's top three-year-olds and likeliest Kentucky Derby contenders. He was ahead by five and one-half lengths at the wire in what was described as a blowout victory. That was my eighth Santa Anita Derby win, and as I was passing the three-eighths pole, one of the markers that tells riders how far they are from the finish, it occurred to me that I would tie Bill Shoemaker's record for wins in that race. I felt exhilarated—and honored!

By the way Point Given handled himself on the track, I could see he was becoming a complete professional. He was stronger now, cooler, more mature, and his acceleration—always impressive—was almost beyond belief. It was no surprise that he was considered the favorite to win the Kentucky Derby, scheduled for the first Saturday in May.

Bob had about a month to hone the horse's already proven skills, transport him to Churchill Downs, and see to it that he became acclimated. Every track feels different to both horse and rider, and every horse responds differently to the way the track feels to him. *How would Point Given react to Churchill Downs's hard, unforgiving surface?* we wondered. Poorly, as it happened.

The colt trained well at Churchill, though some horsemen thought he hadn't changed leads fluidly in his timed morning workout. In the United States, horses are trained to lead with their right front leg on straightaways and their left front leg on turns—the turns are leftward because American races are run counterclockwise. It's too tiring for a horse to stay on one lead for an entire race. He usually changes leads automatically, in the turns and on the straightaways, but sometimes he needs help from the rider.

There are different ways, usually a combination of cues, to make a horse switch leads. For example, coming into the homestretch, a horse will usually switch to his right lead on his own. But if not, as soon as we enter the stretch, I'll turn his head in very briefly, maybe only one stride when we're in midair, without letting the horse change direction. I'll give the reins a quick pull to the right, and that weight shift will cause him to shift his emphasis from the left to the right. I try to turn the horse's head without turning his whole body.

Failing to change leads was not Point Given's undoing in his disappointing Derby finish, however. We had the extreme outside post in a seventeen-horse field, and I moved him early so we wouldn't be trapped in the final furlongs. A field that big can create one big traffic jam. We were well placed as we approached the far turn, but the acceleration I was used to didn't happen. The horse didn't fire. Monarchos went on to win the race by a near record-setting time, and Point Given was a beaten fifth.

Bob had him examined and tested immediately to see if his lackluster showing signaled some sort of injury, but the horse checked out fine. There was nothing physically wrong with him. Was it the track surface, the wildly noisy crowd, or the heavy humidity that threw him off? We'll never know what made him merely show up on Derby day and fail to run the race we had expected.

Despite persistent reports that the horse wasn't sound—that he wasn't the horse he was cracked up to be and had probably run his best race at Santa Anita in April—Point Given came on like thunder in the Preakness. Bob and I had met with Prince Ahmed and agreed that Point Given should come from farther off the pace than he had in the Derby. I took him back after the break, but I knew we had the race going into the first turn. He was carrying himself with an air of confidence I could feel. I was certain this was the same horse I had won on in earlier races, and in truth he was just towing me. We won easily by two and one-quarter lengths.

Three weeks later, when we won the Belmont Stakes, it was by twelve and one-quarter lengths. Point Given ran the race in two minutes, twenty-six and two fifths seconds, the fourth fastest Belmont Stakes run in history—a victory that made his Kentucky Derby loss all the sadder to contemplate. Racing can be a game of luck, and sooner or later every horse gets beaten. This one was beaten on the wrong day.

In addition, every Thoroughbred is fragile, even those as big and rangy as Point Given. The horse lost ten days of training after winning the Belmont due to cracked heels and an abscessed rear foot that had to be protected with a steel-bar shoe. Bob would not have run him again until late August, except that New Jersey horsemen, hoping to get Point Given to run at Monmouth Park, had offered to fatten the Haskell Invitational purse to a record-setting $1.5 million. It was an invitation neither Richard Mulhall nor Prince Ahmed could refuse. They urged Bob to run the horse, and a record crowd of 47,127 fans filled the stands on August 5.

The trainer was nervous; so was I. We both felt that the horse was one workout short of being at his best. We wished we had another ten days, but we didn't. No doubt contributing to Bob's edginess was the fact that we had been at New York's Saratoga racetrack one day earlier to run Point Given's stablemate, Congaree, in the Jim Dandy Stakes. Congaree had run third in the Derby and third in the Preakness, but had skipped the Belmont. I rode him in the Swaps Stakes at Hollywood Park in July, and after we won it, Bob asked me to ride Congaree at Saratoga. He was favored to win the Jim Dandy, of course, which made his third-place showing so painful. Afterward, it was discovered that the horse had wrenched a knee, reaggravating an old injury, and would not race again for the rest of the year. Congaree's loss made the trainer unusually tense about Point Given.

When we are in the paddock together, Bob usually gives me a leg up and says, "Have fun out there." But prior to the Haskell, he didn't say a word. He just turned away. Three minutes before post time, when the horse and I were warming up on the track, an outrider cantered up to relay a message that Baffert had phoned officials at the starting gate. This was unprecedented. Like most trainers, he delivered instructions to me the night before a race, though he often offered a reminder as I mounted. He once chided me for being in a trance before a race, so he was aware how focused I am during the warm-up.

In his anxiety, Bob wanted to remind me to whip left-handed in the stretch so the horse wouldn't lug in, toward the inside rail. The message got garbled; the outrider told me Baffert had said I should whip left-handed coming out of the gate, which made no sense. I thought it was some kind of joke and was furious that anyone would choose to play games just before a $1.5 million race.

Point Given didn't help the situation. He was balky at the gate, refusing at first to load. And when he finally did enter the gate and the race began, he broke slowly, second to last. It was a difficult race; my horse wasn't at his best. That he beat Touch Tone by half a length was a tribute to his strength and stamina. I was angry when I dismounted and became angrier when I heard that Baffert said I had ridden his colt terribly. I was out of control when I confronted him. Everyone within earshot heard my outburst. In colorful language, I shouted something to the effect of, "If you don't like the way I ride, why don't you just fire me! But don't ever do that to me again."

In the winner's circle, Bob was joking and carrying on in his usual jovial way, but I was having none of it. I refused his handshake and bolted back to the jockeys' room, refusing to pose for photographs. A while later, he phoned to apologize, assuring me he had been wrong to say what he did, that he had just seen a videotape replay of the race and was convinced that I had done an excellent job after all. I apologized for having cursed him out. It was boneheaded for each of us to have reacted as we had. The race was really Point Given's show, and we were just part of it. Our confrontation diminished his accolade.

We met in the directors' room at Monmouth Park to shake hands and toast each other with champagne. Several sportswriters were there, but little was reported about our reconciliation. More was written about what the trainer and I had said to each other in anger than about what the horse had achieved, which was unfortunate, as he was the one deserving attention that day. Bob and I behave more like brothers than working partners. We can be very blunt with each other and say just what we think, though usually in private.

Right after the Haskell, Point Given was flown back to California, and when Baffert felt certain the abscessed foot had healed completely, the horse was put back into training. One sizzling workout convinced him the horse was 100 percent fit and ready to compete again. Thus, a decision was made to run him in the $1 million Travers Stakes at Saratoga in late August, and on that day he put on quite a show. He did something he had never done before, absolutely refusing to be led to the start. I had a little bit of anxiety about why he was doing that, wondering if he was in distress or not quite himself. I learned later that he had been getting a lot of starting-gate schooling after his last race. One look at the gate and he must have thought, *Not that again,* and turned away.

The outrider and I tried to get him moving in the direction of the gate without his realizing he was going that way. We put him along the outside fence and took him beyond the ambulance that's always standing by before a race begins. The horse must have thought he was jogging past the starting gate and was perfectly happy doing that, but then we cut behind the gate and one of the starters grabbed the bridle and turned him into his slot. He was taken by surprise, but he stood quietly then performed beautifully. It was another easy win for him—the first horse in history to win four $1 million races in a row. I felt as though he was dragging me throughout the race, just traveling at his own comfortable pace. The way he was running—cruising along like a big ship—I knew the race was over when we entered the first turn. I didn't have any doubts. We won by three and one-half lengths but could probably have won by ten if I had wanted to press the horse.

When we pulled up after crossing the wire, it was as though Point Given hadn't run at all. It seemed that the race had been very easy on him. Of course, I had to keep tapping him and working the reins to stop him from playing with me in the last sixteenth of a mile, and it took a little effort to get him to change leads. Because he was such a big horse, weighing approximately 1,250 pounds, it was awkward for him to shift from one lead to the other. As usual, he had to be coaxed.

Perhaps it was the effort he expended approaching the climax of that race, as he changed to his right lead from his left, or maybe it was the wear and tear of the long campaign that had begun the summer before, but six days after the Travers, when he was already back home in Southern California, his groom detected some heat below Point Given's left front knee. A veterinarian's careful examination, using ultrasound, revealed a strained tendon, an injury that could perhaps be healed by four to six months' rest. But since a strain could eventually lead to a tear, it was decided that he was too valuable and too good a horse—with such an important future as a stud—to risk serious injury. Point Given was retired instead. He ended his career having won nine out of thirteen races and earning $3,968,500 in purses. A few months later he was named Horse of the Year.

For Bob Baffert, and for me as well, the colt's retirement was devastating. I know it may sound odd to say so, but I experienced the same feeling I had as a seven-year-old when my mom and dad came home and announced that my grandfather had passed away: an incredible sense of loss. Bob considered that horse the best one he had ever trained; I thought of him as my Secretariat.

The racing public had come to love him as well, flocking to see him every time he ran. At Saratoga Race Course, his appearance in the Travers Stakes had attracted 60,486 fans. All of us had been looking forward to having him run two more races as a three-year-old, including the Breeders' Cup Classic, in which he would have faced older horses for the first time, and then have a challenging season as a four-year-old. It was not to be. There may never be another horse like him, but I know other Thoroughbreds will come along to grab the spotlight and win our hearts. My belief is that there's always another day in horse racing.

2 Commitments

I don't remember the day it came, but I do remember what it looked like: a brown manila envelope with a letter informing me that I had been elected to the Racing Hall of Fame. That was something I hadn't expected. I was thirty-four years old and had been riding professionally since my teens. I had won more than four thousand races by then, including three Kentucky Derbys, and taken home my 10 percent of some $160 million in winning purses. Still, the announcement came as a surprise.

I had no idea how emotional the induction would be until the day of the event, the first Monday in August, 1997. It was to be a formal presentation, which would take place in a tent set up on the lawn of the National Museum of Racing, directly across the street from the racecourse in Saratoga Springs, New York. The occasion, held annually, spotlights trainers, horses, and jockeys of high achievement—some still active, some retired, some no longer living. Until that day, I had never even been in the museum. I had been by it a number of times when I came to Saratoga to ride, but I had made a pact with myself that I wouldn't enter the National Museum of Racing, until, hopefully, I could be part of the Hall of Fame.

Although I knew that election to the Racing Hall of Fame was considered Thoroughbred racing's highest honor, I almost didn't make it to the ceremony. I was in Southern California, my home base, and that summer had been riding almost exclusively at the Del Mar racetrack, just north of San Diego. Two days before the Hall of Fame event, I got a call from Bob Baffert telling me that jockey David Flores had been injured in a spill and would not be able to ride Anet in the million-dollar Haskell Invitational at Monmouth Park. Could I rearrange my plans and fly back to New Jersey in time for the Sunday race? Afterward, he assured me, I could leave for Saratoga Springs and be there in plenty of time for the Monday morning ceremony.

I felt like a baseball pitcher who had been warming up, getting ready to go into a big game—except that there had been no warm-up. I had never ridden Anet. But in deference to Bob, I agreed to take the mount. I flew to New Jersey on the red-eye and rode the race on Sunday (we took second-place money). Then, traveling with Jay Hovdey, who was covering the hall of fame event for *The Blood-Horse* magazine, I arranged transportation to Newark Airport and boarded a two-engine commuter plane bound for Albany, New York.

The flight was supposed to leave at 8 P.M. but was delayed and didn't actually take off till about 9. Halfway to Albany, I realized that there was absolutely no cooling in the cabin. It was like a sweatbox, something I was certainly familiar with—sweating off excess pounds in a jockeys' room sauna—but not at twenty thousand feet. Finally, the captain's voice was heard on the speaker system. There was a problem, he said; we would be returning to Newark. "Have you ever landed in an airplane with emergency vehicles next to you?" I asked Jay, who was as astonished as I was to look out the window beside me and see fire engines and ambulances awaiting our landing.

Some distance from the loading gate, the plane stopped and two air-conditioning generator trucks pulled up. Huge round plastic tubes were inserted through both doors of the plane to chill it. I assumed that mechanics were also looking after the faulty cooling system onboard. At about 10 P.M., my patience snapped. "I don't know about you," I muttered to Jay, "but I'm not liking this too much." I asked if we could exit the plane via the emergency stairs, and permission was granted. We grabbed our bags; at that time I carried my tack with me, a lightweight saddle plus a heavier one, both in a large luggage carrier. We stepped down onto the tarmac and raced to a car-rental booth inside the terminal.

Jay pointed us toward Saratoga Springs and drove all the way. We arrived there around 3 A.M.; rested or not, I had to be at the museum for the buffet breakfast at 7:30. The trip had been a kind of nightmare, so it wasn't until the ceremony actually began, some time later, that I felt its full impact. My parents, Ron and Barbara Stevens, were there with me; so were my four children: Ashley, fourteen; Tory, nearly twelve; Riley, eight; and Carlie, five and a half.

My daughter Ashley had been to three Kentucky Derbys, her brother Tory—whom we always called T. C.—had attended two, but none of the kids had more than vague ideas of what my career was all about. Divorce proceedings between me and their mother were underway, and family relations were tense. The children hadn't been able to see me race on a day-to-day or even a month-to-month basis. In fact, I'd had almost no ongoing relationship with them until after Toni and I separated, when I began seeing them regularly. For the first time since my youngest daughter was a year old, I was acting like a father again. I began to feel close to the kids. They were becoming important to me.

"It was beyond my wildest dreams that I'd see a son of mine inducted into the Racing Hall of Fame." That's how my mom said she felt that August day in Saratoga Springs. My dad had a tear in his eye; I could see that. In fact, both of them were crying once the significance of the event began to sink in. It was important to me that they know how hard I had worked to reach that particular high point in my career. I thought to myself how gratifying it was to be honored that way, at a fairly young age and while I was still an active rider. I wanted my parents to know that I acknowledged them for all they had given me. It was important that the honor I received would be felt equally by them as well. They had sacrificed so much for all three of their kids, from the time we were small until we left home. My folks weren't rich people, but as a family we were never without. I always thought we were just as well off as anyone else, but learned later that Mom and Dad had really struggled to maintain the kind of life they had chosen and still make it possible for their sons to do all the things we wanted to do.

Craig was the oldest; then came Scott. I was more than two years younger than Scott, and I idolized him. Whatever Scott did, I wanted to do. And whatever he was good at, I wanted to be good at, too. Did I want to be better than him? Always—if only to win my father's respect. Scott and my dad were nearly inseparable; Scott went everywhere with him. I was always trying to please my dad so I could become as close to him as Scott was. Even to this day, I sense that my dad and my older brother have a bond I don't share, having spent so much more time together around horses than I had.

My mother came from an Idaho farming family; her father was a dairyman. The Coopers were hardworking people who always managed to live pretty well. Mom and her two brothers were raised around horses. She was probably riding before she was walking. Horses were part of family life—not just for doing farm chores but also for entertainment. There were frequent rodeos and an occasional match race with quarter horses, when one neighbor said, "My horse is faster than your horse," and you had to race them to prove it. Quarter horses are raced nowadays, but tradition-ally they were bred and trained for roping and cutting and as all-purpose ranch horses.

One of Mom's brothers, Dale Cooper, had been a quarter horse jockey, but an injury ended his riding career. A wooden rail went right through his leg, causing serious damage. He was just sixteen. Mom's younger brother, Gordon—Uncle Gordy to us kids—became a veterinar-ian in the family's hometown, Caldwell, Idaho, where he maintains a prac-tice.

I don't know the last time Mom was on a horse, but she still under-stands the animals. She was the star of Little Britches rodeos when she was ten, and when she was in high school, showed off her riding and maneu-vering skills in barrel races and in queen contests, which were like Miss America competitions on horseback. She tried out for Miss Rodeo of Idaho, but she never won that crown, which was too bad, as she has always been a keen horsewoman.

Mom was the reason Dad became interested in horses. Although he, too, was raised in Caldwell, he didn't grow up around horses. His father was the local fire marshal; his mother worked in a potato-processing plant.

Mom's mother worked there, too, but in a different department. My two grandmothers didn't know each other at the time.

Dad was a top high school athlete. He wrestled, played football and baseball, did every sport, I think. He dated my mom a little when they were sophomores and juniors but had trouble keeping her attention. Being a bit of a hell-raiser, he resorted to extreme measures. The story, as it's been told to me, was that Mom had a 1955 Chevy with a split manifold that produced an engine sound so distinctive her car in motion was always recognizable. No other car in town sounded just like it.

Dad knew this, of course, so one day, while she was sitting in her seventh-period class, he got into her car, found the keys in the ashtray where she usually kept them (it was that kind of town then) and roared up and down the street in front of the school. That got Mom's attention, all right; from then on, she made sure she removed her keys. But Dad was unstoppable; he simply hot-wired the ignition and drove off, making even more noise. Crazy? Maybe so, but his persistence paid off: he and Mom began dating seriously the summer before they were seniors and got married in 1958, a year after graduating.

Dad was always a salesman by nature. He had a number of paper routes when he was in high school, and as a newlywed drove a truck that delivered milk to local restaurants and grocery stores. When my brother Craig was just a baby, our folks moved from Caldwell to Boise. Later, Dad worked for Eddy's Bakery and then Associated Foods, where he eventually became a manager. The house he and Mom bought in Boise was the one I grew up in. It sat on an acre of land, but at that time there were about two hundred acres of wilderness directly behind us, so it was very rural country. During pheasant-hunting season, when I came home from school each day I would round up our dogs, take my shotgun, and go hunting in my own backyard. We lived at the end of a ten-house cul de sac. Since our property had a horse barn, it was inevitable that there would be horses— pleasure horses at first and then Appaloosas. Dad became a good rider and learned to be a good trainer, too.

Appaloosas are stubborn, tough to train and tough to deal with, but Dad was good with them. He started having a lot of success as an amateur trainer, winning local races with his horses as a hobby. There was hardly any money involved; he felt lucky if he could just break even.

Dad never let his hobby interfere with his work, though, at least not at first. When he had three or four horses at the racetrack in Boise, he would be there, in the barn, at 4 A.M. to take care of his animals and get them out for their training. By seven o'clock he was heading home to shower, put on a suit and tie, and get to his office. When he left work at 5 P.M., he would go back to the track for the late-afternoon feeding and to make sure all the veterinary work had been done.

Every horse he raced in those days was one he owned. He was careful about the horses he bought; he studied pedigrees. As he began to win more and more races, other horse owners expressed interest in his success. He didn't ride in these races; he hired riders to compete. The race meets in Boise were very short—just three months long and only in the summer— but it became an incredibly busy time for him when he started being paid to train horses for other owners. Although he sort of fell into this line of work, he fell totally in love with it. That's where his heart was ultimately, but he never dreamed he could make a living doing it.

Mom remembers that at the end of one summer, Dad's boss called him in and said, "Before the next race season, you're going to have to make a decision: do you want to give yourself fully to *this* job or to being a full-time horse trainer?" Dad didn't take this ultimatum to heart, but a year later, right after he had moved his horses to the track, he was called on the carpet: "Remember what I said—you were going to have to make a decision. Now which is it?" Dad replied rather brashly, "It wouldn't take me very long to make that decision." And that was that.

My mother was stunned—and frightened. She had a job; she was a self-trained accountant for the Intermountain Gas Company. But she had three small boys and a household to manage. Would Dad's hobby ever become a meal ticket? Well, she needn't have worried. He became a very successful trainer, moving his horses between Boise, Idaho, Portland, Oregon, and Seattle, Washington. Within a few years, Mom could quit her job and be free to travel with him. By then, owning and training horses had become their way of life.

I was about seven when this transition was taking place. Dad maintained a forty-horse stable at the racetrack even when he was still working at Associated Foods. Eventually, my brother Scott and I got involved. In the summer, when we were out of school, we would get up when Dad did and drive with him to the racetrack. Soon, he would have to leave to get ready for work, but Scott and I would stay on at the track and make sure all of his horses were tended to.

Our older brother, Craig—at that time not known as the most ambitious of the Stevens boys—preferred to make his summers true vacation times. To earn spending money, he mowed lawns and did chores around the house. Years later, he became the hardest-working member of the family, but at that time he was content to do what most teenagers do in the summer: chase girls and hang out with his friends. He was in his own world, and it didn't revolve around horses or the business our father was building.

Dad's workday had turned into a 4 A.M to 9 P.M. routine, and there were more horses than we could logically take care of, but somehow we did it. Scott and I cleaned stalls and bathed horses—not because we were forced to but because we loved doing it. I remember spending every morning until about noon just doing feet. I would take a horse's hoof, clean it out, and paint on the oil that's used to harden the hoof so it doesn't develop bruises or quarter cracks. I would visit every stall, doing all four feet on every animal. Then Scott and I would mix up the feed, including vitamin supplements, mindful that there were different mixtures for different horses. We made sure the feed was ready by the time Dad got back.

He moved on from training Appaloosas to training quarter horses and then Thoroughbreds. He had a little of everything in his barn. Quarter horses run short distances—up to 440 yards, or a quarter of a mile, the distance they were named for. Appaloosas, those spotted ponies the Indians used to ride, combine the speed of quarter horses with the stamina of Arabians. They race similar distances and longer ones, too, up to three quarters of a mile, which is one of the distances that Thoroughbreds run. Training Thoroughbreds, quarter horses, and Appaloosas requires different skills, but Dad mastered them all. Eventually, Les Bois Park, the Boise racetrack, began running sixty/forty meets: six Thoroughbred races and four quarter horse races a day on the same oval.

It was through Dad and my brother Scott that I developed a desire to ride professionally, but it was Mom who was closest to me in the years when I was growing up, perhaps because she always thought of me as her baby. When I was born, she finally realized that she would not be having any girls. "This was it," she insisted. I would be her last child.

I think it was Mom who first noticed me limping, favoring my right leg. I was only six at the time, barely in first grade, but it was clear to her and eventually to everyone else in the family that something was wrong. At first they thought I might be imitating someone I had seen on TV, except that everywhere I went I limped, and when I ran I kind of skipped. Mom watched me play on my own, without my knowing she was watching, and saw that I wasn't faking. She knew that if I was limping, it was because I felt pain. Dad was coaching Little League at the time. One of his fellow coaches was a dentist who referred Dad to a good friend who was an orthopedist in Boise. "Why don't you get an appointment and go there?" the man suggested. "If he knows what's wrong, he'll tell you. If he doesn't, he'll send you to whoever can fix it."

Mom took me herself. The doctor examined my leg, the one that was hurting, and said, "I'll have to X-ray it, but I believe I know what he's got." It was Legg-Calvé-Perthes disease, a rare degenerative hip ailment caused by a lack of blood supply to the bone. Mom says she was so stunned she could hardly comprehend what the doctor was saying, which was that the disease tends to strike kids who are small for their age and overactive. All of us Stevens boys were small; Dad himself was only five foot eight at maturity.

The doctor prescribed a full-length metal leg brace and a built-up shoe, both of which he said I would have to wear for two or three years. No wonder Mom was upset. I was in bed that night when she and Dad were still sitting at the kitchen table. I could hear her crying. "Don't worry, Mom," I told her later. "I'm gonna be all right."

With Legg-Calvé-Parthes disease, the ball joint of the hip actually starts to flatten out as a result of the pressure placed on it from the impact of walking. My doctor said that if it is not diagnosed at an early stage, it can be permanently crippling. The hip bone turns out to be one of the only bones in the body that can be regrown, but in order to do so, no weight or pressure can be placed on it. Once the leg is properly braced, the diseased bone is allowed to disintegrate and become absorbed by the body at the same time that a new bone is forming in the hip socket. I was not permitted to put weight on my right leg until the new bone had grown in; because it was elevated two inches, the shoe on my left foot kept me balanced.

The only time I was allowed to remove the brace and shoe was when I was getting ready for bed. If I had to get up in the night, I would hop to the bathroom—Mom remembers hearing me. I never cheated; I wanted to do everything right. And every month, when she took me in for an X-ray, we hoped we would hear that big changes had taken place. But time after time, the doctor would say, "You're expecting a miracle and it's not going to happen. This is going to take two to three years."

Obviously, I couldn't play ball or do a lot of the things that other six-year-olds were doing, but I did learn to ride a bike with one leg. I went to school, of course, but my grades went down and my disposition soured. Little kids can be very cruel, particularly to someone who's different, and I was a convenient target.

Frankenstein's Shoe was one of the choice nicknames they used on me. I didn't like it, and with my brothers' encouragement, fought back. One thing wearing that brace and shoe did for me was make me tougher. I became a fighter. I learned to defend myself with my fists whenever anyone teased me, and I learned to like fighting. I fought a lot during grade school; it was a very difficult time.

When I look at my youngest son, Riley, I see myself at his age: tireless and hyperactive. No wonder my parents didn't know what to do with me. They were aware of the frustration I felt, forced into inactivity, but they knew that I couldn't get involved in any form of physical play without removing my leg brace, which would have been disastrous. As a four- and five-year-old, I had played pretty vigorously with each toy-drum set I got as a Christmas gift, so my parents decided I should have the real thing.

They bought me a set of real drums; much later I learned it took them three years to pay for it. They also found me a teacher, a man named Hank House who lived at the edge of town and had been a student of Buddy Rich. He was a perfectionist and a taskmaster. My mother was appalled by the abuse that her six-year-old had to take from him. If I wasn't holding my drumsticks properly, I got a nice whack with a stick across my fingers. And if I didn't have my lesson down to perfection when I came to his home, I received a great deal of verbal abuse.

Things got so bad that Mom finally said, "Gary, I'm not going to take you there anymore," but I insisted, "If you don't take me, I'll walk." So we kept going, week after week. There was really nothing else I could do at the time. I knew that instruction in drum-playing was expensive and that it took a lot for my parents to pay for private lessons, so I felt a certain responsibility to them for their investment in me. All I was expected to do was practice for forty-five minutes every afternoon. With both my parents working, I was by myself when I came home from school, and I didn't always like to practice. But I knew that when I went to my lesson, if I didn't perform perfectly, I would get in trouble with my teacher. I'll never forget coming home from school and setting the timer on the stove for forty-five minutes; I couldn't wait for that buzzer to go off while I practiced.

Eventually, Mom heard of another teacher in town, a man who had studied with Hank House, so we switched. My new teacher, Rick Lasbrook, was as good a drummer as Mr. House, and he had a more placid nature. He too was a perfectionist, but he was a lot easier for me—and Mom—to deal with. I remember him laying out four quarters on his desk at the beginning of each lesson and saying, "See these coins. Every time I have to tell you that you're doing something wrong, I'm going to take one away. But if you've done everything right, at the end of the lesson, you can have the quarters." It was pretty basic psychology, and it worked.

By the time I was ten years old, I was playing drums in the drum-and-bugle corps of a Catholic high school that toured the Northwest. We performed at professional basketball games and marched in parades. A year later, I became the youngest drummer in the United States to have mastered the eighteen rudiments of drum-playing. I received a certificate, which I still have, from the National Association of Rudimental Drummers.

Playing the drums, like every other activity I have been involved in, took total concentration. While driving me to one of my lessons, I remember Mom asking, "Are you okay?" My eyes were open, but I was just staring into space, mentally playing the drums. I was preparing myself for my lesson, because I was afraid to fail in front of my teacher. I don't know if anxiety or determination put me there, but I was kind of "in the zone." Mom would say something to me, and I wouldn't hear her.

Years later, when I began wrestling, the same thing happened before a match. I would become so focused, I was almost in a trance. Today, when I'm getting ready to ride a race, I am only aware of the things I *want* to be aware of, and never let anything else intrude. Getting into the zone is an automatic action; I have no idea how it happens. I do know that it's been part of my makeup since childhood.

I took drum lessons until I was sixteen, and by that time I was writing my own music and performing it for my instructor. One day he announced there was nothing more he could teach me, so my lessons ended. By then I was involved in active sports, but I never forgot the experience. Letting me learn the drums was probably the biggest gift my parents have ever given me.

I don't practice anymore, but now and then I'll perform at parties if there is a band and people who remember that I can play get me up on the bandstand. I find it relaxing. When I get around to putting my drum set together and playing, it's like going on vacation. It completely takes my mind off everything else and also brings back a lot of memories of my childhood and what I've learned and experienced in my life since then. I can play for an hour and feel as though I've been away for two weeks. To this day, I consider drum-playing my first love.

My recovery from Legg-Calvé-Parthes disease did turn out to be kind of miraculous, for I was out of the brace and raised shoe after only eighteen months—but not out of the woods yet. My right leg was about two inches shorter than the left one, and Dad remembers that he could put his thumb and fingers around my thigh. There had been a lot of atrophy, and post-treatment therapy was still pretty basic then. My doctor told Mom, "Get a woman's purse, put some rocks in it, and have him lie on the couch; then hook the handle over his instep and have him lift that leg up and down, up and down." It was a painful exercise to perform, but I did it religiously. I also tried riding my bike, but I didn't have the strength to make it go, so Dad brought it into the house and put it up on blocks in the family room. I rode that stationary bike for hours and hours. It didn't take me more than a few months to restore strength to that withered limb, but to this day my left leg is still slightly smaller than the right one.

Six or eight months after I had shed my brace, I got involved in wrestling, and it did the most to boost my recovery. It's a taxing sport, but for young wrestlers the matches are short, and the competition doesn't get really difficult until high school. A longtime fan of the sport, Dad had started my brother Scott wrestling at a young age. Scott was already on the school wrestling team by the time I had recovered from the bone disease. It's not so much that I followed him into the sport but that he took me into it, by his side. He was an important role model.

I loved wrestling and still do. I knew even then that I had natural ability. What I didn't know was how good I was. Coaches encouraged me over the years, and as I approached my junior year in high school, a lot of college scouts were coming to matches to watch me and offering me scholarships. I think I was the fittest I have ever been when I was wrestling. I lifted weights and ran three miles a day. It's been said that, pound for pound, jockeys are the fittest athletes in the world, but I disagree. I think wrestlers are fitter.

My wrestling career faded, however, when I competed in the district finals and dislocated my left shoulder, experiencing the kind of pain that just rips through your whole body. After the injury healed, I got strong again by working the muscles in my shoulders and arms, by lifting weights, and by riding horses.

* * *

I had been on and off horses from the time I was three years old. We had a Shetland pony named Popcorn that my brothers and I rode. She was a rogue. I didn't take her for rides; she took me. Later I rode saddle horses, and as a result of a few riding incidents, developed a little bit of fear. When I was about six, before my ailment became apparent, I went with my parents on a wild-horse roundup at a camp near the Idaho-Oregon border. Other families were there, and at one point a bunch of us kids rode off on our parents' horses. My mount was Candy, my mother's big quarter horse. It was her saddle, too, which wasn't built to fit someone my size. When we had gone out a ways then turned back toward camp, where our folks were having a cookout, my horse took off at a full gallop. I could do nothing but grab the saddle horn and hold on for dear life.

Running back toward camp, Candy swept by my father's 1967 Ford pickup truck, and I bailed out. As I fell, my face hit the truck's outside mirror and I landed on the hood, then slid to the ground, unconscious, with a broken nose. I healed, of course, but was understandably skittish around horses after that, although unwilling to be left behind by my older brother.

But when I was twelve, a Thoroughbred entered my life—and changed my outlook. Golden Ribbon was probably the best horse in our stable at the time. Dad had several Thoroughbreds, but this was the only one I was allowed to ride. Scott got me to do it; Mom and Dad weren't eager for me to start exercising horses. "Let him gallop that horse," my brother urged Dad. "He'll take care of Gary, he'll *teach* Gary." And he did. Golden Ribbon was about six years old, and he behaved around the barn like a docile saddle horse, but once I got him out on the track, he was different. Feeling his power through my hands on the reins and becoming aware of his intelligence—sensing that a relationship was possible through the immediate communication I could have with him—were sensations I had never known before. That was when I began to fall in love with the sport of kings.

I was terrified, that first time, but I had a lot of help from Scott. I had been observing him for quite a while and wanted to appear as confident as Scott looked on horseback, so I let him coach me: "Keep your heels down; keep your center of gravity over the back of the saddle; keep your knees behind the tree of the saddle. You want to protect yourself so you can go *with* the horse rather than off his back if he should duck or dive one way or another."

Not only the horse but the saddle was different from anything I had ever experienced. An exercise saddle is just a large version of a jockey's saddle, which is basically a postage stamp. While you're sitting up there, the pressure you put on your toes is what gives you your seat. What helps you maintain your balance is the horse pulling on the bridle and you sitting against the reins.

My first mile and a half gallop on Golden Ribbon, though an isolated event, was decisive. I climbed on that horse because I wanted to do what my brother was doing. I was hooked immediately, and my fear was gone. But at the time, that was the only Thoroughbred I was allowed to get on and gallop, because at first it was only for fun. According to Idaho state law, a rider who gallops and exercises a horse professionally on a racetrack must be licensed, and no license can be issued until a rider is sixteen. Even if that rider is employed by a parent, he is not allowed on a racetrack.

When I turned fourteen, Scott and I were about the same size and looked a lot alike. I had my own protective helmet by then, but I used to take his cap and pull it down on top of my helmet, and also put on all the other gear he would wear on his morning rides. I would wear his stuff, and Scott would wear something else, so everyone thought that I was Scott—which is how I came to exercise horses when I was only fourteen.

I got away with doing that for about a month and a half, getting on fifteen or sixteen horses each morning for my father. I was working hard but enjoying every minute of what I was doing. Then I got caught, and any rights that I thought I had to gallop horses on an Idaho racetrack were revoked.

At that time, Dad was working for Fred Jacobson, a client from South Jordan, Utah, who had some very good horses in training. Fred, who had known me since I was eight years old, ran his horses at bush tracks in Utah where no license was needed. When I was kicked off the racetracks in Idaho, Fred asked my father if I might want to come to Utah and exercise horses for him that summer. Dad put the question to me and I said, "Yeah, I'd like that. He's got a cute daughter the same age as me." So

I went to Utah, and within a week I not only had several horses to gallop but found myself faced with an assignment to ride competitively.

Stunned, I put in a panic call to my brother in Boise. "Hey, Scott," I said in a quavering voice, "I'm supposed to ride six races this weekend, but I've never been out of the starting gate before. How do I do it?"

My racing career was about to begin.

3 *Getting Started*

Whatever panic I felt at being hired to ride competitively that first time was more than matched by the way Scott and my father reacted. I think they were horrified—and truly concerned for my safety. Neither of them felt I was ready to ride a race, and I probably wasn't. They booked a flight from Boise to Salt Lake City, and when they arrived, Scott tried to explain to me as best he could how to get my horses away from the starting gate.

These were quarter horses, not Thoroughbreds, so each race would be rapid from the start. Quarter horses break from the gate like a six-pack of dynamite; I had never experienced such an explosive jolt before. Complicating matters was the fact that Fred Jacobson had allowed people to believe that I was the leading apprentice jockey in Boise, so trainers were eager to get me on their horses. Everyone thought I was Scott Stevens, and Scott happened to be the top rider in Boise at the time. Fred didn't lie to anyone, but he didn't say anything to discourage them from thinking I was Scott.

That first day, with Scott and my father standing by watching nervously, I rode six horses. I didn't win my first race, but I did win the third one and ended the day with two winners. I don't even remember that first race; I think I've blacked it out. But I know I stayed on and did well enough, and by the end of the day, I was totally in love with the sport. I knew that's what I wanted to do. Money was not a factor then. The purses were small; we were racing for five-hundred-dollar pots. And because

gambling was illegal in the state of Utah, there was no betting—no
that there probably wasn't some wagering going on in the grand

After I won my second race and came back to the jockeys' qua...s, I
was met by an official from the Utah horse-racing board and shaken down
for possession of an electronic device. He thought that since the horses
were running so well for me, I must be cheating—carrying something to
shock my mounts. Electronic device? I was having enough trouble coming
out of the gate let alone using anything extra or illegal. I was just trying to
hold on. The racing official left me alone.

Scott had given me a couple of safety tips for getting past the break,
and I followed them faithfully. He told me to keep my left foot slightly in
front of me and my right foot slightly behind me. Why? Because if a horse
stumbles leaving the starting gate—which is not pleasant but not unusual—my left foot could keep me from being thrown over his head.
Putting my right foot behind me could absorb the shock of going from
zero to thirty miles an hour in a split second, which is how I kept from
falling off the back of a horse at the break. Scott also urged me not to be
tense, because a horse could sense tension and react negatively. "Stay relaxed and loose," he said. "The more relaxed you are, the more likely a
horse will break good for you at the start." His advice has held up throughout my career.

My brother Scott started riding in competition when he was fifteen
years old, although the legal age was sixteen. He could have ridden at fourteen; he was that good. My parents colluded with him to alter his birth certificate so he could ride when the summer season began in May, even
though he wouldn't turn sixteen until October.

That deception might have gone undetected if a former girlfriend
hadn't vented her anger by turning Scott in to the Idaho Racing Com-
mission a few years later. They fined him five hundred dollars. "That's not
bad," he said. "Think of all the money I've made as a rider." But they put
him on probation, fined my parents for aiding and abetting a criminal of-
fender, and also threatened to revoke Dad's training license. Mom remembers them saying Dad was undesirable because he had been party to what
really was a forgery. Everybody was made to feel like an outlaw. The irony

was that Scott was eighteen by then and had already won four jockey championships.

A family friend, Taylor Powell, came to the house as soon as my parents learned that Scott's malfeasance had been discovered. Powell was head of the Jockeys' Guild in that part of the country. When he walked through the door and saw me after greeting my parents, he said, "And I suppose *you're* not old enough to ride either!" In unison, Mom and Dad exclaimed, "Yes, he is!"

But I wasn't riding legally that first summer in Salt Lake City. However, since those races were not supposed to be recognized by the American Quarter Horse Association, my age and the fact that I was not a licensed rider shouldn't have mattered. It was not unusual for riders to start racing professionally before they were old enough; what *was* unusual was for anyone to make an issue of it. But suddenly, my status did become a problem, because it turned out that a couple of futurity trials for two-year-olds were being run, races for big purses in preparation for even more important races to come. So I had to obtain a license.

To get around the law, I changed two letters of my last name, becoming "Stephens" instead of "Stevens," and substituted a couple of digits of my Social Security number, altering my identity so I could ride in qualifying races for a one-hundred-thousand-dollar futurity race that was going to be run two weeks later. After my first day of racing, I went home, and the people whose horses I qualified to run in the futurity offered to pay my airfare if I would come back to Salt Lake City and ride in the big event.

Of course I'd come back—why not? I had been doing well and having a great time. Fred Jacobson had a beautiful daughter who had become my girlfriend. I was living in the same house with her, and it was great: staying up till eleven o'clock watching TV when everybody else had gone to bed. I was growing up.

And then I fell. There has to be a first time. It was in Salt Lake City, right before the start of that one-hundred-thousand-dollar futurity, and I was about a hundred yards outside the starting gate. A horse to the inside of me ducked out very sharply during the post parade, spooked by something he had seen, and made very severe contact with the horse I was riding. My mount was knocked sideways, and I was thrown off. Luckily, we were only going about four miles an hour. The fall stunned me, knocking my wind out, but I didn't get trampled or kicked, and I actually rode in the futurity twenty minutes later. I didn't win, of course; I was up the track somewhere at the finish, but I did compete. When you're fourteen years old, it's amazing how resilient your body is.

I had only three racing days that summer, and I think I won a total of six races. I didn't realize then that I had begun a career, but I came home with an "I can do this" attitude, even though I knew I was two years away from being able to ride legally on a recognized racing circuit.

By then, my brother Scott had won his first championship at Les Bois Park and had established a reputation as a good competitive rider. Quarter horses, Thoroughbreds—it didn't matter what he was riding. Scott had a gift. Even at that point, he didn't have to ponder what he was going to do; there was no question that he could earn a living riding racehorses. I was proud of him, seeing the success he was having and the money he was earning. In the mid-1970s, making $650 or $700 a week riding racehorses was big bucks for a seventeen-year-old kid from Boise, Idaho.

Scott and I are different in many ways. For one thing, his outlook is more traditional—he married the second girl he ever dated—but he has always been special to me. Here was a kid, still in his teens, who was making a good living and had girls knocking at the door, but whenever he went out with his friends, he took his little brother with him. I always wanted to go, of course, but the point is, he took me. I still can't figure out why.

In 1977, he was offered the chance to go to Southern California to work for a trainer named Chuck Taliaferro, who started Cash Asmussen on his riding career and wound up launching another champion rider, Steve Cauthen. But my parents said no. They wouldn't allow Scott to leave home and go to California, even though he was legally old enough to ride. They absolutely refused. Being a parent now, I can understand their concern. Moving from Boise to Los Angeles would be like entering another world, and there was someone they didn't know saying, "Yeah, we're going to take care of your son." My parents couldn't buy into that, so Scott was stuck in Boise most of the time.

By 1979, I too was riding in Boise. I won my first race there in April on a horse called Little Star. Boise is genuine horse country, but not

Thoroughbred country. I was oriented more toward quarter horses, which explains why my first dream after becoming a jockey was not to ride in the Kentucky Derby, although I had heard of it, but in the All-American Futurity at Ruidoso Downs, New Mexico. That was the top race for quarter horses and the country's first million-dollar race. A few of the jockeys who raced there had once worked for Dad. They became role models, as I had known them when they were sixteen or seventeen years old, before they moved on to Ruidoso and the prestigious California quarter horse racing circuit.

After the Boise meeting ended in the summer of 1979, I moved to the old Centennial Racetrack in Denver, a track that no longer exists. My family was with me: Scott, riding racehorses; my parents, training them. It was my first year of riding professionally, legally, and I rode in Denver until November when the wrestling season was starting up in my high school in Boise. I was a junior. My folks gave me permission to go back to Boise a month before their return and live with my oldest brother, Craig, who was attending Boise State University at the time.

He had definitely been the best and most versatile athlete of the three of us, but he didn't have much interest in horses at the time. Craig was a very good catcher in baseball and a very good quarterback in football, but because he lacked size, he had chosen to go the baseball route. He was supposed to be the role model for Scott and me; Dad fancied that he would become another Johnny Bench. But when he was a ninth grader, he got injured in a game and had to have major knee surgery. I think that may have ended it for him; it certainly dimmed his spirits. He was too short to play football in high school but bright enough to go on to college, though he quit after two years to get married.

I have never competed with Craig the way I have competed with Scott, but he has followed my career and schooled himself to understand Thoroughbred racing. Craig was really talented. I think it was more than just an injury that changed his life. He had been very close to our grandfather on Mom's side. Being the eldest, he had more exposure to Grandpa Cooper than Scott and I had, and Grandpa never made the kind of demands on him that Dad did. He was uncritical and caring, and suddenly at sixty-three, he died of leukemia. I was shocked and upset—I didn't know what death was and had never lost anyone before—but Craig was really devastated. In many ways, he had been as close to Grandpa as he was to Dad, although he was constantly trying to please Dad, which was one reason sports were so important to him.

Dad had hoped Craig would play pro football or baseball, and pushed him very, very hard—until the injury occurred that crushed Dad's hope and ended Craig's ambition. I think the reason he didn't want to be directly involved with horses and tried so hard to find another direction is that, from a young age, Dad had steered him so hard toward horses. Craig was always being dressed in cowboy outfits, cowboy boots and hats, and being told that he should ride this horse or that one.

My brother wanted nothing to do with that world. Today, however, he keeps up with the sport in his own way. He has come to love horse racing as a spectator sport and knows more about horses than I do. He also understands blood stock and breeding. He could have had a career buying and selling racehorses if he had wanted to, but for many years he has been happy and content living in Boise, making daily milk deliveries for Triangle Dairies, a company Dad once worked for.

I stayed with Craig until my folks came home from Colorado. I had gone back to Capital High School and, once again, become involved in competitive wrestling, which was my only other love at the time. Everything was fine until I hit the district finals, which would determine who would go to the state finals. There I was bested by a guy who should never have been able to beat me. I still don't know how he did it. In this, one of my worst matches, I also dislocated my left shoulder. But worse than the pain I experienced was the disappointment I felt, not being able to go on to state.

Dislocating my shoulder didn't have to end my wrestling ambitions, but in losing that match, I felt as though I had failed a lot of people—my wrestling coach more than anyone. I was a very anxious competitor then, and still am. It wasn't fear of wrestling that troubled me, only fear of failure. I drove myself into a nervous knot in the weeks before the big match.

I was actually overprepared—to the point that I had absolutely zero energy when I walked out on the mat. I had won twenty-two matches and was undefeated going into that tournament.

Losing the tournament was a humiliation I had to face realistically. Because of the injury, I was afraid I would never be healthy enough ever to wrestle again. In another match a year or so later, I probably would be put in the same wrestling hold that had caused the injury, so my chances of completing the next season as a wrestler were minute. As it happened, I had grown so in love with horse racing by then that the time seemed right to shift completely from one sport to the other.

Losing a key match and dislocating a shoulder not only signaled the end of my wrestling career, it also marked the end of my formal education. I quit school two months later. I had been a decent student, earning mostly A's and B's to ensure that I'd be allowed to wrestle, but by my junior year in high school, I was being pulled in two other directions: toward wrestling and also toward riding. I knew I would have to stay in school if I advanced to the state finals, but since I hadn't, I took an alternative course, which had been in my mind for awhile. Many times since then, I have regretted what I did, for I immediately went from a kid's world into a man's world, and I came to miss being a kid. All of my friends would not only finish high school but go on to college. I often am embarrassed that I did not.

When my oldest son, T. C., announced that he wanted to quit high school before his senior year to become a full-time horse trainer, I felt hypocritical but was adamant in saying no. "What about *you*, Dad?" he asked, challenging my decision. I could only tell him that I was one in a million and lucky to be where I was.

I know that when I announced my plan to leave school my parents were very upset, and I felt I had let them down even then. First, Scott had dropped out to embark on a riding career, and then I did the same. Until then, no one in our family had ever failed to finish high school. Scott promised to get his high school diploma, and did so dutifully, taking one class a week until he qualified to take the test.

About that time, I got a phone call in Boise from the same man who had tried to bring Scott to California, Chuck Taliaferro. He made me a similar offer to come west to work for him, and once again my parents said no. They were not going to let me do it—until Scott interceded. I'll never forget my brother going into a room alone with Mom and Dad. They came out saying, "Okay, you can go, but there are some ground rules." First, I was to devote 100 percent of my time to what I was doing, which was an easy promise to make. Second, I was to complete my education, getting my high school equivalency. To date, I haven't done this, but I will someday. A promise is a promise.

It's not that Mom and Dad were easygoing, but they wanted their sons to do what they knew we loved. Mom still says she was devastated when I quit school. The Stevens boys were never indulged by our parents but always encouraged—Craig, in particular. Mom and Dad gave us more freedom than I have ever known three children to have, but they knew we respected the freedom we were given and realized that if we went out of bounds, we would lose everything we had gained. We were basically good kids, although we weren't angels. As close as we were, the three of us fought constantly among ourselves, like most siblings. Craig, the oldest, was always trying to antagonize me, but I knew that he would be there for me when I needed him. Always.

Nineteen seventy-nine was a turning point. I was given the same professional opportunity that Scott had been offered, and he talked Mom and Dad into letting me go forward with it. When I went to work for Taliaferro, he was into Thoroughbreds in a big way, but he had started out with quarter horses. Like a lot of successful trainers, he eventually returned to his roots—to the Lazy-E Farm in Oklahoma, which is probably the most successful quarter horse breeding and racing stable in the United States.

Chuck died of cancer in the early nineties, but his spirit remains with me. He was responsible for shaping the next phase of my racing life.

Growing Up

Scott and my dad had bought me a 1955 Chevy pickup with a Corvette 327 engine. It was a hot rod when I got it, and I wish I still had it. It would be worth about forty thousand dollars today. At the time, it looked great, but I think it got about six miles to the gallon and was showing its age. It was an impractical toy that wouldn't have made the 550-mile trip to Southern California. I traded it in, a straight-across swap, for a 1974 Ford Ranchero, a modified pickup truck with a bench seat in the cab and a camper shell on the back. It was the reliable vehicle that would take me southwest.

I loaded the back with my clothes and the few pots and pans my mom had pulled together for me—she actually thought I was going to cook. My departure had her blessing, but she had a hard time controlling her emotions. Her youngest was leaving the nest. Dad's good-byes would come later, for he was driving to California with me. We headed south, through Winnemucca, Nevada, and then along the outskirts of Sequoia National Park until we reached Bishop, California, at the edge of the Mojave Desert. We spent the night in a motel there and did some sightseeing before crossing the desert—desolate country, not a place where I would want to run out of gas—and completing the trip the next day. We arrived in Arcadia around eleven o'clock at night. Dad found us a Motel 6 on Colorado Boulevard, which backed up to the parking apron of the Santa Anita racetrack. We could see it from the highway as we drove into town. The lights were on, but the stands were empty—grandstands that on important race days could hold more than maybe fifty thousand people, compared with

Boise's Les Bois Park, which held only two thousand. Seeing Santa Anita that first time was the most humbling experience I had ever had.

It was April 1980, and I was just seventeen. I had dropped out of school and made the kind of naïve career decision that a kid that age would make. Had I known how difficult things were going to be and what it was going to take to achieve the kind of success I envisioned—how lucky I was going to have to be to be in the right spot at the right time—I'm not so sure I would have made that choice. I'm positive that even if I had stayed in school, I would have wound up doing exactly what I've done—except that I would have completed my education.

My first twenty-four hours in the Los Angeles area added up to a kind of wake-up call. Dad was scheduled to fly home to Boise the next day, so we had a little time to look around and get a feel of the place together. We headed for the ocean at Redondo Beach, which was about fifteen or twenty minutes from Los Angeles International Airport. Along one street, we saw TV-news vans and camera crews with cameras poised and lights switched on. I remember Dad saying something like, "Oh, look, they're making a movie." Although I had done most of the driving till then, he was behind the wheel of the Ranchero, so he pulled over to the curb and parked. We got out. There was a large group of people lined up, waiting. We waited, too. Across the street, there was a five-story parking garage, and soon we were aware of armed policemen up on the roof. Suddenly, we saw a guy running toward us down an alley; the police saw him too and opened fire; he was shot dead in front of us, only yards away. I had never seen anything like that. I thought to myself, *That stuff I see on* Starsky & Hutch *is the real stuff!* What we weren't aware of was that a bank was being held up, and the cops had been tipped off.

When the police ambulance arrived, the crowd dispersed. We climbed back into the Ranchero, and I drove my dad to the airport. It was a weekday and fairly quiet, but not serene. On Century Boulevard, about two miles from the airport, we were at a stoplight when I saw a man running across the street with somebody right behind him, giving chase. The running man jumped up on my car and ran across the hood. I was paralyzed. Within the course of one hour, I'd seen one man die in front of me and another one use my vehicle as part of an escape route. No wonder, then, that after dropping Dad at the airport, I drove straight back to the motel and locked myself in my room. I was alone for the first time and scared to death.

I couldn't sleep. It was all I could do to wait until 4:30 A.M. when it was time for me to get up, dress, and get myself to the racetrack. I didn't know where to go, so I went to the main-stable gate. I had appropriate I.D., since I had obtained my apprentice-jockey's license the morning after we had arrived. Since I was under eighteen, Dad had had to sign me over to Chuck Taliaferro as my legal guardian. This was no shock. My folks had agreed to the arrangement because by then they were fully aware of Chuck's great reputation for bringing along young riders. After several phone conversations, my folks finally felt confident that I was going to be well looked after by Chuck and his wife, Linda. I too had telephoned Chuck a couple of times prior to coming west. He was easy to talk to and rather nonchalant: "Aw sure, anytime, come on down, we'll put you to work." I knew he would make me feel welcome when I found him.

The guard at the gate looked at my license and gave me directions to Chuck's barn. As I walked there, I began to see the legends I had heard about and often seen on TV. First there was the Whittingham barn, and that revered trainer, Charlie Whittingham. Then along came D. Wayne Lukas on his lead pony. It was unreal. I found my way to Chuck, and he put me straight to work. He had about thirty horses in his barn, which Linda managed while he was at the track. The two of them were pretty much partners in the business, just as my parents were in their training operation, so I was at ease with them from the start. They invited me to come to dinner at their house that night.

"Where would I live?" they wondered. My idea was that I was going to bunk in the tack room just off the backstretch at Santa Anita, but Chuck wouldn't hear of it. He didn't like the atmosphere, sensing that it might not be healthy for me or safe. I think he was concerned that I might befriend the wrong people and get mixed up in drinking or drugs, and he didn't want me in that environment. He took his role as my legal guardian seriously.

For the next two months, until I got my own apartment, I lived in the Motel 6 and was very homesick. The room had no telephone, but there were pay phones on the bottom floor, directly below me. Each evening, I would go downstairs and call my parents. I remember crying as I told them how much I wanted to come home. They urged me to stay; it must have been heartbreaking for them, especially my mom.

I began riding races almost immediately but didn't think I was doing very well. I wasn't winning. I had twenty-seven second-place finishes in my first two and a half months in California but had expected to be doing much better. "Why not get an agent?" Chuck suggested a few weeks after I arrived. But getting one took time.

Every rider has to have an agent, of course. If you're a top rider, you need an agent to pick mounts for you, to separate the good horses from the bad. If you're starting out, as I was, you need someone to promote you and get you mounts, someone willing to hike through the stable area of every single barn every day to get work lined up for you—mostly morning workouts, for which jockeys are not paid. You're basically begging for mounts. I finally found someone willing to accept the challenge and help me become established. Ron McClellan was the brother of a very successful agent who represented Chris McCarron, an established rider. Ron worked for me for about a month, then decided there was less work and more potential gain in representing Frank Olivares, a journeyman rider, so I was without an agent again.

I felt discouraged; I was also a shy kid, quiet and not very assertive. Chuck Taliaferro said he knew someone I should talk to, a former trainer living in absolute boredom since his retirement. Bobby Mitchell owned Bonnie Acres, a ranch in the Bradbury Estates in Bradbury, California, about ten miles from the Santa Anita racetrack. He was best friends with Steve Cauthen, who had won the Triple Crown on Affirmed in 1978, and had a lot of good connections with horse owners and trainers. Since Mitchell was a mature gentleman, Chuck thought he would be another good father figure for me. I don't recall if Chuck made the call or if he forced me to pick up the phone, but Mitchell agreed to work for me, and within a short time, I went from riding two or three horses to riding eight races a day.

According to our arrangement, Chuck had first call on my services, but if he didn't have a horse for me to ride in a particular event, Mitchell was allowed to find another mount for me. I may not have been winning races, but I was earning probably five times more money than I had made the summer before in Boise. The seconds and thirds I racked up were adding up to a lot. Still, I wasn't satisfied. I wanted to go home. I was disappointed that in two months of riding in Southern California, I hadn't won a single race. I felt alone, despite the support I was getting, and inexperienced, not really up to the demands of what I was doing. Suddenly, I had questions— about my future and about what I wanted out of my career. The painful homesickness I felt was a clear signal to me and to everyone around me that I had a lot of growing up to do.

One morning, Chuck called me into his office and closed the door. He said he knew how unhappy I was; I said yes, I was, and that I had decided to go back to Boise. While I sat there, he got on the phone and told my dad, "Don't let this kid come home. It'll be the biggest mistake he's ever made if he leaves. He can ride; he's doing well; he's expecting things too quickly. He's got to be patient." Later, when we spoke on the phone, Dad insisted, "You're *not* leaving. You're staying until you win one race." On a Saturday about a month later, I not only won one race but three of them. My first was on a pickup mount. Either because of injury or a scheduling conflict, a jockey withdrew and his horse became available. And Jerry Fanning, the horse's trainer, chose me as the replacement.

It was not advantageous for him to do that. If an apprentice is substituted for a journeyman rider, the weight allowance is waived. I would not get the five-pound allowance I was accustomed to, and Fanning knew it but he wanted to use me anyway. My horse finished in a dead heat for first with the horse Sandy Hawley was riding. We both were awarded first-place honors, and I came back two races later to win one for the trainer Larry Sterling. Then I won a race for Chuck. All on the same day.

The next day, I rode four horses and packed my things. I told Chuck I was leaving, heading back to Boise. He was a little upset with me, convinced I was making a mistake. Dad was upset with me, too, for quitting after only three months. But I was glad to be going home. I didn't think I would be coming back.

I didn't know it then, but in retrospect I can see that those three months gave me the best experience I could have had at that stage of my career. I was able to ride with some of the best jockeys in the world and absorb a great deal just from watching them. I marveled at Laffit Pincay's power and strength; I admired Bill Shoemaker's finesse; I thought Darrel McHargue's seat on a horse, his stature, was poetry in motion. Those were the riders that I tried to shape my style after. I wasn't riding enough horses, or really good horses, to learn much myself. To really learn tactically what you need to do—where you need to be in a race—you have to ride good horses.

Before leaving California, I sold the Ranchero and bought a brand-new limited edition Pontiac Trans Am—gray with an orange firebird on the hood. That was a symbol of success for me, and I was proud of it. I packed it with everything I owned, including Mom's pots and pans, and left in the wee hours of the morning. I drove home nonstop, about a thirteen-hour trip, happy at the prospect of being close to my family again. I'd had a taste of being on my own, but I'd never been that far from home for so long. I wasn't ready for it. I found I wasn't as capable of taking care of myself as I thought I was. But I think the experience prepared me for what I've had to do so many times since then: sit in a hotel room by myself. A lot of my adult life since then has been spent doing just that. I don't mind it anymore; actually, I've learned to enjoy it a little.

Adding to the homesickness I felt in California was the fact that I missed my girlfriend, Kim McReynolds. We had started dating when we were thirteen years old, even though we went to different schools. I played football at Fairmount Junior High; she was a cheerleader at Foothill. We had broken up before I left home but had been exchanging letters, writing to each other a lot when I was in California. When I came back to Idaho, I found out that she already had another boyfriend. That took a little luster off my homecoming.

I didn't move back in with my parents. My brother Scott had his own trailer at the trailer park by the Les Bois Park racetrack, where he was the leading jockey at the time. He was my mentor as far as the basics of riding are concerned and to this day doesn't hesitate to give me constructive criticism if things aren't going too well. I was not only his roommate; I was his shadow. I think, at least I hope, he enjoyed my being around all the time. He not only shared his home with me, he shared his agent. Ray Bryner, a horse trainer now, became my agent, too.

My California experience gave me a powerful boost in expertise, so when I returned to Boise, I was able to ride ten horses every afternoon and also work fifteen or twenty horses in the morning. The racing season was well underway when I got to Les Bois, but in the month that remained, I won a lot of races, putting to good use much of what I had picked up in California. When the season ended in late August, Mom and Dad took their string of horses to Portland Meadows in Portland, Oregon, and I went along with them. I was a professional jockey, no longer a schoolboy, and needed to work. I would ride the Stevens horses in races, of course, but would need other mounts as well, so I hired another agent.

Butch Fillingness wasn't really an agent; he was Dad's Portland blacksmith and an all-around horse person. His first priority was making a living as a blacksmith, and he was good at his trade, the best blacksmith on the grounds. As such, he had access to a lot of trainers. That's how he ran my business as an agent. While bent over, shoeing a horse, he might ask a trainer, "Hey, why don't you put my jock on a horse?" Butch was a great guy, but he didn't know much about being an agent. At first, I wasn't riding many horses, and I wasn't winning on a regular basis either. Other than my father, the only other trainer I was riding for was Vaughn Cunningham, an ex-jockey who had a large stable in Portland. At that time, in Portland as in Boise, an agent received 20 percent of a jockey's earnings. Now, pretty much everywhere, it's 25 percent.

I was in Portland when Mount St. Helens erupted in 1980. Most of the smoke and ash was blown northeast, toward the Yakima Valley, but we did get quite a bit of ash. My Trans Am was coated with about four inches of it, and we didn't race for nearly a week because of the heavy ash accumulation on the track. It was like a war zone.

A few days after arriving at Portland Meadows, I was in the track kitchen playing a video game when I spotted a girl shooting pool with a couple of guys. I had seen her before, galloping horses in the morning. She was a cheerful young woman, far more outgoing than I was at the time, and I was attracted to her. I found out that she was Toni Baze, whose father, Carl, was a trainer and whose older brothers, Mike and Gary, were jockeys. Her first cousin, Russell Baze, was a prominent rider in Northern California. They were a racing family.

It took a lot of nerve for me to ask Toni out that first time, and I think the way I asked her was to say, "Hey, I'm goin' to a movie tonight. If you want to go, too, you can come along." She did, and we started dating. She was as interested in racing as I was and soon took a big interest in what I was doing. Part of her appeal, I guess, was that she came to believe in me, in what she believed I would be capable of doing in my career. We dated for only three months before I asked her to marry me.

It was Toni who urged me to get another agent. "Who's gonna take me on if I'm not doing any good?" I asked. She said she would ask her dad to talk to Ray Kravagna, an agent who represented two jockeys who were among the top five in Portland at the time. He wasn't eager to work for me but did so as a favor to Carl, Toni's father. The change was immediate—and dramatic. In my first three months at Portland Meadows, I had won three races. Period. But in the first month after Ray became my agent, I won forty-five. With him behind me, my career caught fire. Portland had night racing, and I starting riding ten races a night. I was riding quarter horses and Thoroughbreds and by November was no longer an apprentice.

According to rules set up by the Racing Commissioners International and recognized by all racing jurisdictions in the United States, a rider loses his or her apprentice status after winning fifty-five races or riding one year—whichever comes *last*. The reason: If you have ability, you're going to rattle off those fifty-five wins pretty quickly and could realistically end your apprenticeship in only two months. At that time, if you didn't have much talent, you could maintain your apprenticeship up to five years. Now, I believe there's a limit. After three years, you automatically become a journeyman rider, but should probably think about finding another profession.

Becoming a journeyman didn't mean getting a pay increase. Through the 1930s and forties, a jockey was paid whatever a trainer felt the rider was worth, and much of the time, for a great many riders, it was slave labor.

Now, a rider earns 10 percent of the purse if he comes in first, 5 percent if he is second, third, or fourth. This is in addition to a basic fee, based on standards that vary according to the level of the track. At class-A tracks such as Santa Anita, Hollywood Park, Saratoga Springs, and Churchill Downs, for example, a standard jock mount for a purse below ten thousand dollars is eighty-five dollars. For million-dollar races like the Kentucky Derby, the standard mount is over two hundred dollars. Since the first-place winner of the Kentucky Derby earns six hundred thousand dollars, the jockey takes home more than sixty thousand dollars—nice pay for little more than two minutes' work.

When apprentices lose their five-pound weight allowance, they tend to go through a dry spell—a time when some make it and some don't. With me, just the opposite happened. I had already had my dry spell. Now, with Kravagna as my agent, my career took off. I think one reason I had become a better rider is that I was stronger. Losing my apprenticeship meant that I could eat more. I could legitimately gain five additional pounds. I had been dieting really hard to maintain my apprentice weight of 108 pounds; now I could go up to 111 or 112. My weight has crept up a little every year since then—weight control has been a battle from the time I started riding. Most of us have that problem. There are only a few natural lightweights left riding.

Nowadays, I struggle to ride at 115 pounds, and to keep to that weight I try to eat moderately. I eat very little breakfast and a very light lunch, but I usually eat a good dinner. If I overdo it, as all riders do from time to time, I make myself throw up. But I don't do that nearly as much now as when I was younger. The older I get, the better care I take of my body. I'll fast when I have to, but I hit the hot box every day—three days a week I do steam and two days I do the dry sauna to break up the monotony.

On an average day, I'll come in weighing 114 or 115 pounds and usually pull two pounds before I ride. These represent water weight and come off very quickly—usually within forty-five minutes, including a ten-minute break. I'll normally sit in the hot box for about twenty minutes to get a good sweat going, then come out and get in what we call the cooling-out room. It's not room temperature in there—it's usually about 90 degrees Fahrenheit. Once you've got a sweat going, you don't need a lot of heat to continue to sweat comfortably. But once I stop sweating, I'll get back into the steam room or sauna for another fifteen minutes. I actually prefer the steam room; the sauna's dry heat tends to dry out the joints and skin. If I were to sit in a sauna every day, my skin would get scaly. One of my tricks, while sitting there, is to rub baby oil all over my body to keep my skin from getting dry and peeling. It also helps me sweat.

Hot box visits are part of my daily routine. Unless I go into the jockeys' room at least two hours before I have to ride and sit in the hot box, I don't feel comfortable. That's what my body has become accustomed to. Of course, I lose weight as I ride, so after every race, I come back and drink water, to make sure I keep sufficient fluids in my body throughout the day. If I feel myself cramping up, I take a low dosage of potassium.

I weigh myself maybe forty times a day. Obviously, I have to weigh in before and after riding a race, but I also get on a scale every morning and night. It's the first thing I do when I get up and the last thing I do before going to bed. I am constantly tracking my weight; it can vary as much as five pounds within a day.

In February 1981, when the season at Portland Meadows ended, the scene shifted to Seattle, as most of the top stables in Portland were also prominent in Seattle, at Longacres, a track that doesn't exist anymore. Boeing acquired the site in the nineties and planned to build offices and a jet simulator for training. The problem was that they hadn't done their homework. Longacres was sitting on national park land where they couldn't build. So nothing really happened. The facility is used mainly for storage and the racetrack itself is overgrown with weeds. A new track, Emerald Downs, was built in Seattle to take its place.

Portland Meadows was on a much higher scale than Les Bois Park, and Longacres was a cut above Portland Meadows, but a lot of Seattle trainers would bring their horses to Portland for the winter, some right near the end of the season, to give their horses one prep race before shipping them to Longacres. A few of these trainers urged me to go on to Seattle, too, instead of returning to Boise. I wanted to go, but Ray felt I wasn't ready. "There are a lot better riders in Seattle than Portland," he said. "You need another season of experience." He urged me to go back to Boise and ride there that summer.

I didn't like hearing that at all—I was really annoyed—and I proved him wrong. Vaughn Cunningham was running three of his horses on opening day at Longacres, horses that I had ridden and won on at Portland Meadows. He wanted me to go to Seattle and ride those three horses, which I agreed to do, and all three horses won. I had a couple of second-place finishes, too. All in all, it was a very good day. As I came back to the jocks' room after my three wins, who should be waiting for me but Ray Kravagna, who begged me to stay. "You can't go back to Boise now," he said.

"Yes, I can," I insisted, "I'm not good enough to ride here. I'm going back to Boise to spend the summer there. I'll see you here in Seattle after Boise's season is over." I thought that I would hit the last month of the summer season at Longacres and then go directly from there to Portland Meadows. Back in Boise, I had a very good summer, finishing as the track's second-leading rider—after my brother Scott. In June, Toni and I returned to Seattle to be married. Her folks lived in Kent, a suburb of Seattle. The day after our wedding, the two of us drove back to Boise. We were both eighteen, and our lives stretched out before us. I felt confident, at last, that in terms of the sport I had chosen, I could do anything. I felt I had made it.

5 *Northwest Conquest*

$\mathcal{M}$y wife and I were on our own at last—no more living with parents or siblings. But as we needed to be mobile, I bought us a thirty-five-foot house trailer with two tip-outs that would let us expand our living room and bedroom about 50 percent whenever we settled in at a trailer park. We had a washer and dryer and a waterbed, but we no longer had the Trans Am. I traded it in for a three-quarter-ton Chevy pickup truck so we could pull the trailer when the season in Boise was over. Losing the sports car, the first of many I would own, was painful but necessary. Knowing that I would be moving from one track to another, it seemed so much easier to have our house *with* us than to have to search for digs when we got to a new racetrack. We knew there would be trailer parks convenient to the tracks whereever we worked.

And both of us worked. While I was riding, Toni would leave our trailer, which was right at the racetrack, and go over to help Mom and Dad in their barns. Meanwhile, Ray Kravagna was on the phone with me often, wanting to know when I would be getting to Seattle. He had horses lined up for me to work and ride, trainers and owners he wanted me to meet. As cool as he had once been about my prospects in Seattle, he was red-hot to have me there now, and I certainly wanted to be there, too.

During the last week of Boise's racing season, in August 1981, I was riding in a quarter horse race. Just as we were pulling up after crossing the finish line, a horse in front of me fell. My horse stopped abruptly and I went down and was knocked unconscious by the impact. I was taken by ambulance to St. Alphonse's Hospital to be examined, complaining that my shoulder hurt. X-rays were taken, and I was told that nothing was wrong. I could ride the next day. When I got home, I could see I was black and blue around the collarbone area and was a little alarmed to see that the discoloration traveled down my body toward my abdomen. I tried to ride the following day, and I did ride one race, but found the pain too much. I went back to St. Al's to be reexamined. That's when they found the fractured collarbone; they hadn't even looked the first time.

Collarbone injuries are common among jockeys. I've had at least four since then, and a veteran jock like Pincay has probably had more than a dozen. I've also broken every finger on each hand, including my thumbs, and have had to ride with them broken. It's difficult to splint them up, and you can't ride that way, anyway. I certainly wasn't going to let this collarbone fracture slow me down very much, despite the discomfort, so I took five days off while we packed up our trailer and hooked it to the truck. I didn't know what I was going to do when we arrived in Seattle, but I was determined to press ahead, as though nothing had happened. No one knew I had been hurt, and I didn't tell anyone. Kravagna didn't know until I got there. My body was still discolored and I was still in pain, but I went to work right away. I rode with a figure-eight brace for collarbone injuries. I started winning races despite the pain, which along with the black and blue marks gradually diminished during the next three weeks.

I think that, to be successful, every professional athlete must learn to play in pain. There may be days when you have a little flu and don't feel 100 percent, but you've got to go out and get the job done. If I ever felt that I was going to be a detriment in a horse race, or be a danger to someone, I'd never go out. I have learned that the best thing our bodies create is endorphins. With every serious accident I've had, I didn't feel pain at the moment—it was like being loaded full of morphine. With that collarbone fracture, I didn't feel any real pain until the next day. Many times, during the five or so years leading up to my retirement in 1999, my knees would act up. I would break into a cold sweat just heading for the starting gate. Then I would get to the gate and start focusing so much on the race that when the gate snapped open, I would plunge into the heat of competition, not feeling anything. After the race—that's when I'd feel it.

I'm in some degree of pain all the time. When I wake up in the morning, my lower back hurts. When I get out of bed, my right leg hurts, my left leg, too, and both shoulders. I turn the water on in the bathtub and make it pretty hot. Then I lie in it for about five minutes before getting out. I used to run three miles a day, but no more. I stay fit now by working: riding races in the afternoon and galloping horses in the morning, a half mile to a mile each. I figure I ride about twenty-two miles a week, all told. I work my ass off; then on my days off, I play golf. I gallop horses not only to stay fit but also to learn about the horses my agent wants me to ride. I don't get paid, but exercising horses paves my future.

There was only a month of racing left when I reached Seattle that September, just in time for the rainy season. Sometimes it would pour for three days straight, and the track would be so thick with mud that it might take a week for the shadiest parts to dry out. Imagine sixteen inches of sticky, gummy mud. Racing continued, however, but riding was particularly perilous—not so much each race itself but those moments right after a race ended, when the horses were going from a gallop to a jog. A tired horse, pulling up in that muck, was likely to stumble, and after every race, one or two horses did—from exhaustion and not being able to pick up their feet. As a rider, you would hold your breath and pull back on the reins with all your might, although you knew your horse would probably stumble anyway. It was you against the horse, trying to pull his head up and keep him balanced.

There was a downpour that lasted a week when I first got to Seattle. I was named on only a couple of horses the first few days, but one by one all the jockeys at the top of the ranks started abandoning their horses, either because they didn't want to ride in the rain or thought it would be unsafe to ride. I picked up mounts right and left and started winning races at an unbelievable rate. In one month of racing, I won something like thirty-five events, an unheard of number of wins in such a short period of time for someone like me, who had never run on that particular surface and in that company of riders.

I wouldn't say I was at my best, but I was getting the job done and keeping my injury fairly well hidden. The trainers certainly weren't aware of it. This was the first of many times in my career that I rode with pain, and it proved to me that I could be competitive even with an injury. It showed me I had a toughness I hadn't known was there.

In October when the season ended, we drove our trailer down to Portland and set up housekeeping right on Union Avenue, literally a stone's throw from the backstretch at Portland Meadows. I think there was an overlap; the winter season had been under way for about a week when we got there. Toni began exercising horses. She was still an apprentice; never a daring rider, she was always safe on the racetrack. Carl Baze, her father, had moved his horses from Seattle to Portland. Her family had a home in Battle Ground, Washington, just across the Columbia River, about fifty miles from Portland. That's where Toni had gone to high school.

The season in Portland was the most successful meeting I'd had up to that point. I was named the leading jockey for quarter horses as well as Thoroughbreds. There were two quarter horse races a day; the rest were for Thoroughbreds. In April 1982, we returned to Seattle as planned. Mike Chambers, Bud Klokstadt, Nub Norton, and Bob McMeans were among the top trainers in Seattle, and I pretty much picked up their stables. They, and men like Marion Smith—we called him "Million-Dollar Smitty"— had a big influence on my career because they gave me a lot of support. My goal, as the summer season began, was to become the leading jockey at Longacres.

I wasn't disappointed. I was not only the top jockey, but with 220 wins, I set a new record. I actually broke the record that had been set by Gary Baze, my brother-in-law.

I don't remember the exact date that it happened, but I do remember that at some point, Toni and I had an argument about something. I also remember that I was having a horrible day; the horses didn't seem to be performing well for me. It was probably just after the fifth or sixth race and I was walking back to the jocks' room. Toni was standing at the rail, and she beckoned to me; she said she had something to tell me. "What's that?" I wanted to know. "I'm pregnant," she said.

I was shocked—happy, yes, but also a little scared. I didn't know what to say. I was nineteen, and all of a sudden I was going from happy-go-lucky, with no responsibilities other than to myself and my wife, to having to think about providing for someone else, too. Even though I thought of myself as an adult, I really was still a kid, not grown up at all. Toni was happy—I think women mature a lot quicker than men do—and there was comfort for me in that. Her happiness gave me strength and assurance.

Both of us knew we would need more living space when we moved back to Portland, but we weren't prepared to invest in property or anything that suggested permanence. Not yet. Toni and I picked out a custom mobile home instead. It was a sixty-five-foot-long, double-width model with all of the amenities I could afford at the time: sunken living room, sunken bathtub, three bedrooms. It was plush. Then we located a mobile-home park just across the Columbia River in Vancouver, Washington, about twenty-five minutes by car from Portland Meadows. I had earned about one hundred thousand dollars racing in Seattle that summer. That was a big change in my income, considering that in Portland, I was used to bringing home about fifteen hundred dollars a week. I was still very careful about money; that's the way my mother raised me.

Our daughter Ashley was born in Vancouver on January 27, 1983, at the height of Portland's winter racing season. I was doing well on the track, but life at home was difficult. Ashley was not a good sleeper. I would get home from the evening's racing program around 12:30 A.M., wound up, my adrenaline still flowing from racing. Winters in Portland were cold and damp, so I'd be freezing, too. The baby would be crying; I was getting little sleep. Then, of course, I would have to be back at the track by 7 A.M. for morning workouts. I was putting in a lot of hours. The schedule was punishing, but the achievement was great: I set a new record for wins at Portland Meadows that winter, more than two hundred.

Ashley was only a few weeks old when her mother and I began taking trips to Seattle on my days off to look for a home. We wound up buying a brand-new three-bedroom condominium in Renton, about five miles from the Longacres race course. We moved in when the Seattle summer season rolled around and sold the mobile home in Vancouver. As I had advanced a level or two by then, I decided that, instead of returning to Portland at the end of the summer, I would be going to Bay Meadows in San

Francisco. My agent also felt that it was important for me to take the next step up.

In Seattle, I broke my own record for wins that summer, and in September, as soon as the season was over, I headed south to the Bay area, leaving Toni and the baby behind, near her family. She was fine about my leaving. After all, I would be coming home as often as I could—certainly for Thanksgiving and Christmas—and would have a chance to earn even more money than I had in Seattle. I would be living simply; I planned to share a room at the Hillsdale Inn, near the Bay Meadows racetrack, with her brother Gary.

San Francisco was new territory for me, but what gave me confidence was that many of the stables I had begun riding for in the Northwest had moved south to California, for the winter. I went to Bay Meadows with horses to ride and without a real need to look for other mounts. I knew that even if my agent didn't pick up new business for me, I would be all right. There would be conflicts, of course, but it would be Kravagna's job to decide whom I was going to ride for. As it happened, I did pick up several new stables in the Bay area, even though trainers knew I would be returning to Seattle in April, when the Longacres season started up again.

I had a very successful wintertime at Bay Meadows. I was racing against a new caliber of riders, a better colony of jockeys than I had ever ridden with since my first stay in Southern California—men like Chad Schvaneveldt, Chris Hummell, Paul Nicolo, and, of course, Russell Baze, who had become the leading jockey at the time. Proving to myself that I could be very competitive and ride with these guys was good for my confidence. I was learning a lot.

Back in Seattle, I was leading jockey again for the 1984 summer season; my 256 wins broke my own record. I was also under a little pressure. Ray Kravagna had begun urging me to go to Southern California for the fall and winter, rather than back to Bay Meadows. He sat me down one day and said, "Look, Fernando Toro is getting up there in age; Bill Shoemaker is getting up there in age; Laffit Pincay is getting up there in age. Now, these guys are gonna quit at some time, and this might be our opportunity to get our equipment going in the big time." He was convincing, for I knew that Santa Anita, Hollywood Park, and Del Mar were class-A tracks, like Belmont Park and Churchill Downs in the east. What I didn't know, of course, was that Shoemaker and Pincay had many more riding years ahead of them, but that didn't matter then. Trainers I knew and rode for, including Bob McMeans and Million-Dollar Smitty, were going to Southern California, each with a barnful of mounts, so there was reasonable assurance that I would get work.

"We've got sixty horses going down there," Ray insisted. "This may give us a chance to show people what we can do. We'll at least have these horses to ride, even if we don't pick up any outside mounts, After all, we've had a great year; we've made a lot of money. Let's go down there for the winter. Think of it as a working vacation. You're gonna be down there in Southern California, and you'll ride through April. Then you'll come back to Seattle for the season up here."

It didn't take much to convince me to take this "working vacation," for there was another attraction, another event that was luring me south. The very first Breeders' Cup races were to be held at Hollywood Park in November 1984, and I knew it would be a red-letter day in the fall racing season. Bob McMeans had a horse he wanted me to ride, Got You Runnin, in the Juvenile Fillies. This would be not only my first Breeders' Cup experience, but also my first exposure on national TV. My family and all of my friends at home would be seeing it.

Riding in the Breeders' Cup would also be my first opportunity to compete with Angel Cordero, Jr., a jockey I had never met, though I had grown up watching him ride on TV. He was a competitive jockey known to take great risks, not only to himself and his reputation but also to horses and other riders—a reputation brought home to me when I rode with him that day. Cordero was in a heated battle with Chris McCarron for first place in the national standings that year; each wanted to best the other for the top-money title. This only added to the expected pressures of Breeders' Cup day. When the starting gate sprang open, Got You Runnin jumped out quickly; I knew my filly had a lot of speed. Cordero was on the front-runner, but we began moving up on the outside to challenge for the lead.

We were only about fifty yards out of the gate when Cordero began dropping over, moving closer and closer to the path my filly and I were taking. I knew that Cordero liked to ride tight—to be real close to his nearest rival—but that day, he wasn't riding close so much as he was coming over to join me. I kept thinking to myself, *He's going to stop coming over, he's going to stop coming over,* but the fact is, he didn't. By moving me farther and farther out, he would force my filly to run farther to cover the same distance on the track, so I held my ground and we clipped heels: my filly's front feet actually connected with his horse's hind heels, and my horse stumbled. It's amazing how the mind works at such times, for I found myself thinking, *This can't be happening on national TV!*

Mercifully, when Got You Runnin went down, she didn't fall. She picked herself up right away, but we were well up the track when the race ended. The racing stewards, watching the race unfold, lodged an inquiry, and Cordero was summoned to a hearing the following day. Depending on its outcome, he could receive a penalty—a fine or a temporary suspension from riding. Cordero, at his disarming best, turned to me immediately. "Hey, Poppy," he said—he called everybody Poppy—"you know I didn't do that on purpose. Can you come with me to the stewards and help me get out of it?" I felt trapped. Who was I, just a kid getting started, to say no to Angel Cordero? I said I would go and knew that I would have to lie for him. He didn't want a suspension; it would cost him the national money title. He was a seasoned rider, and I, at twenty-one, was still virtually a novice. A lot was at stake for both of us, and I was really scared.

We went into the hearing together. One of the head stewards looked at me and he looked at Cordero. Finally, he said, "Gary, if you don't want to be here, you don't have to be," so I gladly got up and left. Cordero did receive a penalty: a five-day suspension that put him about a thousand dollars behind McCarron for the money title. Even so, I was angry, but it was impossible to stay angry at Angel for long.

The truth is, what he did to me that day at Hollywood Park, he did to other riders all the time. He was the type of guy who could do anything to you on the track, and you would be boiling mad when you came back. But he would always look at you, pleadingly, with some kind of excuse, and you couldn't stay mad at him for more than ten seconds. He could completely rape you out on the racetrack and you'd be upset, but when he came back . . . you just couldn't stay angry. He retired from riding at the end of the eighties and eventually became a jockey's agent. After my winning ride on Point Given in the 2001 Belmont Stakes, he came to our hotel to cele-brate with Bob Baffert and me. That gesture was classic Cordero.

It turned out that my agent was right in suggesting I go to Southern California, despite my initial run-in with Cordero, and at the same time he was wrong. What was supposed to be a six-month working vacation in the Southland turned out to be a whole new phase in my life. I didn't know it then, but I would never go back to the Northwest to race.

6 *Southland Sojourn*

*A*rcadia, California, is known not only for Santa Anita Park racetrack but also for its ancient oaks. They are considered landmarks; it's illegal to cut any down. The Oak Tree Racing Association also makes its home in Arcadia. Every autumn, it leases Santa Anita for a thirty-day season before racing resumes at Hollywood Park, in Inglewood, for about a sixty-day period, until the winter season gets under way at Santa Anita around Christmastime.

I was looking forward to going back to Southern California. I was twenty-one, relaxed in my life, with money in the bank. I figured I would go down there and give it a shot—see what happened in the wintertime. Toni and I had purchased five acres of land in Renton, Washington, and hired an architect to design a four-bedroom house for us. We planned to break ground the following March. That was to be our permanent home.

Toni had become pregnant again the previous winter. On September 11, 1984, our first son, Tory Chad Stevens, was born. He was just a few weeks old when we set out for Southern California. There was a great deal of chaos involved in the move: we hadn't arranged in advance for a place to live but assumed we would find an apartment as soon as we arrived. Not so. Some apartment complexes had a no-dogs edict (we had left ours temporarily with Mom and Dad in Boise); others wouldn't allow children. Everybody seemed to have a reason why we couldn't have an apartment, so we camped out at the Santa Anita Inn for a month until we finally landed a rental in Monrovia, adjacent to Arcadia. It would be several months before we found a house to buy on Fifth Avenue in Arcadia, about three miles from the racetrack.

Meanwhile, my return to Southland racing had a promising start. The very first horse I rode was Sharper One, and he was set for the feature race on a weekday afternoon. Charging Falls, a very good sprinter, was the 3–5 favorite; I think Sharper One went off at about 10–1. I had a lot more confidence in this horse than the handicappers or the bettors; winning that race was great for me. In my first week, I think I rode ten horses and won on six of them. That picked people's heads up.

On Saturday the following week, Pat Valenzuela took off all of his mounts, the start of a growing problem that would plague him for the rest of his career. Trainer Mel Stute had four horses scheduled to run that day and had hired Valenzuela to ride each of them. I had no mounts lined up for any of those races. Stute had taken notice of me and told the clerk of scales to go ahead and put me on those horses. That was the break I needed. All four of them won. I had a four-bagger at Santa Anita, which was just about the ultimate.

Within about three weeks, I knew I wasn't going back to Seattle, so plans for the house in Renton were scrapped. We just held on to the property. When the Oak Tree meeting ended, I found myself fifth in the jockey standings, which for a neophyte was kind of incredible. I had similar success at Hollywood Park. By the time the new year began, I felt certain that I would be the leading rider in Southern California in 1985. I believed that success breeds success, and the more I won, the more I was going to win.

My first really significant win was in the San Luis Obispo Stakes, a Grade II race at Santa Anita, where I rode a horse named Westerner. His trainer was Lazaro Barrera, the man who had trained Affirmed. Winning that race cemented my relationship with Laz forever. I was riding for Charlie Whittingham and D. Wayne Lukas at the time, but Laz was the first top trainer to give me carte blanche to ride any horse in his stable. It really helps business when a Hall of Fame trainer like Laz Barrera starts choosing you on a regular basis. All of the other trainers and owners become aware when you've earned the confidence of a great man willing to give you his best horses. At that time, Laz had one of the most successful training stables in the United States. Wayne had started using me on some of his lesser horses by then, too. Ray Kravagna, my agent, had to work hard to keep the Lukas and Barrera horses separated, but I would say that Laz had more impact on my career than any trainer I have ever ridden for. He gave me my first shot at the big time. We never, ever had a falling out.

In April, Wayne phoned my agent to ask if I would ride one of his star three-year-olds, Tank's Prospect, in the Arkansas Derby. With a half-million-dollar purse, it would be the biggest race that I had been asked to ride in terms of prize money; it was also a major prep race for the Kentucky Derby. Riding for Wayne at that time was an important career boost. Raised on a Wisconsin dairy farm, he had been coaching high school basketball when, like my father, he began training quarter horses as a sideline. Eventually, the racetrack replaced the basketball court as his focal point, and he moved from training quarter horses to Thoroughbreds. He was a fast-rising star in the early eighties. In 1990, he would become the first trainer to saddle winners of $100 million; in 1999 the first to score $200 million.

I was ecstatic about riding Tank's Prospect in the Arkansas Derby, despite rumors I began hearing that the horse had problems. I remember walking out of the jockeys' room at Santa Anita carrying my equipment, the day before I was supposed to leave for Oaklawn Park. "Where are you off to?" Darrel McHargue asked. "The Arkansas Derby," I said proudly. "Who are you riding?" When I told him, he shook his head: "What are you goin' to ride him for? He's got no chance." McHargue had ridden Tank's Prospect in his previous race and either hadn't chosen to ride him again or had been taken off the horse by the trainer, for whatever reason. "Watch yourself," he said.

No rider takes such a warning casually. When a jockey tells you to be careful, it usually means that he has ridden the horse you're about to ride and something might not be right. The horse might not be sound. It's kind of an unspoken rule: if you ride a horse you don't like the feel of, the next time that horse runs, you tell the rider to be careful. *Be suspicious, look after yourself.*

Despite McHargue's warning, I flew to Oaklawn Park in Hot Springs, on the heels of bad weather. The track was muddy. Even so, Tank's Prospect warmed up well and moved out swiftly when the race began. I was in midpack, coming into the stretch, but I knew I had a handful of horse. I was stalking the front-runners, the same kind of trip that I've had winning all of my classic races. Tank's Prospect went on to win by daylight. Had I known who was going to greet me in the winner's circle that April day in 1985, I would have been a lot more impressed. It was the governor of Arkansas and his wife, Bill and Hillary Clinton.

But the thought that crossed my mind as I flashed under the finish line was that in three weeks, I would be riding my first Kentucky Derby. That was a dream come true—the dream of every young kid who chooses to become a jockey: *Maybe someday I'll ride in the Kentucky Derby.* At least for me, the dream wasn't so much winning the Kentucky Derby as wanting to experience it. I was eager to know what it was like.

I wanted to treat it like any other race, but the press wouldn't let me. Once it was confirmed that I was going to ride Tank's Prospect in the Derby, newspaper and TV reporters descended on me. I was bombarded. It was the first time I had been exposed to that kind of press. I also felt the hot breath of competition, for when I returned to California, I found that every top jockey, from Angel Cordero, Jr., to Chris McCarron, was trying to get the mount on Tank's Prospect for the big race.

Eugene Klein owned the horse. He was the previous owner of the San Diego Chargers, and he had the reputation of being a very difficult boss, a man who made many harsh and rash decisions. Lukas told him that I had ridden his colt perfectly in the Arkansas Derby and that I fit Tank's Prospect to a tee. "That's fine with me," Mr. Klein said, and with his sanction, Wayne said he would give me the opportunity to ride the colt at Churchill Downs. Despite the talk that I was going to be replaced, which I was hearing the week following my Oaklawn victory, I secured the mount. Wayne told my agent that I had the call for the Kentucky Derby. It was a contract signed with a handshake. You can't renege on it, for if you do, you'll be called before the stewards and there will be problems.

Toni and I took a red-eye flight to Louisville, Kentucky, two days before the Derby. In the three weeks prior to the race, I was getting a lot of press, but it was nothing compared to what I would get in later years when I was riding a legitimate favorite. Tank's Prospect had a chance to win the Derby, but he wasn't the bettors' choice.

On Derby Day, I remember being in the jocks' room about twenty minutes before we walked out to the paddock. We had already weighed in for the race. Bill Shoemaker came up to me and said, "When they start playing 'My Old Kentucky Home,' you're going to get a lump in your throat and have tears coming down your cheeks. Don't worry about it. It happens to me every year." I thought to myself, *That's not going to happen to me,* and I climbed aboard Tank's Prospect; we circled the paddock, then walked out onto the racetrack. The band started playing "My Old Kentucky Home." People in the stands were singing. Suddenly, I found myself thinking how far I had come from Les Bois Park. I thought about my mom and dad and everything that had happened to me in my life, from the time I was a kid, and here I was at Churchill Downs for the first time, on national TV. It was a pretty special feeling. The tears came, just as Shoemaker had said.

Now I knew I had to compose myself. As the song ended and the pre-race warmup began, I started focusing on what my strategy would be. Basically, I wanted a forward position, to be in the first pack of horses, though not on the lead. Tank's Prospect broke a tad slower than I would have liked. I didn't get the exact position I wanted, but I was all right. I was between the front pack of horses and the second flight. I thought I had a good stalking position, but I didn't have a feeling of confidence that day. The colt didn't give me the same signals he had given me in the Arkansas Derby. Turning into the stretch, I knew we weren't going to win. I was riding hard, but the horse was staying pretty much where he was. He wasn't giving me a good feel, the way he was striking the ground. I didn't like what I was experiencing—an odd kind of unbalance.

When I rode him in the Arkansas Derby, Tank's Prospect had had the most magnificent strides that I had ever felt underneath me. He was completely balanced then, and it was almost as if his feet weren't touching the ground. Now he was hitting the ground very hard, but there was nothing I could put my finger on—no specific weakness that I could detect in his left-front or right-rear leg, for example. He finished seventh. I came back after the race with no excuse. I felt I had given him a good ride and had given him every opportunity to win the race, but the win just wasn't there. The magic of the Kentucky Derby wasn't with me that day, but I knew one thing when the race ended: this wasn't going to be my last Kentucky Derby. By riding in the Derby, I had reached one goal; now, I felt that this was a race I would have to win. That was the attitude I had when I left the track that day.

After I returned to California, I was riding a filly named Deal Price for owner Leonard Lavin of Glen Hill Farms. I won four consecutive races on her, and when word reached us that Wayne Lukas was going to skip the Preakness and run Tank's Prospect three weeks later in the Belmont Stakes, that suited me fine. I hadn't liked the way Tank's Prospect had felt to me on Derby Day, and skipping the Preakness was a way to avoid a conflict: my next ride on Deal Price—at Hollywood Park—was to occur on Preakness day. My agent and I gave the filly's trainer, Hap Practor, a commitment.

Three days later, Wayne announced that he was going to go ahead and run Tank's Prospect after all. He said he had found the colt's problem, though he didn't say specifically what it was. As far as he was concerned, the animal was training great. At that point, I couldn't cancel my commitment to ride Deal Price, so Pat Day picked up the mount on Tank's Prospect.

I rode Deal Price early on Preakness day. The fact that I won that race didn't soothe the feelings I was about to experience. I remember sitting in front of the TV in the jocks' room with a group of riders watching the Preakness Stakes unfold at Pimlico. Three-eighths of a mile from the finish, I heard myself say, "The son-of-a-bitch is going to win!" And he did, of course. I hadn't wished him to run poorly, but I knew my not being there was going to make me look bad. Indeed, everyone assumed—and it had been announced on TV—that Gary Stevens had been replaced by Pat Day. That's how the change was reported; no one except those closest to me knew the full circumstances. What came across was that, with Pat Day on his back, the horse had improved measurably in the two weeks between the Kentucky Derby and the Preakness.

Three weeks later, Pat Day rode Tank's Prospect again in the Belmont Stakes. The colt was favored to win, but an eighth of a mile from the finish line, he suffered a tendon injury and had to be vanned off the track. It was his last race. I'm just speculating, but it's an educated guess that the colt had injured himself in the Kentucky Derby and the trainer got one more good race out of him in the Preakness. Having to run a mile and one-half against top three-year-olds in the Belmont aggravated a serious problem that may have been building up.

Tendon injuries are really serious. When someone asks a trainer what's wrong with his horse, and he says, "Oh, he's got a little tendon on him," it's like being told a woman is a little bit pregnant. Either you have a bad tendon or you don't—you're pregnant or you're not. A tendon is in-elastic tissue that connects muscle to bone. In a horse, it runs down the back legs, and when it tears it's more than just sore. In humans it's like straining the Achilles tendon and is extremely painful. The Achilles tendon supports the whole structure of the leg from the knee down.

An athlete will *tell* you when something is wrong. With a horse, it often takes a practiced eye to figure it out. Only someone with years of experience can spot a tendon that's torn, and only when the horse is standing still. Then you can see that the tendon is bowed; it actually curves out where the tear occurs. Once a tendon tears, the horse's racing years are history. Very few horses come back to the track after suffering a bowed tendon.

When Point Given strained a tendon after a dramatic Travers at Saratoga in the summer of 2001, his trainer and owner were criticized for making the decision to retire him. A lot of people said, in effect, that Bob Baffert and Prince Ahmed were too wrapped up in the money aspect of breeding—why didn't they just give the horse four months off and try him again? The reason was that Point Given had suffered a strain that might not have healed correctly, or at all, if not given the proper amount of time off from training and running, and there was no telling how much time would actually be needed. Many horsemen will tell you that once there is a strain, it doesn't matter how much time you devote to healing, the problem is bound to recur. A strain means there is a weakness that is probably going to turn into a tear, which would most definitely be career-ending and could be life-threatening as well. Point Given was much too valuable to take such a risk.

I was saddened and distressed by what had happened with Tank's Prospect, but I had learned by then to look ahead and not sulk about an unhappy situation. There were other things for me to focus on, other races for me to ride. When Hollywood Park finished up in July, I made my first visit to the Del Mar racetrack, near San Diego, which I had heard so much about. I had looked forward to being there and had a very successful meet. It started out a bit slow, but by the end of the meeting, I think I wound up the third-leading rider, which was the highest rank I had achieved till then in Southland racing.

Toni and I were living in Solano Beach, a little town right next door to the racetrack. Our rented condo was on top of a cliff overlooking the Pacific Ocean. It was a beautiful place. Both children were with us. We had an Olympic-size swimming pool at our disposal, tennis courts, beach access, everything. We were starting to live a little bit of the high life. For us, it was a really nice, enjoyable summer. The disappointment of not riding in the Preakness faded in the bright California sun.

7 *Hitting the Fence*

$\mathcal{W}$e returned to Arcadia, California, between the end of the Del Mar racing season and the start of the Oak Tree meeting at Santa Anita. Usually there's a break of about nineteen days. When racing resumed, it was my goal to be the leading rider in the thirty-day meet, and I started out well with several winners the first week. I was in first place with a lot of momentum behind me. It seemed things were just getting better and better.

I was supposed to work a horse for Laz Barrera at 8 A.M. one morning, but Mike Chambers asked if I could change my schedule. Mike, a trainer friend from my Seattle racing days, told me, "There's an old trainer named Marlon Horton in the barn behind mine who has a few horses. He says he has this nice filly that he thinks can really run. I've watched her train. Could you do me a favor and get on this guy's horse for me? See what you think." I said that, of course, I would. I got permission from Laz to work his horse at 8:15 and arranged to work for Mr. Horton at 8.

His filly's name was Irish Kristen, and she had never run a race before. Mr. Horton wanted to get her qualified out of the starting gate, which meant that she had to have two registered workouts coming out of the starting gate before she would be allowed to run in her first race. I mounted and took her over to the gate. When I went into the gate, Tucker Slender, the starter, told me, "You'd better put your whip in your left hand. They had this filly over here yesterday, and she tried to turn the wrong way up the racetrack when she came out of the gate. So get your stick in your left hand and be ready for her."

"Yeah, yeah, yeah," I said, but I did put my stick in my left hand. When the gate opened, Irish Kristen blasted out. There was traffic coming toward us, other horses being trained. The riders were waiting for me to come out of the starting gate and join in the flow of traffic; this was planned as a timed workout. Official. When the filly flew out of the gate, she made a left-hand turn to go the wrong way up the racetrack. Her hard left happened about halfway across the gap where the six-furlong chute met up with the main track. But running at quarter horse speed, she was going too fast to make a complete left turn. I wanted to get off but didn't. I don't know if I froze in my seat or just couldn't get off. Throughout my career, I've had a hard time jumping off a horse going forty miles an hour.

When Irish Kristen hooked left, my saddle shifted to the right side, and now both of my feet were caught in the stirrups and I *couldn't* get off. When she hit the inside rail flush with her chest, I flew off full blast. She was unhurt, but I was just ripped into the fence. From the time we left the gate until the moment I hit the rail took about four seconds—that's how fast we were going. If we had run a full quarter mile, we probably would have been clocked at 21.4 seconds; in an actual race, a 24-second quarter mile is like par in golf; in a workout, 21.4 seconds is almost unheard of.

The last thing I remember was going off one side of Irish Kristen and slamming into the rails. I blacked out. I don't know how much time passed, but when I briefly regained consciousness, I was already strapped to a gurney to be loaded into an ambulance. Two riders were there with me, Sandy Hawley and Jack Kaenel—"Cowboy Jack" Kaenel. They had gotten off their horses and I remember hearing Jack say, "Oh, my God, he's got blood coming out of his ears." I knew what had happened to me, but I didn't know what was going on. As the attendants went to put me in the ambulance, my right arm was hanging behind me and got caught on the door. Then Sandy was shouting, "Hold on, hold on, you got his fuckin' arm caught in the door." They put my arm on my chest and slammed the ambulance doors. That was the last thing I remembered.

I woke up in the Intensive Care Unit at Methodist Hospital, and Toni was there with the doctor. They asked me if I knew what had happened, and I said, *"Yes, my horse hade a heff-hand hurn out of the hate."* The doc-

tor looked at Toni and asked, "Does your husband have a speech impedi-
ment?" She said, "He never did before." A CAT scan of my brain was or-
dered immediately. The doctor then asked if I knew what time it was, and
in some kind of jumbled language, I said that it had to be about 9:30. After
all, I had planned to work that filly at 8 in the morning, so by then it had to
be at least 9:30. Yes, they said, it *was* about 9:30, but it was 9:30 at night. I
had been unconscious for thirteen hours.

That conversation was the first thing I recalled after being put into
the ambulance. Then I was unconscious again. When I awoke, the extent
of my injuries was explained to me. My right shoulder was dislocated, and
I was going to need surgery. My right knee was basically destroyed—cartilage, ligaments—and would need surgery. And that was the good news.
The bad news was that the inner eardrum of my right ear had been punc-
tured and I had suffered a severe concussion. My doctor described it as a
mini stroke, which was why my speech was affected. Other doctors examined me to determine the extent of my head injuries. They didn't know if
my speech would ever come back. The good thing, they said, was that I
was still alive, but they didn't know if I was ever going to ride again.

Then a weird thing happened. It seems that one of the public handicappers had been filming workouts at the track that morning—not unusual
for a professional—and had captured my accident on videotape. It was
October, when the baseball playoffs took place. When I regained consciousness that first evening at Methodist Hospital, the playoffs were on
TV. The news came on, and then the sports segment, which showed my accident as part of the news. Talk about strange! I thought somebody had
had a hit on me or something, but it was chance that the handicapper
caught that moment on video. The video allowed me to see my own accident, but I couldn't see how I fell or what I hit. Obviously, I had hit the
fence with my right side.

I spent thirteen days at Methodist Hospital in Arcadia, then was trans-
ferred by ambulance to Centinela Hospital in Inglewood. By that time,
Dr. Robert Kurland was involved. He was a renowned orthopedic sur-

geon and also a good friend of Angel Cordero's. He was affiliated with Centinela Hospital, which is why I was sent there, but because of the swelling in my head he couldn't operate on me right away. It took two days for me to stabilize before the surgery. I was placed under anesthesia and both surgical procedures were done at the same time: right shoulder and right knee.

I was started on rehab almost immediately. It was brutal. Dr. Kurland had a physiotherapist named Clive, who was a slave driver. He was as tough as a football coach, the Vince Lombardi of therapists. Within a week of my operations, he had me on a stationary bike; he also had me lifting very light weights, about one ounce each, to strengthen my right arm. He told me it was going to be at least six months before I could ride, *if* I was ever going to ride again.

I worked my tail off, probably doing too much. I've always been like that. If I was told to do twenty minutes on the stationary bike, I did forty minutes. If I was told to do three sets of ten arm lifts, I would do twenty sets. I really, really pushed myself; I wanted so much to get back to riding. Of course, there were still doubts in people's minds about whether I was going to ride again. People at the racetrack believed I was washed up, but I wouldn't hear of it; there was no way.

I was at Centinela Hospital about ten days and within a few weeks was back at Hollywood Park, but just as a visitor. My speech didn't come back for about six months, and I really had to work at it. Even to this day, when I get tired, I'll begin slurring my words and they become a bit jumbled. My tongue gets a little thick on me at times. A slight lisp that's audible now and then was caused by that accident.

I had been out of the hospital about four months and frequently visiting Hollywood Park when Laz Barrera came up to me and said, "When're you gonna be able to ride?" "Probably in another month," I replied. I hadn't even started galloping horses in the morning yet. "Next week," he said, "I'm running a filly for the first time that I think will win the Kentucky Oaks, and I want you to ride her."

"Laz," I insisted, "I haven't even been on a horse, you know. I'm not going to be ready!"

"Believe me," he said, "this filly is somethin' really special. I want you to ride her. All you gotta do is hang on."

So being the way I am, I told him I would do it. I think I worked about five horses in five days. I wasn't really scared—there's an old saying that if you're scared and can admit you're scared, it's time to quit riding—but I was apprehensive. I still couldn't raise my right arm all the way above my head, and my right knee was very, very stiff; I couldn't bend it more than 85 percent of the amount that was needed to ride. I had started hardcore rehabilitation so that I *could* be back riding in a month, so in terms of my muscle tone and cardiovascular functions, I was fit. But as I hadn't been riding, I knew my timing was going to be off, and of course I was still very sore.

Laz continued to be insistent; that's how much he thought of me. I went ahead and accepted the mount. The filly's name was Tiffany Lass, and I won on her. She came back immediately and won the Landaluce Stakes at Hollywood Park, and from there was shipped to a barn in New Orleans run by Laz's brother, Luis Barrera. At the Fair Grounds, she won an allowance race, then went on to win the New Orleans Oaks. Ricky Frazier was riding her in that one. Her next race was going to be the Fantasy Stakes at Oaklawn in Hot Springs. Laz said he wanted to take Frazier off of her and bring me to the race in Arkansas. That didn't go over very well with Frazier or his agent, but it happened. Tiffany Lass won the Fantasy Stakes, so her next race would be the Kentucky Oaks, which was the filly equivalent of the Derby and in 1986 probably one of the greatest races I'd ever been in.

We were in a head-and-head battle all the way down the stretch, although I can't remember who was second. Few winners ever remember who finished second, but according to official records it was Life at the Top that day. The Kentucky Oaks was my first Grade I victory. For me to win a major race like that the day before the Kentucky Derby really put me on the map.

* * *

I remember the first time I rode Tiffany Lass, coming back to racing after my accident. I was in the jocks' room, in the shower, by myself, still feeling apprehensive. I had won the race but still didn't know if I was ever going to be what I had been physically. I had lost a lot of confidence. Bill Shoemaker came in. He saw me in the shower, struggling to lift my right arm. "Don't worry," he said. "You're gonna be all right. In two months, you're gonna be back where you were." He was right. I was back near the top of the standings and never really looked back.

The accident had been painful and debilitating, but all in all a good experience for me. It taught me that I was resilient and made me realize that I would probably have to experience many falls throughout my career with as many races as I was riding. I was learning to endure pain and to be patient about healing. Most of my injuries have been the result of wear and tear, the daily rigors of riding. But, year-round, the law of averages has dictated that I would have my share of spills and that coming back from injury was going to be part of my life.

From that time on, I knew I could rebound from anything.

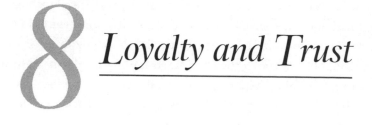

8 *Loyalty and Trust*

*L*az Barrera was and continues to be an important part of my life. If I ever idolized anyone in Thoroughbred racing, it was Laz. I didn't actually ride for him until I had settled in Southern California in 1984 but had met him on my first brief stay there, when I was still an apprentice. He once said that he'd remembered me then, but I don't think he did. Saying that was just a Laz mannerism. He could paint these beautiful pictures that weren't always true to life. Putting it into perspective, I can imagine going fishing with Laz and seeing him catch a twelve-inch bass. By the time you'd get home, he would be telling everyone he'd caught a swordfish. He could concoct elaborate stories.

When I first came to Southern California, I rode horses for Laz's son Albert, who was also a trainer. I remember being in awe that I was riding a horse for Laz Barrera, because at that time Laz was very powerful. He had a lot of horses in his stable, and every time he led one in to be saddled, that horse had a good chance of winning. I don't remember the name of the first horse I rode for him, but I do recall that it was in an allowance race and that the horse was not favored to win. He had raced several times and was not running very well. When I won on that horse, it was a highlight for me.

What struck me most was being hired by a man responsible for training a Triple Crown winner. Affirmed had won the Kentucky Derby, Preakness Stakes, and Belmont Stakes in 1978, one of only eleven horses so far to have performed that feat. I was in awe of Affirmed, too, although I never actually saw him race. I watched his Triple Crown campaign on

TV, of course, and developed a high regard for his rider, Steve Cauthen. I'll never forget seeing Cauthen pictured on the cover of *Sports Illustrated* under the headline THE NEW $6,000,000 MAN. When he appeared on *Time* magazine's cover, with a cigar hanging out of his mouth and a tear coming down his cheek, I thought, *Man, this kid's only a few years older than I am, and look what he's done!* Cauthen retired from racing after riding successfully in England, which is where I finally rode with him. He'd really had an impact on my decision to become a jockey.

What sealed my relationship with Laz Barrera occurred after I had ridden a couple of winners for him. I had the mount on his horse Westerner in the San Luis Obispo Stakes at Santa Anita in 1985. The colt was not favored to win. Laz was out of the country at the time, on a Mediterranean cruise. When he returned, he told the story of how two women from Idaho, who were also on the ship, had learned somehow that Western and I had won the San Luis Obispo. I don't know how they got word that we had, but they were the ones who passed the news to Laz. Our relationship was solid when he came back from that cruise. From then on, I was his number-one rider. He was the first hall of fame trainer I rode for, the first big-time racing professional who showed enough confidence in me to put me on his best horses—not just his allowance-type runners, but graded-stakes winners, the top horses in his barn.

Laz's loyalty didn't really show itself to me, however, until the following summer at Del Mar. Bill Shoemaker had been riding a horse for him named First Norman that was scheduled to ride in the Del Mar Derby, one of the big stakes races of the season. Shoe had had to sit out a temporary suspension imposed by the racing steward because of some infraction, and he was not available to ride First Norman in an important prep race. I rode him instead and won on him.

It was customary for a rider of Shoemaker's stature to expect to assume the ride again when that horse ran his next race, even though another jockey had won on him. But Laz gave me First Norman in the Del Mar Derby. It was a pretty straightforward race, and I won it easily, but for me, getting to ride First Norman was a true sign of Laz Barrera's support.

Another trainer who had been a loyal supporter was Mike Chambers, with whom I'd had a long-standing relationship since my Seattle days. The friendship had even survived his request that I work Irish Kristen for Mr. Horton. In 1985, Chambers had a horse named Hilco Scamper that he said was the best horse he had ever trained. Then a two-year-old, Hilco Scamper had won his first race in Seattle under Gary Baze. Then Russell Baze rode him. When Mike brought him to Hollywood Park for the Hollywood Juvenile Championship, he put me on him. We won that race and other juvenile events that year, because Hilco Scamper was one of the fastest sprinters I'd ever ridden. He had more natural speed coming out of the starting gate than any quarter horse I'd been on. He was not only quick out of the gate, but responsive as well—you could do whatever you wanted with him. He was strong, and also a very honest horse.

An injury he incurred at the end of the racing season interrupted Hilco Scamper's career, keeping him out of competition during his entire third year. When he came back to the track as a four-year-old, he couldn't compete at the top level, which included the best sprinters in racing at six furlongs. He was raced against quarter horses, instead. I rode him twice against them at Los Alamitos, near Anaheim, California. Those races were part of a match series for mixed-breed horses. They raced the standard quarter horse distance, 870 yards, and Hilco Scamper won the series. But the horse was significant to me mainly because of my relationship with Chambers.

Tsunami Slew was another ground-breaking horse for me, far different from Hilco Scamper or any other mount I'd had. His sire was Seattle Slew, a previous Triple Crown winner, and he had Seattle Slew's temperament: he was hot-blooded and not the easiest ride in the world. I knew that no one had been able to get along with him, but when his trainer, Eddie Gregson, asked me to work him one morning, I said yes. When I came back after the workout, I asked Eddie how this horse was ever beaten. He just smiled at me and acknowledged that the horse and I got along very well. Knowing that I recognized Tsunami Slew's ability, Gregson put me on him. After I'd won one race with him, I was given the mount in the Eddie Read Handicap at Del Mar, which may have been my first Grade I win—a quality victory. We won it wire to wire, leading all the way.

Tsunami Slew was a free-running type of horse. Before a race, I would warm him up without the usual accompaniment of an outrider on a lead pony. When he was around other horses, regardless of gender, he would become very studdish. He would get nervous, begin to sweat, and refuse to concentrate. He would get so twitchy and use so much energy, he would tire himself out—basically running his race before the starting gate even opened. That's why I worked him alone on the track. I was supposed to ride him in the Breeders' Cup at New York's Aqueduct racetrack, but 1985 was the year I hit the fence. The accident kept me out of Breeders' Cup competition that year. In 1986, Breeders' Cup racing took place at Santa Anita. It proved one of the most lucrative but disappointing days I'd ever had. I rode in every race but the Sprint, coming in second and third much of the time, but I didn't have a single win. The only real contender I had was Precisionist in the biggest race of the day, the Classic. I had won on him in a major prep race. I had also won on Turkoman, the post-time favorite. Both horses had been Chris McCarron's mounts, but he was recovering from a broken leg and wasn't able to ride.

Twenty-four hours before the Marlboro Cup Race at Belmont Park earlier that fall, I had received a phone call at Del Mar, asking me if I could fly east to ride Turkoman the next day. I jumped on a plane for New York, rode Turkoman for the first time and won. I picked up the mount on Precisionist the same way, because of Chris's injury. Both horses were pointed toward the Breeders' Cup. As both were still his mounts, I knew that whichever one he chose *not* to ride, I would be riding in the Classic.

My choice between the two horses would have been the same as McCarron's: Turkoman. I had more confidence in him, but after Chris made his choice, I committed to ride Precisionist. About a week before the event, Chris reinjured himself. He knew he would still be in too much pain to ride the Breeders' Cup, so Pat Day got the mount. I was sick that I wouldn't be on Turkoman. I think the trainer, Gary Jones, was sick about it, too, because Turkoman was a horse that not only needed to be ridden with patience but also with a strong finish. He was a very physical ride. Jones knew that Turkoman and I were a good fit. Having committed to ride another horse, however, I couldn't get off. Precisionist was completely the opposite of Turkoman. He was a speed horse trying to maintain his speed and needed to be ridden with finesse, not physical prowess. The race began, and Jerry Bailey, on a horse named Herag, made the lead going into the first turn. That kind of shut me off. I had to steady a bit, coming off of heels, and that pretty much took me out of the race. I was boxed in on the rail and never really got loose until the head of the stretch. Then as soon as I did, Laffit Pincay on Skywalker came along on the outside and passed me; then Turkoman came from a long way back to finish a fast-closing second. I have always wondered if, had the circumstances been different going into the first turn, I might have won the Classic on Precisionist. I'm certain I would have won if I'd been on Turkoman—he was much farther back than he probably would have been, had I been on him. But that's hindsight, of course.

I still think back to my second Kentucky Derby, in 1986, and recall how certain I was that I was going to win it. I was riding Wheatly Hall for trainer Jack Van Berg. Coming into the stretch, we were about six lengths off of the lead. Bill Shoemaker was right next to me, riding Ferdinand. Being on the inside, toward the rail, he'd had a ground-saving trip the whole way. We were about a quarter of a mile from the finish, when he drew alongside me. There was a wall of horses in front of us, and an opening with room for one horse. At that point, Ferdinand had more acceleration than Wheatly Hall, so Shoemaker beat us to the punch. I actually had to steady my horse to keep from clipping heels with the horses in front of us, while Shoe got through the gap and went on to win the race. I finished sixth that day. In the aftermath, Wheatly Hall went pretty much unnoticed; no one ever talked about his performance. But to this day, I feel that if I had been the one to get through the opening, we'd have won the race. We didn't, of course; that just shows how lucky you have to be to win the Kentucky Derby. And you get only one chance a year.

Nineteen eighty-six was one of the first years I found myself having to choose from among several top horses for big races. I've had to do that often since then, and a lot of times, politics are involved. For example, one reason I'd rather have ridden Turkoman in the Breeders' Cup races was that Gary Jones, the trainer, had about seventy-five horses in his care, whereas Ross Fenstermaker, Precisionist's trainer, had only fifteen. Often, when I choose one horse over another, racing handicappers assume that I've made my choice based on what, in my eyes, is the best horse. That's not always true. Much of the time, I'm basing my decision on whom I'm riding for at the time.

Just before my temporary retirement in 1999, I was riding a lot of horses for Bob Baffert. I knew that often I wasn't riding the best horses, but I made this choice, knowing I had to make the Baffert camp happy. Similarly, prior to the Breeders' Cup races in 2001, I had to choose between Gander and Macho Uno in the Classic, a difficult decision. My heart was telling me to ride Gander; my brain was telling me the correct move was to ride Macho Uno, because I felt that his owner, Frank Stronach, was more likely to come up with another champion than Gander's trainer, John Terranova. Obviously, if I had been convinced that either of those horses had a stone-cold lock on winning the Classic, that's the mount I would readily have chosen. But I was trying to be a realist; it looked as though either of them would have to be very lucky to win (and neither did). Instead I based my decision on what I thought was going to do the most for my future. That's how I make a lot of these decisions.

Usually, before I ride a horse I do my homework, and my agent does his homework, too. I study films all the time and keep track of what's happening at the major racetracks around the country. I look to see which horses are improving and which are regressing. When there is a big race somewhere, I'll watch it on TV. I look carefully at most of the top horses just in case I happen to pick up one of them as a mount. When I ride European horses, I'll usually get tapes of their racing performances prior to riding them. My homework involves not only the horses I'm riding but the competition, as well. I want to find out, *What do I have to know about this horse to beat him?*

Despite the disappointments and the layoff caused by what was—and remains—the most serious injury of my career, I actually had a good year in 1986. I earned more than I ever had before—six or seven million dollars in purses, at least—but it took most of that year for me to fully regain my confidence. That was the mental challenge; the physical part was the gradual absence of pain. I finally stopped hurting. I was no longer taking medication or getting physical therapy. I stayed fit and kept my weight down by working: galloping horses in the morning and riding in the afternoon. I would get up, go to the track, work seven or eight horses, go straight to the jocks' room, ride seven or eight races, go home, and go to sleep. That was my life and how I had chosen to live it.

My memory of 1987 is clouded by my recollection of Bedside Promise, a really neat horse based in Northern California. I went to Bay Meadows many times to ride him; we won several big races together. He was six or seven, an old campaigner that wasn't supposed to be as good as he was: a horse that hated to be beaten. He was an overachiever with a great personality, and he was such a fighter when he raced. He would give everything he had and then some, which ultimately was his undoing. He basically killed himself running.

We were at Bay Meadows riding in what was being used as a prep race for the upcoming Breeders' Cup Classic. Bedside Promise was the odds-on favorite to win; there wasn't much competition for him. But from the moment the race began, I felt him struggling underneath me. I didn't know why. He was traveling fine, but he wasn't giving me a feeling of confidence. We were laying second when we turned into the homestretch, but he just wasn't making his typical aggressive moves. Throughout the race I kept thinking, *Okay, he's going to start taking charge and we're still all right.* But when we hit the eighth pole, it was clear he wasn't giving me the fight that he normally gave me. We finished second.

As we galloped out after the race, he felt as though he were drunk underneath me. I got him pulled up, and I jumped off just as he collapsed. I had a pretty good idea that he'd had a heart attack; instead he had ruptured an artery. His aorta. He bled to death, right on the track, within thirty seconds of my getting off of him. It's never easy to swallow when a horse breaks down and dies or breaks a leg and has to be put down. But Bedside Promise's death really hit home because he was such a fighter and had such a tragic end.

I've had other horses do that since then. It is a strange, unsettling feeling. You sense that something is awry, but you don't know what it is. I remember riding a filly for the trainer Willard Proctor and feeling something odd happening in her hind quarters. She was almost staggering as she ran. She was one of the favorites in the race, and we were laying second, but three-eighths of a mile from the finish, I pulled her up because I thought she had broken down. As I slowed her pace to a trot, however, she seemed sound and it appeared that nothing was wrong. I got off her back and felt like a total ass. *Ah, Willard's gonna kill me for pulling this filly up,* I thought. I walked off the track and found out three races later that, on the way back to the barn, about a quarter of a mile from the racetrack, the filly had keeled over because she was bleeding internally. She just bled to death.

As a jockey, you learn to trust your instincts. If you feel something is not right, you are probably right. Your instinct is to pull the horse up as quickly as possible to prevent further injury. As with the Proctor filly, sometimes I've pulled up horses that don't appear to have anything wrong with them, yet I've felt something was not right—especially with a horse that I've ridden in the past. I know what his action is; I'm aware of how he normally moves. All horses move differently, of course. Some have a rocky way of going, not the prettiest action. There are other horses that move smoothly, but all of a sudden, they feel different to you. They're not hitting the ground the way they have in the past, and it's a warning signal that something is wrong. Maybe it's the way the horse is carrying his head. Or his stride may be a little bit shorter, something a person standing on the ground might not see with the naked eye, but I can feel distinctly. If I've been on a horse before and know what his stride generally feels like, I know within a few seconds of jogging that horse if his stride is different compared to the last time I rode him.

I sometimes have felt like an ass for pulling up a horse even though he appeared to have nothing physically wrong with him, but nine times out of ten, the next time that horse raced something did happen to him physically. Within twenty-four hours, it would show up. When you pull up a horse, you immediately tell the trainer why. Over the years, through experience with the trainers you've ridden for, you have built up such rapport that they trust your instincts. They respond to your action by summoning a vet, having X-rays taken of every joint, examining the horse with something like a fine-toothed comb. When they take every precaution, they usually find something.

Some trainers will just change jockeys if you tell them what they don't want to hear. That's one of the things I hate about this sport and about the relationship between jockeys and some of the trainers who hire them. There are certain trainers who refer to us as pinheads. They think of us as just passengers on their horses' backs. They insist that we don't know anything, and they won't listen to our opinions. That's very frustrating. The reason I feel so strongly about equine soundness is that I'm putting my life in a trainer's hands every time I climb on a horse. To do that, I have to have a certain amount of trust.

There are some trainers I would trust with my life, and others in whom I have no trust at all. So I mainly trust myself. If a Bob Baffert, Richard Mandella, Jack Van Berg, Wayne Lukas, or Neil Drysdale tells me, "Look, this horse is going to feel funny to you when you warm him up, but he always moves like that," I'll believe him. But there are other trainers who might say, "Look, this horse is going to feel a little funny, but don't worry about it," then *boom,* a warning flag goes up, and I say to myself, *Uh-uh,* because I know the guy doesn't care if I wind up in the hospital that afternoon. All he wants me to do is win a race and put some money in the bank. He doesn't care at what cost. A trainer like that will only get me one time. I'll never ride for him again.

All horses can get body sore from traveling or maybe from working on a track they don't handle well, or perhaps they slipped and pulled a muscle. That's what I have to work through in the prerace warmup. Most of the time, I'll be jogging a horse, trying to warm him up for a race, and he may start out a little stiffly. But by the time I gallop a half mile or so, he'll have worked out the kinks and be moving well. If he doesn't work out of it and the stiffness gets worse, that's when you scratch the horse—take him out of the race. You go to the state veterinarian, who is always on the scene, and tell him, "This horse isn't traveling right and I don't want to ride him."

There are always surprises, of course: a sudden misstep, an unde-tected weakness. In the mid-nineties, I was riding a horse named Coup d'Argent in a big race at Belmont Park. The horse was absolutely sound. His stride was perfect as the race progressed, but suddenly he took a bad step. We were at the quarter pole, just entering the stretch. I was beginning to think we had a chance to finish third, and the next thing I knew I was lying on the ground.

Coup d'Argent had fallen. I fell with him, and another horse went over the top of us. There had been no warning; I hadn't felt anything. The horse just dropped out from under me, as though he had been shot with a gun. He had shattered the cannon bone in one of his legs. The wind was knocked out of me, and I guess I was in a state of shock—he had been going so fast and the fall had happened so quickly. Fortunately, I was uninjured, only shaken and a little bruised, but the horse broke his neck when he fell. He died right there on the track.

I never ride with fear. The only real fear I experience now is looking back to when, at sixteen or seventeen, I was riding without really knowing the difference between a sore horse and a sound one. Today, even on horses I've never ridden before, if something isn't right, I feel it instantly and say so. Someone may want me to do a morning workout on a horse I've never been on before. In the middle of a warmup, I may stop, take him back to the barn and say, "Something's not right. You're going to have to get somebody else to work this horse." A trainer will ask what's wrong, of course, and I may not be able to pinpoint it. "It might be on the right-front side," I would say. "I don't know if it's an ankle, a knee, or a shoulder, but something's off on the right front. And if you ever want me to ride this horse, you'd better fix it." I couldn't have said anything like that when I was sixteen or seventeen; I would not have known enough—*felt* enough— to be able to protect myself. I hadn't learned the lessons I know now.

Today, when a horse is on some drug or medication, I may not have been told but I can feel it. I'm definitely against all race-day medications. I would prefer that there was zero tolerance for drugs of any kind on race day, whether it's Lasix, given to prevent a horse's lungs from bleeding under stress, or even Butazoladin, a mild-pain reliever, like aspirin. The reason I feel so strongly about this is that for horses, as for athletes in other sports, the war on drugs is still evolving. Every time a test for some new drug is developed, there is somebody out there trying to develop a synthetic drug that won't show up in testing. In any game you play, there are always going to be cheaters; somebody is always trying to beat the system.

The testing procedure is still imperfect. When a urine sample is collected, a lab runs a test. If the test results are cloudy, indicating that the sample contains something foreign that is not an allowable medication, the next step is to try and find out what the drug is. Each test for a specific drug costs a certain amount of money, so to run a battery of tests to determine the nature of that drug can be expensive. Unless the test is for a specific drug—nowadays, Clembuterol seems to be the drug most often tested for—a test may be cloudy when the results come back, but the technicians don't necessarily know what caused it. The report is not marked "positive" because the drug has not been identified and to do so would be a cumbersome expense.

Horseracing today is not always a level playing field, which means I have to be more alert than ever to behavioral change. If there is a definite distinction between the way a horse has performed for me in a prior race or a previous morning workout, I know something is wrong. Say, I've ridden a horse ten times and suddenly I'm getting a sense I've never had before. I consider it a negative change because the horse's behavior is affected, and I assume his performance will be, too.

There are certain allowable drugs that I call smokescreens. It's purely speculative on my part, but I think that these drugs mainly cover up some other drug being administered. I have no proof, of course, but it's my belief that Lasix can be a cover-up for something else, just as Butazoladin can be. If a horse has suffered a broken knee and has been given some kind of drug, he may not feel the pain as I'm riding him. And because he's experiencing no pain, he may feel all right underneath me as I continue to ride. That pain, if he felt it, would stop him from running; not feeling that pain, he's going to snap that knee off, not only putting my life in danger but that of everybody else who is behind or around me on the track.

It's a scary feeling, being on a horse that breaks his cannon bone at thirty-five miles an hour. You may sense it two strides before the break occurs—a change in the horse's stride that doesn't feel right. You know something is about to happen, but you can't pull the horse up; he's still running strong. The horse doesn't even know he has a broken leg. The pain has

The Stevens brothers, all decked out on Easter Sunday, in front of our house in Boise, Idaho. I'm on the left, Scott is in the middle, and Craig is on the far right.

Playing center at a young age helped me perfect my future riding stance.

The Capital Eagles (H.S.) wrestling team photo. I'm kneeling, second from the left.

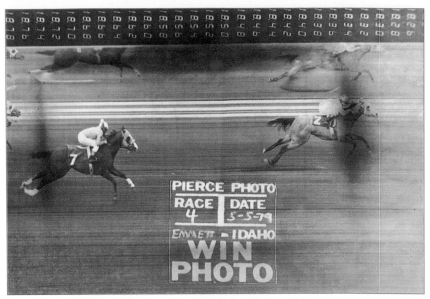

My first "official" win came on May 5, 1979, in Emmett, Idaho, on a quarter horse,
Sweet Dancin April.

By 1981, I had moved my tack to Portland Meadows. Here I am aboard Miss Silver Streak,
getting an early-career win.

My wife, Nikki, and I on our wedding day in 1998 at the Arboretum in Arcadia—just across from Santa Anita Park.

My kids came out to Santa Anita in 1996 to celebrate my acceptance of the George Woolf Memorial Jockey Award. From left to right: T.C., Carlie, Riley, and Ashley.

©Vicki Vinson

My mom, Barbara, and my dad, Ron, after I had received the George Woolf Memorial Jockey Award in 1996.

A celebration for the prestigious Dubai World Cup, which I won aboard Silver Charm in 1998. From left to right: Bob and Beverly Lewis (owners of Silver Charm); my dad, Ron; and Catherine and Frankie Dettori.

I grow 'em big, don't I? Me with my son, T.C., sharing a typical laid-back Del Mar moment in 2001.

The "other" Serena's Song (left) and Silver Charm, in my front yard, just a few miles from Santa Anita Park. I've named all my dogs after horses I've ridden.

The Boise crew in an impromptu high school reunion in 1997.

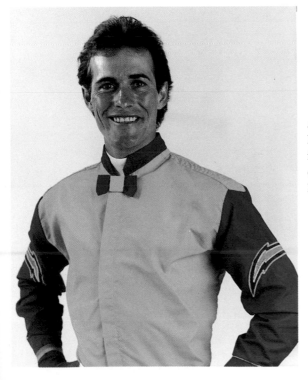

A publicity still from the 1988 Kentucky Derby. Do I look nervous in the San Diego Chargers silks of Winning Colors's owner Eugene Klein?

Crossing the wire at Churchill Downs in 1988 on the D. Wayne Lukas–trained filly Winning Colors—my first Kentucky Derby victory.

Check out the legendary spires of Churchill Downs, as Thunder Gulch and I cross the wire in the '95 Derby.

On the first Saturday in May in 1997, I found myself in the Churchill Downs winner's circle once again—this time aboard the Bob Baffert-trainee Silver Charm.

Silver Charm won one of the most dramatic Preakness Stakes in recent memory. Heading into the stretch, we're sitting second to rival Free House. Touch Gold is down at the rail, and Captain Bodgit looms boldly under Alex Solis (in the red cap).

I couldn't resist doing a Frankie Dettori "flying" dismount after winning the 1998 Dubai World Cup.

been masked by the drug he's been given, so he runs *through* the pain, which means that when something goes wrong, it *really* goes wrong.

I believe it's permissible for Lasix shots to be given on race day, but only up to four hours before race time, and there is a similar restriction on when a horse can be given Bute, either intravenously or in tablet form, and how much, based on the level of Lasix that may also have been given. It's all become scientific stuff, and most of the drugs being administered today are legal. But I feel certain that, more than I would even want to know, some drugs that shouldn't be given are being given covertly—which explains why I so strongly favor zero tolerance for drugs on race day. I must make it clear, however, that I have the utmost faith in the integrity of Thoroughbred racing. I believe it is being policed better than any other sport today.

9 *Winning Fillies, Valiant Colts*

"*T*he walk of a hooker, the looks of a queen." That's what Wayne Lukas once told me he sought in any top filly he wanted to acquire or train. His meaning came clear to me two days after Christmas 1987, the opening day of Santa Anita's winter season, when he asked me to ride a promising two-year-old filly, Winning Colors. (She would turn three on January 1, the day when all Thoroughbreds advance a year in the record books, regardless of their actual birth date.)

It was a six-furlong allowance race, not a particularly important contest, except that she won it very impressively. She was precocious and she had attitude—she was a fiery mount going to the starting gate. Once the race began, she was lightning in a bottle. I had never experienced the kind of athleticism she showed me. Her very first race had been at Saratoga that summer, and it marked her maiden win. I had known little about Winning Colors. I had never ridden or worked her until race day, but I was riding a lot of horses for Wayne by then, so I was the logical choice for his star filly.

After the race, I came back to the jockeys' room and said to Jacinto Vasquez, who had the locker next to mine: "I'm going to win the Kentucky Derby on that filly!" He said that I was completely crazy. Admittedly, mine was a presumptuous boast, considering that only twice in history had a filly won the Kentucky Derby. In racing, as in most sports, female athletes rarely compete directly with males. Where this filly was concerned, however, I had a strong gut feeling. I was sure she could face male competitors easily. For one thing, she was bigger than most of them, standing nearly seventeen hands tall, nearly the size of Point Given. For another, she was extremely focused, very professional when she raced, and she was tough. I could see that she intimidated other horses. I knew she could at least hold her own with the boys. She was a handful, not particularly pleasant to be around, and if you were within ten feet of her, the safest place to be was on her back. She would kick anything in her path.

I found out later that early in her training, she had been extremely difficult when it came time to bridle her. You couldn't just put the bit in her mouth and pull the head stall up over her ears in the normal way. She would rear up and flip over backward; she didn't want anyone messing with her ears. Her handlers had to disassemble the bridle, then rebuckle the pieces when the bit was secure. She never tried to threaten other horses during a race, but would not hesitate to bite the lead pony on the way to the starting gate. Breaking out of the gate, she was always agile; she could out-break any other filly or colt. When she left the gate, she was in front—and usually stayed there.

I rode her to victory again in the La Centinela Stakes, then rode her in the Grade I Las Virgenes, coming in second to Goodbye Halo, a filly trained by Charlie Whittingham. When she came back to beat Goodbye Halo in the Santa Anita Oaks, Lukas pointed her to the Santa Anita Derby. It was the last big West Coast prep race for the Kentucky Derby, and it would be the first time Winning Colors would run against colts. It wasn't a problem; she won with little coaxing from me.

Regarding the Kentucky Derby, we left her options open. Lukas entered her not only in the Derby but also in the Kentucky Oaks, a fillies race that is run traditionally the day before the Derby. He wanted to be covered in case she got a poor draw for post position or something was not 100 percent right leading up to the Derby. Race week got underway at Churchill Downs, and we drew post eleven, which would put us beyond the center of the large Derby field. We were happy with the position, but to be honest, we were not that concerned about post position because of the way Winning Colors ran her races—always out front. In the Kentucky Derby, her win was practically handed to her on a plate. To me, it seemed almost effortless. She jumped to a three-length lead going into the first turn but was really just cruising. I had a light hold of her mouth, and she was pricking her ears back and forth, telling me she was comfortable with what she was doing. Nobody challenged us, so I was able to control the pace and go as fast or as slow as I wished. According to Lukas's instructions, I was to wait till the end was in sight, at the three-eighths of a mile pole, and then ask her for her best so we could open up an insurmountable lead.

Winning Colors was responsive and had a long, fluid stride and an abundance of natural speed. Although she went off at short odds, few serious handicappers felt that Winning Colors could stay the course of a mile and one-quarter race, particularly when running against quality colts like Forty Niner and Private Terms. And Forty Niner, with Pat Day aboard, did come at her in a rush. At the three-eighths pole, negotiating the final turn, I asked for her best and her acceleration was incredible. But in the last fifty yards, she was getting very tired—that finish line couldn't come soon enough.

Winning Colors had a habit of wanting to lean, or lug in, toward the rail when she was tiring, and I knew I couldn't let her because the track surface along the rail was deep and slow. It's not where you want to be, coming into the stretch, especially with a fast-closing colt like Forty Niner coming on. The last twenty-five seconds of the race were the longest twenty-five seconds of my life till then. We were alone until about five strides before the wire—that's how fast Forty Niner was coming and how quickly we were stopping—but Winning Colors held on to win by a neck. It was my first Kentucky Derby victory, the thrill of a lifetime.

Lugging in was one of Winning Colors's quirks, probably the result of her training. Wayne's exercise people seemed to like working their horses right on top of the inside rail. So, being creatures of habit, his horses wanted to be on the rail when they ran, which could make it difficult for a jockey trying to maneuver his mount. If a horse has had twenty-five workouts before running a race and every workout has been on the rail, that's where the horse wants to be when the gate snaps open. If I'm on that horse's back and all of a sudden I'm trying to move that horse out, the animal doesn't want to react to me, thinking, "Hey, I'm supposed to be down on the fence."

Winning Colors wasn't that bad, though. She wouldn't lean in until she got tired, but frankly, I'd rather have a horse that lugs out than lugs in. If you get into traffic, you can at least move out and go around all the oth-

ers. If you have a horse that lugs in and he or she is running with you behind a wall of horses, the only way to get by them would be to sprout
wings. If you can't pull a horse out around the traffic, you're finished.

For the Preakness Stakes, two weeks after the Derby, Pat Day was given
instructions to go out on Forty Niner and hook my filly so she wouldn't
have an easy time of it. He packed me something like six horse-widths out
around the first turn and kept pushing me wide. Down the backstretch, we
were out well beyond the middle of the track, maybe eight or nine horses
wide approaching the final turn. This was fair racing strategy, but following it cost both Forty Niner and Winning Colors the race, for it left the rail
wide open. A colt named Risen Star came through on the inside and won
for fun. Winning Colors was third. Forty Niner finished seventh, some
fourteen lengths behind the winner.

In racing, the rule of thumb is that every length of ground you lose
going wide adds up to three lengths of distance in a mile and a quarter
race. So if you are racing five wide at that distance, you lose fifteen lengths.
Since the Preakness was a mile and three sixteenths, Winning Colors probably traveled a mile and a quarter.

She was a tired filly when she went into the Belmont Stakes three
weeks later. She had lost a considerable amount of weight, a lot of her fitness, and most of her edge. She seemed lethargic going to the gate that day
and didn't run much of a race. She just seemed hollow. After that, she was
given a rest, but we came back to ride in the Maskette at Belmont Park and
the Spinster at Keeneland. She was beaten both times; obviously, she had
not recovered completely from the rigors of the Triple Crown—a taxing
marathon for any three-year-old, male or female. In truth, I don't think
she was ever the same filly again after the Kentucky Derby. That day, she
went over the top but never repeated her winning form, which confirms
my belief that most horses have only one super, super race in them. Afterward, they never find that form again.

Winning Colors went right from the Spinster to the Breeders' Cup
Distaff at Churchill Downs, where she raced against fillies and mares. It

was a cold day with enough of a downpour to make the track muddy. We rode the race pretty much the way we had ridden the Derby, heading into the stretch with a commanding lead. Then, as before, she began to falter in the last fifty yards, and the undefeated Personal Ensign nailed her right at the wire. It was a photo finish that took several minutes for the stewards to decipher; the film showed that there was only about a sixteenth of an inch separating us from a dead-heat tie for first place.

I went into a tailspin. As great as I had felt after winning the Kentucky Derby, I was at the complete opposite end of the spectrum after the Breeders' Cup. For months, I was depressed, trying to figure out what I could have done differently, but I knew that Winning Colors was not the same for the Breeders' Cup as she had been prior to the Kentucky Derby. It was my belief that, had she been as good in the fall as she had been the previous spring, Personal Ensign would never have beaten her. But that changeability is what makes horse racing; that's the harsh beauty of our sport.

In 1995, the year I won my second Kentucky Derby, on Thunder Gulch, I was also riding another special filly: Serena's Song. I had ridden her to victory in two sprint races at Hollywood Park in 1994 and was offered the mount in the 1995 Oak Leaf at Santa Anita, which was a mile and one sixteenth. I chose not to ride her because I didn't feel she could win if she ran a step beyond six furlongs. Boy, was I wrong!

Corey Nakatani picked up the mount, and she won by more than two lengths. He rode her a lot after that while I was on Thunder Gulch, but I did win on her that year in five stakes races, including the Black-Eyed Susan and Mother Goose Stakes. She was a consistent filly; every time she ran, she gave me her best.

Over the years, I've gained the reputation of being able to make horses relax, to settle going into the starting gate. And I've also become known for being able to get along with fillies, female horses under four years old. I've had a lot of success with fillies and not just normal ones— high-strung fillies that have a lot of energy. They can be dangerous; the best of them have to be treated like ladies. You can't manhandle them. There's a fine line between trying to get them to do what you want them to do and making them think it's their idea that they're doing it. I approach a filly differently from the way I deal with a colt. I have no idea what I do physically as a rider, but I am somehow able to get along with nervous horses, which is what fillies are. Basically, I'm just aiming to be as quiet as I can on their backs. I guess I try to follow some words of wisdom that Bill Shoemaker used to describe himself as a rider; he said he tried to stay out of a horse's way and be a passenger as much as possible. In other words, let the horse do its job.

I try to make a filly happy. I basically let her get away with as much as she wants to get away with, up to a point. When we reach that point, I let her know she's wrong. Let's say I'm going to the racetrack in the morning or heading for the gate and my filly keeps reaching over, nipping at the neck of the lead pony or trying to actually bite him. I'll let her do that a little bit, though it may annoy the rider of the lead pony. I'll just let her have her way. If she doesn't feel like trotting to warm up, I'll let her walk as far as she wants to until it's her idea to trot. If she wants to gallop a little faster than I think is appropriate, I'll let her do that, too, until she thinks she's gotten away with something. Then she'll tend to respond to what I want her to do. If I let her do a little of what she wants to do, I expect something from her in return. It's definitely give and take.

If I'm riding a filly known as a run-off, a front-runner that usually uses herself up too early in a race, and the plan is to rate her—take her back off the pace—I may let her get away with whatever she wants going to the starting gate. But when the gate opens, I'm going to take a firm hold of her. I don't let her know I'm in charge until the race is on. Some fillies will fight me, and if they do, I try to be as firm as I can without upsetting them and hope that the next time I attempt to do whatever I've tried, they'll remember it and work for me.

When they've responded to something I've asked of them, whatever cue I've given them, as soon as the race or the workout is over, I give them as much praise as I can. I pet them, talk to them, tell them how sweet they are. They listen; they respond. They like to know they're special for doing what I've asked. I make them think they're queens. It's almost like giving a dog a treat after you've taught him a new trick. Colts are like that, too. Fillies may be more sensitive than colts most of the time, but certain colts lack confidence, and you can't be harsh. Others are big and stout, like the colts sired by Storm Cat. As soon as you get on their back, you have to let them know who's in charge.

Just as Winning Colors was difficult to ride, Steinlen was a lot of fun. He was certainly one of the best milers I've ever ridden, and for me good turf milers are the most thrilling to ride. Mile races are usually run tightly—to win one, you need a ground-saving trip. The horses enter the stretch in packs, running in close quarters. If there's a small opening, you've got to have a horse brave enough to go through it, one that has the acceleration to get there quickly. For me, the highlight of a racing day is getting to ride an exceptional miler.

The only way I can put these thoughts into perspective is to compare the ride with driving a Porsche. You've got one hand on the steering wheel and one hand on the gearshift knob, and you're cruising along in fourth gear. Suddenly, you need to pass somebody and you downshift into third; then with all this new horsepower underneath you, you just zoom! To be more specific about what I'm feeling and seeing on horseback, for me the ideal one-mile turf race is coming into the stretch no more than three lanes off the rail, behind maybe three or four horses. I'm right on their heels, so that when something does open up for me, I can be there in a split second. In other words, I'm looking for any daylight I can see within this wall of horses, and when it appears, I'm able to accelerate and grab it in one and a half strides.

Steinlen, though a delight to ride, didn't have the prettiest action; he was really rough hitting the ground, and he ran with his head in the air, instead of outstretched, in a balanced position. To give him a morning workout, you wouldn't have thought he was worth very much. As a matter of fact, he was uncomfortable to work. The first time I did, my back hurt, because with a horse that's not pulling you, not in the bridle and not pulling on the reins, it's very hard to stay balanced. A horse that's running with its head in the air and not pulling on you puts a lot of strain on your back. The effect is almost like standing on your tiptoes for a minute and a half, crouched down and not holding on to anything.

I did not have the mount on Steinlen exclusively. Jose Santos rode him a lot on the East Coast; I rode him in the West. Adding to that odd arrangement was the fact that he was trained by Wayne Lukas, who was not known for training horses to run on grass. The first time I rode Steinlen in a race, he was plugging along in mid-pack, not giving me a good sensation or a feeling of confidence. I remember coming into the stretch and a small opening between horses appearing in front of us near the rail. I thought, *I'll test it, and I'll test him to see if he's willing to go through there.* I asked him to run, and the acceleration was amazing, like breaking out of the starting gate, even though he was already at a full run. He turned out to be the epitome of a quick finisher. I've ridden only two other turf horses with that turn of foot. One was Exbourne, a horse I rode in 1991; the other was Irish Prize, which I rode ten years later. I handled Exbourne with enormous confidence. We could be fifty yards from the finish line, three lengths behind whichever horses were in front, but if any daylight opened up ahead of us, I knew we would win by a length and a half. Exbourne would do that.

There was one occasion, at Hollywood Park, when we were trapped behind a wall of six horses and there seemed no way Exbourne could win. But with only fifty yards left in the race, he got loose and won by a length and a half. Victory in a mile on the grass—there's no other moment so thrilling.

I'll have to admit that I eventually lost confidence in Steinlen and stopped riding him. We were in a race and he was behaving as he did in the morning. He showed no enthusiasm and was kind of scratchy, hitting the ground, placing his feet very gingerly. I didn't know whether he was suffering from bruised feet that day, but I did feel that he was over the hill, a horse that had seen better days. When I quit riding him, Santos took over, and he went on to win the 1989 Breeders' Cup Mile, running a spectacular race.

I'm definitely fallible. As many times as I've been right about horses, I've also been wrong in my judgment of how good they are. They may be having a bad day or are just not responding to me. Whatever the reason, I have to swallow my pride or my ego and say to the trainer, "Look, this horse just isn't performing for me anymore." What often happens is that the horses get tired of me or I get tired of them. The horse may be one of those tricky animals you get your best performance out of the first time you ride them. Why? Because your style is unique; you may be doing something totally different from what the previous rider has done, and that takes horses by surprise.

Let's say I suddenly hit a horse left-handed, and it's the first time the horse has ever been struck that way. It catches him by surprise. Now, I've almost tricked him into running for me, so the next time I ride him, the horse is expecting me to do the same thing. He is very intelligent; most horses are. He is probably waiting for me to do what I did, so he can refuse to respond. It's almost as though he has turned around, given me the finger, and said, "Fuck you, I'm *not* gonna do that." When a horse knows what I'm going to do before I do it, that's when it's time to change jockeys.

For any rider, and particularly for a young jockey, I think you've taken a big step forward in your career when you've learned to admit you are fallible. I also think that, as a horseman working with trainers and owners, you need to have a really open relationship to get the best out of the horses you're riding or working with. You need to be able to communicate with trainers without worrying that you've insulted them or their horses; you need them to know that, right or wrong, you're trying to get the most for the people you're riding for. You're trying to win everybody money, and if that means taking yourself off of a horse, you hope that gesture will be appreciated.

Early on in my career in California, a number of trainers didn't grasp what I was up to. But over the years, they've come to realize that I really *am* working with them, that I'm trying to make things work *for* them. This has turned out to be a big plus for my career, because so many people have come to trust my judgment and the sincerity of my opinion.

Nineteen eighty-eight was not only the year I won my first Kentucky Derby but also the year I won the Hollywood Gold Cup, the most important race at Hollywood Park. But the incident that took place then still sticks with me today. The horse I rode was Cutlass Reality, and his was a rags-to-riches story. Until then, he had achieved only moderate success, a horse that would pick up pieces of prize money in not even top-notch events, but mostly in minor stakes races on the East Coast, at Monmouth Park and the Meadowlands in New Jersey, and sometimes at tracks in New York. He was sent out to California to train with Craig Lewis, and somehow under Craig he underwent a transition—from so-so horse to superstar.

I remember going down to Craig's barn and being told that he'd just acquired this horse that he really liked. "He's training great," Craig told me, "but he's got a reputation for being a cheater." A cheater is a horse that doesn't give you 100 percent all the time. For whatever reason, he holds back. Another way of describing such a horse is to say he's common. I might come back from riding a race and if the horse has not given me his best effort, has been holding back consistently, I'll tell a trainer, "This horse is common." That's about as degrading a comment as you can make about a horse; it's almost racist to call a horse common. Usually, when you refer to horses as common, it means they're always going to be cheaters, never giving you their best effort. You're going to have to out-think them or cheat them yourself—trick them into winning a race.

When I was about to work Cutlass Reality, Craig told me about the horse's reputation but insisted that this was the best horse he'd ever trained. The horse had been raced mostly on the grass, not often on dirt. Craig decided to race him on the grass one more time. We got a moderate performance out of him; he won, but not impressively. Then he was entered in the Californian, a prep race on the dirt for the Hollywood Gold

Cup. Craig felt that Cutlass Reality probably was a dirt horse rather than a turf horse, which could have been why he hadn't been putting forth his best efforts. I went along with this because Craig was so high on him and also because I was aware that he had never run nearly as well on grass in the afternoon as he did on dirt in the morning. Craig was right about the horse; he turned into a very good grade-1 competitor.

In the 1988 Hollywood Gold Cup, Cutlass Reality and I were the bettors' third choice, behind Ferdinand with Bill Shoemaker, winners of the 1987 Breeders' Cup Classic, and Alysheba with Chris McCarron, eventual winners of the 1988 Classic. Chris was on the lead; I was laying second, just stalking Alysheba, with Shoe to my inside, going down the backstretch. Chris is not a rough rider by any means, but he likes to float horses out. He'll take every advantage he can, and he does so smoothly—trying to force another rider to either take back or go wide, basically to make that rider do something he doesn't want to do: lose ground. Chris started floating me wide at about the five-eighths pole. I was three-quarters of a length behind Alysheba, and Shoe was about a length and a half behind me. We were halfway down the backstretch. Alysheba floating us wide created a big space along the rail for Ferdinand to come through, so I hollered up to Chris to watch the fence. He immediately looked behind him and dropped down to the rail. We had Ferdinand trapped.

There was nothing illegal about that action, except that it's kind of an unspoken rule among riders not to communicate things like that during a race. It probably would not have mattered that day. Ferdinand wasn't going to have any impact on Cutlass Reality; no one was going to beat my horse. The rest of the race went very easily; we won by almost seven lengths. I was ecstatic. It was my first Gold Cup victory, a huge achievement for me at the time.

I did my post-race interviews and came back to the jockeys' quarters to watch a rerun of the race on closed-circuit TV. Suddenly, Shoe entered the room and came up to me. I'd never seen him so upset with a fellow rider. "Boy," he said, "don't you ever fuckin' do that again. You were *way* out of line!" Then he turned and went in to shower.

What he said really hurt me; I felt tears in my eyes and a lump in my throat. For Shoe was a man I really idolized. Moreover, I knew I had earned his respect as an up-and-coming rider. Now I feared that in one gesture I had blown away all of the respect I had gained.

Later, he came back and apologized for the outburst.

"You don't need to apologize," I said. "I was wrong. I'll never do it again." And I never did.

10 *Building on Success and Sadness*

$\mathcal{N}$ineteen eighty-nine was the year my second son, Riley, was born. It was also the year I built my dream home, which in retrospect may have been the most foolish thing I have ever done. The property was in Arcadia, not far from Santa Anita Park, and its three-quarter-acre site initially included a four-bedroom house. It was a ranch-style house, and it was beautiful, only about two years old, but barely a year after we moved in, we started knocking around the idea of making it larger. We had the resources, and with three small children we had the need.

What started out as a thirty-four hundred-square-foot house on one level became a sixty-nine hundred-square-foot two-story mansion, with five bedrooms, maid's quarters, and an office, plus a separate guest house. Outside, there was a rock-rimmed swimming pool that looked like a pond, a rock-clad diving cliff and a three-tier waterfall. Inside, there was a huge loft that I turned into a game room, complete with pool table, card table, pinball machine, and a bar big enough to serve twelve. My only other design contribution was the master bathroom. It had a Jacuzzi and a steam room with built-in TV, so I could sweat off the pounds and be entertained simultaneously. A practical plus to having a steam room at home was that I wouldn't have to visit the weigh-in room at the racetrack so early; I could pull down my weight before leaving the house.

It was a total transformation. We all but leveled what had been there; only one wall was left standing. A remodeling project that was supposed to be finished in six months took twice that long, and cost nearly three times as much as we'd planned. We moved into a rental house nearby and stayed there a year while reconstruction went forward. I spent nearly all of that time having horrible second thoughts about watching a perfectly sound home being replaced by something that seemed a bit over the top. Our family life became discordant. There were constant arguments about what we were going to do and what we weren't going to do. That, I think, was when our marriage began to fall apart. The financial pressure I was under to support this undertaking really got to me. I kept thinking that what we were doing was a huge mistake.

Fortunately, my career was progressing at the time we began work on the house. I was riding good horses from respected barns and for some of the country's top trainers, including Wayne Lukas, who had begun using me a lot. I learned a great deal then, too, not only about handling Thoroughbreds in challenging races, but also about the fallibility of my own judgment.

I remember the spill I had on Imaginary Lady, a very good two-year-old filly I rode at Santa Anita. It was the first race of her life, I believe, and there were problems right from the start. Wayne's saddling theory is that the weight of the rider and saddle should be kept off of a horse's back as much as possible and, instead, be thrust forward, onto its shoulders. This is a fine theory until you get a horse pulling on you so hard that the saddle moves up on the animal's neck and you have absolutely no control.

Moving Imaginary Lady to the starting gate, I was getting really upset, thinking: *Why does Wayne keep setting these saddles so far forward? He knows I hate it.* Sitting a saddle way up on a horse's withers is not the most comfortable place for a rider to be; it is also not very safe. *What if this filly breaks slow, then wants to rush up with me?* I wondered. *The saddle's gonna go straight up on her neck and I'm goin' to drop myself.* Then I thought, *Nah, that's not gonna happen,* and I did nothing about it. I probably could have taken her to the gate, dismounted, and had the saddle placed where I liked it, but I knew that Lukas was unhappy when a rider did that. He's never liked having a saddle reset after he put it in a specific spot. *All right,* I thought, *I'll leave it.*

Sure enough, Imaginary Lady broke slowly; we were in the one hole, the post position beside the inside rail. The horses outside of us moved ahead immediately and crossed over in front of us. Going into the first turn, the filly had reached full speed and was running off with me. I went to take hold of her and slow her down when she clipped heels with a horse in front of her. She stumbled, my saddle slipped forward, and—*boom*—down I went. There were horses behind me, but all of them missed me, so I wasn't hurt, just shaken up—and furious. *If I could hit that son-of-a-bitch right now, I would!* I muttered to myself as I lay on the racetrack. I never did, of course.

Imaginary Lady wasn't hurt either. I rode her successfully several times in big races after that, including the Grade II Princess Stakes at Hollywood Park. Wayne and I both hoped that she would turn into another Winning Colors, a horse she physically resembled. That didn't happen. With hindsight, I can say for certain that Winning Colors was unique; I may never have another mount like her.

Riding an unraced filly or colt in a maiden race is daunting, particularly a one-mile race, as that one had been. On most tracks, the first turn comes up quickly, and it's difficult to get an inexperienced horse to switch over to the left lead at the turn, especially if you're down on the inside and in tight quarters, as Imaginary Lady and I were that day. The horses in front are already dropping into the turn by the time you've caught up. If you're three-quarters of a length inside of a horse, with no room to maneuver, or give your horse the extra space it needs to change leads, you can find yourself in dire straits.

Cuddles was another Lukas-trained two-year-old that I was successful with, despite extraordinary circumstances. Before riding her, in the fall of 1990, I'd had a spill at Hollywood Park, a much more serious one than my fall on Imaginary Lady. I was on a filly for trainer Steve Young in what was just an everyday claiming race. We led a field of eleven by three lengths and had gone about a quarter of a mile when my filly fractured both front legs. She went down and so did I, with the whole field behind me. I was kicked in the tailbone and struck by several horses. One of them stepped on my right arm.

That happened on a Wednesday. I went to the hospital. All the X-rays on my back and tailbone were negative, but I learned that I had fractured my elbow. Even so, I was determined to ride Cuddles in the

Hollywood Starlet, a half-million-dollar Grade I stakes race held three days later. I talked to my physician and asked if it would be possible for me to ride that weekend. "Well," he said, "I can come in twenty minutes before the race and inject you with cortisone and a local anesthetic that will pretty much block out the pain for about thirty minutes. But if I do this, you may have problems down the road: instead of being out four weeks with a fractured elbow, you may be out eight weeks if you ride that race."

"But that's what I want to do," I insisted, so on race day, I let him give me the injection. A lot of people knew I had been injured. I was getting plenty of flak from the turf press. So was Wayne, from reporters critical of his choice of a jockey who was possibly not 100 percent. But Wayne had a lot of faith in me, and I had faith in myself that I could get the job done. The race ended as a furious stretch battle between Cuddles and the filly Russell Baze was riding. I won by a nose, then sat out the next six weeks.

What was amazing about that race was that, from the eighth pole to the wire, I used my right arm to hit the filly about sixteen times to keep her alert and focused. But I didn't feel a thing. Granted, the arm had been anesthetized, but something else happens in a situation like that. Whether it's an arm that's hurting or an ankle that may be swelling up because a horse has banged it going into the starting gate, the moment that gate opens, I feel nothing. I don't experience any of the pain I would normally feel because my adrenaline level has amplified about a hundred times. Adrenaline and the body's natural endorphins are probably the best pain-killing combination around.

Another memorable Lukas mount I rode was On The Line, a warrior, just like Bedside Promise. He was a quick horse. His trainer and Gene Klein, his owner, were eager to stretch him from sprint to classic distances, except for one problem. At the end of his three-year-old season, he had broken an ankle, which was surgically repaired before he could race again. On his return, after a long rest, I was asked to ride him in a sprint race at Santa Anita, and when I first saw him my heart sank. The horse had six screws in his injured ankle, and the joint was huge and ugly. To me, it seemed impossible that On The Line could walk, let alone run, but I knew he had been in a couple of races after coming back from his injury and that Lukas wanted me on him.

In the walking ring after I had mounted, On The Line felt as though he was hobbling. It might not have been visible to anyone on the ground, but to me a limp was apparent. I thought, *There is no possible way that I'm gonna ride this horse. There is no way he can run. This is insanity. He's gonna hurt himself. . . . I'm gonna hurt myself. . . .*

We walked onto the racetrack and the horn-blower started playing the call to the post. My horse's ears went straight up, and he suddenly started prancing with me. No more limping. There was nothing wrong with him. *Holy cow!* I thought and started warming him up. I warmed him up a lot, to make sure he was safe to ride, that he really was moving all right. When the race began, he rushed out of the starting gate and proceeded to run six furlongs in just over a minute, eight seconds—not a record but damn close. His next few races, including the Grade II San Pasqual Stakes at Santa Anita, were run that way. He would warm up very stiffly, then run like a champion. He was all heart, with a great willingness to run.

His story had a tragic end, however. At the Breeders' Cup races at Florida's Gulfstream Park, he was entered in the Sprint, and I thought he had a good chance to win it. We had drawn a middle post position; far outside of us was a horse named Sam Who, with Laffit Pincay aboard. Leaving the gate, Sam Who angled in sharply and made hard contact with On The Line. We were running on a very uneven surface that day. Horses were taking missteps, often slipping and sliding.

After the contact was made, On The Line balanced underneath me, but he didn't feel right. I had ridden three previous races that day, and all three of my mounts had given me that seem feeling early on of slipping and sliding on the racetrack. I just assumed that On The Line wasn't handling the track, though he *was* pulling on the bit. I mean, he was really pulling underneath me, telling me how much he wanted to run. So I went ahead and rode him, and his action stayed the same. He kept slipping and sliding with me.

By the time we had gone three-eighths of a mile, I knew there was something seriously wrong. On The Line was hitting the ground poorly, so poorly that I told myself, *He's blown an ankle; I've gotta pull him up.* But I couldn't pull him up right away; I couldn't slow him down enough until we were at the eighth pole, right in front of the grandstand. I jumped off and looked down, and there was blood squirting out of his right front leg. When Sam Who hit him, he'd struck On The Line with one of his hoofs and severed a tendon, cutting it in half. Veterinarians tried for about five days to save the horse's life, but they wound up having to euthanize him.

There's always pressure on a jockey riding a difficult horse or one with odd quirks or habits, but for me riding Criminal Type for Wayne Lukas involved unusual pressure, even though he was a pleasure to ride. He was a great racehorse, clearly headed to be Horse of the Year in 1990, so each time I rode him I felt that the only way he could be beaten was if *I* made a mistake. I rode him only once—in the Whitney Handicap at Saratoga—replacing his regular rider, Jose Santos, who had been suspended briefly. Criminal Type was mature, having begun his career in Europe racing on grass, and because he was an Alydar offspring, he had been difficult to train. Wayne did a tremendous job managing that horse. It was a pleasure to accept my cut of the winner's purse for essentially taking an afternoon stroll around the park.

By 1990, after six years of riding Breeders' Cup races, I think I was 0 for 36. I had earned loads of seconds and thirds but had never actually won, so I approached Breeders' Cup day 1990 with a big monkey on my back. By then I had started to ride a few horses for Sheikh Mohammed of Dubai. His French trainer, André Fabre, asked me to ride In The Wings, a horse that came to the United States with a strong reputation. I knew I would have a good chance of winning the Breeders' Cup Turf with In The Wings, but deep down inside I wasn't feeling very positive. In fact, all I could think was, *What's gonna go wrong this year? I'll probably run second and third all day!*

On race day, I got a call from my father asking me what I thought of my chances. I said, "I ride a very good European horse in the Turf. If we get the right trip, I think I can win it." He told me, "Son, listen, you're a great rider. You've proven yourself. You've won a Kentucky Derby, and you've ridden in Breeders' Cup races before. Just go out there and have a good time. More than anything, enjoy yourself."

So I did. While warming up In The Wings before the race, I kept telling myself, *Relax, let's just have fun with this. Don't put any pressure on yourself; if the horse is good enough, you'll get the job done.* The trainer had instructed me to let the horse come away from the gate at his own pace, then let him place himself wherever he wanted. When we reached the stretch, he said, I should have plenty of horse, whenever I felt it was time to go for it. Fabre also warned me that when In The Wings got out in front, he tended to want to play around, as though he thought he had already done his job, and would try to pull up with me. He cautioned me to try and time my ride so I wouldn't get the lead too early.

When we hit the furlong marker, with an eighth of a mile left to run, With Approval was in front of us with Craig Perret aboard. I knew we had With Approval anytime we wanted him, so I never really asked In The Wings to run until the last sixteenth of a mile. When I did, he gave me brilliant acceleration and went on to win by half a length. It was a $2 million victory, and a big, big relief for me to finally get my first Breeders' Cup win.

Another important race for me that year was the Arlington Million at Chicago's Arlington Park. My horse was Golden Pheasant, which Charlie Whittingham had asked me to ride. I rode him first at Del Mar in the Grade I Eddie Read Handicap, a one and one-eighth mile race that California trainers often used to prep for the one and one-quarter mile Arlington Million three weeks later. I had worked Golden Pheasant in the mornings and felt, frankly, that he was over the hill. He seemed lazy; he would trip on anything; he didn't pick up his feet. Every time he stumbled, it jerked my back. It was hard keeping this horse enthusiastic; he didn't seem to care about training. The first time I sat on him, I decided that I didn't care to ride him. I couldn't say that, of course. After all, his trainer was Whittingham, racing's Bald Eagle, a hall of famer who may have been the greatest trainer of all time. *How can I tell this man I don't want to ride his horse?* I thought.

I didn't. I rode Golden Pheasant in the Eddie Read, and we finished third. He ran unimpressively. He stumbled with me as we pulled up after the race, and my stomach was practically up in my throat. *Man,* I thought, *I do not want to ride this horse again.* But Ray Kravagna, my agent, said he had already told Whittingham I'd ride the horse in the Arlington Million. "But I don't feel comfortable on him," I protested. "Listen," said Kravagna, "I've already given Charlie a commitment, so you *have* to ride him. Just be careful, and take care of yourself."

We flew to Chicago, and I knew a hundred yards out of the gate that we were going to win that day because Golden Pheasant behaved so differently. He started pulling me right away. His win was a tribute to Whittingham's mastery. The trainer knew just how to point toward specific races; he would never ask his horses for their best in prep races, but knew he would have them at their peak for the big day. He had used the Eddie Read to fine-tune his horse for the Arlington Million, and Golden Pheasant won it easily.

Whittingham's next big goal for his horse was the $2 million Japan Cup in Tokyo a year later. Before being shipped, Golden Pheasant was scheduled for a prep race, a one-mile event during the Oak Tree meet at Santa Anita. I rode him there, and once again he felt very uncomfortable to me, finishing a lackluster third. Two weeks later, I gave Golden Pheasant his final workout before going to Japan and got the same feeling I'd had the last time I'd worked him. To me, once again, he seemed very lazy.

"Ray, we're wasting our time," I said to my agent. "This horse has absolutely no chance of winning the race." Ray replied, "You didn't trust Charlie before, and look what happened! We owe this to him. He's been good to us. Let's go!" So, with strong misgivings, I flew to Tokyo for the first time, and Golden Pheasant won the Japan Cup the same way he had won the Arlington Million.

Whittingham was known for giving his horses lengthy layoffs, and Golden Pheasant had obviously suffered some physical problems I didn't know about. There were long lapses between major races, which suggested that the horse had been ailing and needed time to recuperate. Needless to say, I never asked Whittingham what these problems were. All I knew was that this was another horse that hated to train in the morning and loved to race in the afternoon.

In 1990, Laz Barrera told me about Mister Frisky, a horse that had just arrived in his barn from Puerto Rico undefeated. *Yeah, yeah,* I thought, *an undefeated horse from Puerto Rico—that could be anything.* But I didn't refuse to ride him because he was Laz's horse, and Laz had fallen on hard times by then. At some point in the late eighties the California Racing Board had announced that one of Laz's horses had turned up morphine-positive. He was later exonerated when it turned out that the "drug" had actually come from a poppy seed bagel the horse had eaten. This horse was a pig. A garbage collector. He would eat anything that happened to be in front of him.

The mistake would have been amusing if it hadn't taken about three years to resolve, during which time Laz's reputation suffered. His spirits sank, and he seemed to age dramatically. He had always been a proud man. He never cheated, didn't need to, for in my view he was the ultimate horseman. But at the time he was exonerated, there were no longer any top horses in his care and very few horses in his stable, so having Mister Frisky really jump-started his career again. I could see that this horse reinvigorated him. Why not? Mister Frisky came to the West Coast with an unblemished record.

A horse so special to Laz would become a very special horse to me. I won three races in a row on him, including the Santa Anita Derby, and went on to Churchill Downs as the favorite to win the Kentucky Derby. He arrived in Louisville with a streak of sixteen wins behind him, tying a record that was set in the forties by Citation and that would be tied again in the nineties by Cigar. But turf writers in North America didn't recognize that streak, because eleven of Mister Frisky's victories had been in Puerto Rico, which they figured didn't count. Those wins should have counted, though, because Mister Frisky was an important horse. I thought he had an excellent chance to win the Derby.

I flew to Louisville a week before the race to give the horse one final workout, and I felt the workout was erratic. Rumors had been rampant that he wasn't training well in the weeks leading up to the race, but such rumors are not unusual. Everyone wants to knock someone else's horse. Even so, I wasn't overly pleased with the way he worked. He didn't perform badly, just not the way I'd expected. I tried to think positive: *It happened to be a bad day for him. I've still got a hell of a shot to win that race.*

On Derby day, I warmed him up and he seemed tense and nervous with me, as though agitated. He wasn't comfortable with his surroundings, which I wrote off to the noisy crowd: *There's probably a hundred thousand people here—no wonder he's upset!* I thought. But he ran a mediocre race and finished eighth, a real disappointment. When I was pulling him up afterward, I heard a whistling sound in his breathing, something I had never heard before. I told Laz about it, and he had the horse scoped. Horses are usually scoped to detect internal bleeding; a vet runs a tube tipped with a microscope down the horse's throat to see what's going on. With Mister Frisky, the scope found nothing. He scoped clean: no pharyngitis, no infection. Everything looked fine. So Laz decided to run him in the Preakness, two weeks later.

He ran a very brave race but finished third, and throughout the race, I could hear that same whistling sound—more evident now than right after the Derby. He pulled up in a lot of distress and had a very high temperature. He was scoped again, perhaps more thoroughly this time, and a wood chip was found lodged in his trachea. It seems that because he would eat the straw that was normally used to cushion a horse's stall, wood chips were always laid down in his stall instead. Obviously, that hadn't stopped him from eating his bedding. He had eaten wood chips, and one had been inhaled.

No one knew how long that wood chip had been in there, but it took an operation to get it out, leaving behind a big ulcer and permanent damage to the horse's breathing apparatus. Mister Frisky never ran again, though he went on to have a fairly successful stud career. With that horse's retirement from racing, Laz Barrera was back in the emotional doldrums and his health slid into permanent decline. It was as though Mister Frisky was the final candle to have been blown out.

11 _Trainer Differences_

One of the most important races I rode in 1991 was the Longacres Mile in Seattle. It was the Northwest's premier race, the one I had heard about even more than the Kentucky Derby when I was growing up in Boise. I had ridden it at least four times while I was working at that track but had never won it. Now, after traveling back to Seattle from Southern California, I would win the race on a horse named Lois Cyphre. That race would have particular resonance—not only because I finally won it but mainly because that was the last time the race would be held there. Longacres was to shut down permanently at the end of the racing season, and the Longacres Mile would be shifted to the new Emerald Downs racetrack.

Two other important races that year were the Beverly D at Arlington and the Wilshire Stakes at Hollywood Park. I won them both for Bill Shoemaker, who had retired from racing and become a trainer. My mount in each of these races was Fire the Groom, by far the best horse that Shoe had in training. She was a large filly, the size of a colt, and extremely good looking, and she had an exceptional turn of foot. In the Wilshire, we were blocked behind a group of horses and had nowhere to go, but she displayed amazing speed coupled with the strength and ability to get herself out of trouble.

Shoemaker used other jockeys, of course, but I felt that it was a feather in my cap that he wanted me to ride for him, considering that I had contributed to his loss on Ferdinand in the 1988 Hollywood Gold Cup. I felt I had lost his respect then, so when he selected me to ride his best horse, I felt very special. There's an old saying in racing that ex-jockeys never become good trainers. For me, that's an old wives' tale that has no validity. Shoe, for one, went on to become a very successful trainer after his riding days ended.

Bruce Jackson was another trainer who had earned my respect, and his horse, In Excess, turned out to be one of the best horses I have ever ridden. Jackson had purchased In Excess in England, where he had been racing, and brought him to the United States with the hope of making him a top turf horse. Working with him in the morning, it didn't take the trainer and me very long to figure out that the horse was as talented on dirt as he was on grass, which was a bit unusual in a horse initially trained abroad. He proved an incredibly versatile performer. I won the Grade II San Fernando Stakes at Santa Anita on him and three prestigious Grade I races in New York. He seemed destined to be Horse of the Year in 1991, but bad management—in my opinion—cost him that title.

In Excess had had a hard campaign, which began taking its toll. He had developed quarter cracks in his feet, and I felt his efforts were tailing off as the end of the year was approaching. It was my feeling, and the trainer's as well, that he would be named Horse of the Year whether he ran in the Breeders' Cup—and won—or bypassed that event altogether. We felt that the only way In Excess could lose the coveted title was by failing to win whatever Breeders' Cup race he ran in.

The most logical spot to enter him was the Classic, but the owner, who insisted on entering him even though the horse wasn't 100 percent, decided that the Breeders' Cup Mile was going to be a much easier spot than the Classic. He felt confident that the Mile would be an easy win for In Excess, and that by pulling in another big victory, the horse would secure Horse of the Year. I rode him that day; we were favored to win. But contrary to the owner's prediction, the race was very tough, and In Excess finished out of the money. It was a dismal loss. What the owner failed to realize is that there are no easy Breeders' Cup races. Each one is as difficult to win as the one before it and the one that follows.

Performing so poorly in what many people considered an easy task for him put In Excess out of the running for Horse of the Year honors. To the media, it was only a fluke that he had come in first in all of the races he had won that year. I have always felt that if the owner had been straightforward and honest with the turf press, saying that bad feet would keep his horse out of the Breeders' Cup, In Excess would have been named Horse of the Year, and that title would have guaranteed his future as a money-earning stallion. What happened, however, is that when he retired, no one was interested in him. He stood in California for about a year, but for stud fees that may have been as low as five thousand dollars. In 1993, I learned that In Excess was for sale for $1 million, and I urged my business manager to try and pull together a syndicate to buy him. I was confident he had the potential to become a very good stallion, but people thought I was crazy, so I never did get the syndicate together. Mike Pegram wound up making the purchase. The future owner of Real Quiet and Silverbulletday acquired In Excess, and the horse turned out to be one of the best sires California has ever had. I think his stud fee is twenty-five thousand dollars now. Needless to say, the $1 million purchase price would have been paid for over and over again.

My instincts have been pretty good in terms of predicting good sires. These predictions have been nothing but educated guesses, but I always base them on my assessment of a horse's build, action, and temperament. These are the characteristics that deserve to be passed along from generation to generation, and over time I have been a good judge of which horse was going to excel at stud. What influences me most is a horse's temperament. He should have an aggressive attitude and a will to win. I think it's possible to have the fastest horse in the world, but if he lacks determination, and heart, you've got nothing. The most successful stables in the world have built up their racing barns through breeding their best horses and selling the offspring. In Thoroughbred racing, money is made at the auctions and in the breeding barns—more money, long term, than on the racetrack.

I suspected that Silver Charm was going to be a very good sire, just as I felt certain about Thunder Gulch, the stallion that sired Point Given. Another horse I felt strongly about was Bertrando, a colt I rode in 1993 that I thought would bring me my first win in the Breeders' Cup Classic. Bertrando was a massive black animal with a great temperament. He was a true racehorse and gorgeous. He also became a fine stallion.

Bertrando had what I can only describe as a John Wayne swagger. When he was walking to the starting gate, it was like, "I am the daddy. I *own* this racetrack. The rest of you running against me have *no* chance." That was the feeling he gave me. I really loved riding that horse. He had versatility as well as great speed. He could run six furlongs in a minute, eight seconds, or a mile and a quarter in two minutes flat. His performance was push-button easy, for he could really carry his speed. I could use him hard out of the gate to establish the lead, then take hold of him to slow down the pace. When the other jockeys figured out that the pace had been slowed, they would press their mounts up to about his shoulder, and I would let him pick up his speed a notch. With Bertrando, I could play cat and mouse throughout a race—right up to the quarter pole. Then I would ask him for his best, and he always gave it to me. He was fun to ride.

In the 1993 Breeders' Cup Classic, when Bertrando finally got the lead, I felt confident that he had put away every other horse that I had been concerned about and had a clear shot to win the big purse. Then, about fifty yards from the finish, along came a horse with Jerry Bailey onboard wearing silks I didn't even recognize. His horse flashed by and beat us by two lengths. I was stunned. The horse's name was Arcangues, and as I learned later he was trained by André Fabre. But riding back, after the race, I didn't even know the horse's name, only that the tote board said that he had gone off at ninety-nine to one. That's the biggest number a tote board can show. Since Arcangues, a horse that never raced again in this country, had paid $269.20 on a $2 bet, his actual odds must have been something like 133 to 1. No wonder I felt doomed never to win a Breeders' Cup Classic.

Bertrando's trainer felt similarly doomed. Bobby Frankel had entered horses in thirty-six Breeders' Cup races over the years, but it wasn't until 2001 that one of them won. I have done a lot of business with Frankel and have always considered him one of racing's great trainers, but he is a difficult man to ride for. For one thing, he's a poor loser. Yes, it's true, if you show me a good loser, I'll show you a *loser*. Even so, he's not a gracious winner either. After all the races I have won for him over the years, he has never once said "Nice ride" or "Thank you" afterward. But if I got beaten, it was a damn sure bet that he would berate me.

Frankel has always loved to own his riders. He loves to have one or two jockeys riding all of his horses so he can control them completely. Control means it's so well known that you're riding for him that no other mounts are offered to you. The result is that if and when he fires you, you're left out in the cold with no clients to ride for, because he has so completely dominated your racing schedule.

The trainer-jockey relationship is sealed with a handshake or a phone call. There is no contract, only an understanding. You ride race by race, and though you may think you're locked in solidly with a particular trainer, he may get angry and fire you for whatever reason, and you've got to go out and build up a whole new clientele. I am always happy to ride some of Frankel's horses, but I won't commit to riding his whole stable.

Trainers are all vastly different characters, and working with them is one of the most challenging aspects of a jockey's life. You've got to know how to deal with different personalities and be able to switch on one attitude for one trainer and switch it off when confronted by another. On a single race day, you might be riding a race for Bob Baffert, who likes to tell jokes in the paddock—it's his way to unravel tight nerves. You might be facing a million-dollar race, but with Bob the atmosphere can be very light. You kid, joke around, have a laugh. Then maybe twenty minutes later, you're riding a race for D. Wayne Lukas, and you've got a Vince Lombardi on your back. You have to adjust quickly, just like an actor.

For me, riding skills add up to just 25 percent of being a great jockey; being a good politician is probably 50 percent of it, and being a good actor is at least 25 percent. In dealing with certain trainers, you have to tell them what they want to hear—you have no choice. I have been very fortunate with most of the trainers I have had to deal with. They respect my opinion and expect me to shoot straight from the hip. Being completely honest did hurt me early in my career, but in the long run it has helped me a lot.

Wayne Lukas has probably done more for my career money-wise than any other trainer, and during the years when I was riding his best horses, he did much to raise my stature as a rider. He was a visionary trainer and also a great motivator. I would go out in the paddock fully prepared to be riding a horse that had no chance of winning; I had probably worked that horse in the morning and decided it had no talent. I was committed, so I wouldn't back out, even though I felt certain the horse couldn't run. But by the time I was up in the saddle and leaving the paddock, Lukas would have me convinced I was riding the second coming of Secretariat—and that the only way the horse could be beaten was if I screwed up. He is probably the best motivator I have ever met anywhere in any business. Having once coached high school basketball, he learned to use a lot of the motivational skills he had developed to put jockeys in the right frame of mind and also to persuade owners to buy racehorses.

One day, he asked me to give one of his horses a test run. The workout was terrible. The horse made a lot of noise, huffing and puffing, and I sensed he was having trouble with his breathing. After the workout, Lukas accompanied me back to the barn, riding his lead pony. "What do you think, jock?" he asked. I said, "I think we're screwed with this one, Wayne. He can't breathe." He said, "Well, don't be so sure about that. We can make some changes; we can operate on his throat."

The walk and talk to the barn took about five minutes. After I had unsaddled the horse, Lukas looked at me and smiled: "Come to the office with me. I want you to hear this." I walked with him to his office and sat there while he got on the telephone. He was talking to a potential owner about a horse he wanted the man to buy. "He's got a gorgeous stride," he told the man. "He's got a great pedigree; I think he's got a great future. We can get this horse for $150,000, and I think if we don't move now, somebody else is gonna make the buy."

I didn't know what horse he was talking about, but by the time he hung up, *I* wanted to buy the animal. "Man," I said, "who *is* this horse? Is there any chance I can get in on the deal?"

"It's the horse you just worked," Wayne replied, and told me the client had agreed to buy him. The best part of that story is that the horse went on to win six or seven races. I never rode him; after working the animal, I wouldn't have paid $100 for him, let alone $150,000. But he raced for three or four years and wound up making about $300,000. Lukas did well with him and did equally well for the owner.

A turning point in my relationship with Wayne occurred in 1991 because of the horse Farma Way. Here was a horse that was always very stiff, physically, prior to a race. His strong suit was his speed from the gate, but he required a lot of warming up. He was capable of establishing a forward position early on and more or less dictating the pace, but he was not an easy ride because he could go too fast too soon. There was always a fine line between getting him away from the gate in good order and going too fast. There was also a danger of not warming him up enough so that he was left behind at the start. He would not run in behind horses; if he got dirt kicked in his face, he was useless. I won with him in the San Antonio Stakes at Santa Anita, the Santa Anita Handicap, held that year on my birthday, March 6, and the Pimlico Special, which took place a week before the Preakness. Then came the Suburban at Belmont Park, a stakes race that would have a negative impact on my relationship with Farma Way, and also with his trainer.

He was stiffer than usual that summer day, so I was faced with a dilemma: should I warm him up a lot, which would loosen his body but might also make him too aggressive, or just soothe and relax him and take the chance of having him break slowly and be left at the starting gate? I think I had drawn the number-two inside position, a few slots down from Craig Perret, who was riding another speed horse, one that had been shipped in from Canada. I decided that it was important to get Farma Way out of the gate in good order, so we wouldn't be shuffled back in the field with nowhere to go, and I warmed him up a lot more than I had wanted to. His motor was really running, as though he thought he was going to sprint six furlongs instead of run a mile and one-eighth. The result: he bolted ahead like a quarter horse and ran off with me.

When I'm on a speed horse and there are other speed horses in the race, I am always a lot more comfortable being the *outside* speed; that position gives me more options. It's much easier to get a mount to rate, or relax, from the outside; the horse doesn't feel claustrophobic or closed in. If I'm the guy on the inside and the outside speed gets a half-length advantage on me and crowds me toward the fence, my horse tends to feel unsettled. Feeling unsettled, he tends to want to do too much, and it becomes almost impossible to get him to relax and ration his energy—he's in the race to make the lead. But if I'm on the outside, I have room to move away from that other speed horse and take back half a length, letting the other horse set the pace so I can save all I can for the final eighth of a mile.

In the Suburban, I was going head and head with Craig Perret, who was trying to slow the pace down but couldn't. Both of our horses were very competitive. Both wanting to lead, they set suicidal speed fractions down the backstretch and both caved in at about the same time, setting up the win for still another horse. Perret and I were reduced to being passengers, and we knew we were going to be heckled when we got back. Racing fans in New York can be tough, particularly when a jockey is riding the favorite.

I have always been able to accept responsibility when I have made a mistake in a race, and have taken pride in being able to come back, face the trainer honestly, and say, "I cost you the race," if I had failed in some way or done something I shouldn't have done. Farma Way was a badly beaten fourth that day, but I didn't consider it my fault that he had gone so fast, with not enough left to fight off a challenge from a late closer. It wasn't as if I had been down on my belly scrubbing as hard as I could with my stick to make my horse run such cruel fractions. Once he was off and running, I was unable to slow him down or give him a breather at any time in the race.

Even so, I rode back with hurt pride when the race was over; I was very embarrassed. The first person to greet me was Lukas's son, Jeff, an assistant trainer, who shouted some obscenities, which really surprised me, as I had never heard that kind of language coming from his mouth. I was already upset—upset at the outcome of the race and upset that people were booing me. I told him to go fuck himself and walked to the scales for the weigh-out, which is done to make sure a rider and his tack weigh the same before and after a race. Then I headed for the tunnel leading back to the jocks' room. That's when I met Wayne himself, who was standing with a group from the media corps, all with pens and pads at the ready to get the hot quotes Wayne had obviously promised they were going to get. And he really lit into me. Publicly. No, I didn't tell him what I'd told his son. I just said he needed a new rider for his horse. Then it came out in the news-papers and the *Daily Racing Form* that Lukas and Stevens had had a big blowup.

Actually, I already had been telling my agent that I didn't want to ride for Wayne Lukas anymore. I had been riding good horses for him but had begun to receive a lot of pressure from him. He was becoming very difficult to ride for. I was beginning to feel that, no matter what the cir-cumstances, if I didn't win a race for him, it was going to be my fault. I was always to blame. That year, it seemed that when I didn't win, there was a stamp on my forehead that said "scapegoat." The feeling had been grow-ing in the weeks leading up to that race in New York. I felt that I was be-coming excess baggage and had an uncanny sense that the next time I had a questionable ride I was going to be fired.

I have always been a pretty good judge of character and could sense when someone was getting ready to fire me. I tend not to operate very well under such conditions. In Wayne's defense, I remember that he too was under a lot of pressure. He was going to the yearling sales and spending forty to fifty million dollars a year on his clients' behalf, sometimes invest-ing three, four, or five million dollars on one particular horse. If that horse didn't turn out to be a champion, Wayne's neck was on the line. He was se-lecting these horses; he needed performance.

Concerning my own performances, I am perennially hard on myself. I don't think I should make mistakes. I have been at the top of my game for a number of years, and people pay me big money *not* to make mistakes. When I do my homework, study the films and the *Racing Form*, and go off to New York on a red-eye flight because someone has given me a guaran-tee against the purse money to go out there and perform like the best in my business, then I *should* be the best in the business. If I do make a mistake, I am my own worst critic. I guess I've been like that in everything I've ever done, whether it's playing golf on my days away from the track or playing the drums when I was a kid.

It was the same with wrestling. When I was beaten in a match, it was never because my opponent was a better wrestler; in my mind it was be-cause I hadn't prepared well enough or wasn't as fit as I should have been. I am a little difficult to be around in that way because I am so hard on myself. I tend not to leave my work at the office. If I have a bad day at the racetrack, I tend to bring it home with me. I go out there to win every race that I'm in. Most owners and trainers know the kind of pressure I put on myself.

I remember that whenever Wayne thought he got a bad ride from a jockey, he would tell the agent, "I'm suspending your jockey for six months," which meant you weren't going to ride for him for the next half year, and he would stick to his promise. When the six months were up, you could go back and ask him for rides. He suspended me at times for as long as three months. He suspended Angel Cordero; he suspended Pat Day and Laffit Pincay. He suspended the best of us. After being publicly berated after my ride on Farma Way, I told my agent that I wouldn't ride for Lukas for a year. "He suspends jocks," I said, "so I'm suspending this trainer. I'm not riding for him."

And I didn't. We would still speak cordially to one another in the morning, but it was probably two years before I rode for him again, and then it was just a few horses at first. I was not among his number-one riders again until 1995.

12 Hong Kong Calling

*M*arch 17, 1992, was a memorable day for me. A day earlier, I had been to a party given by Ray Kravagna, no longer my agent but still a close friend. It was an old custom of his to host a gathering around St. Patrick's Day at a pub in the basement of a bowling alley in Arcadia. This was mainly an excuse for a group of racetrack people to get together each year. There was always a pool tournament—we would draw our partners' names out of a hat—and since there was only one pool table, the tournament, which started at noon, would last pretty much all day. We drank beer; we laughed; it was always a good party.

I got home around seven thirty in the evening and wasn't in the greatest shape in the world. Toni greeted me with the news that our baby was about to be born. It would be our fourth child, so she was in a position to know. Fortunately, she didn't go into labor until about ten o'clock that night, so I had some time to get my senses back before we left for the hospital. Toni had had a very difficult pregnancy. There were a lot of problems, some of which had landed her in the hospital emergency room. She had gone into early labor six months out; the baby was breech, so Toni's abdomen had to be manipulated so the baby could be rotated. At one point, we thought we had lost the child. There was no heartbeat, but it did come back, and Toni's pregnancy resumed on a normal course.

There was a couch in her room at the hospital, so I was able to get some sleep while she was in labor. The baby, whom we would name Carlie, didn't arrive until about six thirty the next morning, St. Patrick's Day. I was in the delivery room wearing scrubs, expecting to be an interested observer just as I had been with my other children. When the baby's head appeared, the doctor suddenly turned to me and said, "Come on, come over here."

"What do you mean?" I asked.

"You're going to deliver this baby," he told me, and his nurses immediately pulled surgical gloves on me. My heart was going ninety miles an hour, but I followed the doctor's instructions and there were no problems. The baby just popped out into my hands. It was a pretty neat feeling to be the first one to hold Carlie when she entered the world.

She was a child we both had wanted, as Toni had been trying repeatedly to become pregnant. Our first two children were older; we felt that having a fourth child would create a potential sibling arrangement for Riley, who was going on three. Also, we hoped that having another child would help patch together a marriage that had already begun to fray at the seams.

Toni and I had married when we were both very young. Although our marriage seemed right at the time, over the course of the next dozen years or so, what with bearing and raising four children and running a household—a job in itself—Toni's interests changed. She developed an agenda that was totally different from mine. We came not to like each other's friends—mine were from the racetrack, most of hers were not—and, little by little, found ourselves growing apart. As time passed, our lives changed dramatically. We were both simple people raised in small towns who had suddenly become high-profile people earning more money than either of us had ever thought possible. Additionally, I made a lot of mistakes after the first years of my marriage—I admit that. I don't think I really started growing up until I was about thirty.

A lot of what happened had to do with my traveling, my schedule of being away, sometimes on a moment's call. Deep down inside, I felt what I was doing was wrong: flying off so frequently, devoting myself so fully to my career instead of being there for my wife and our children. I guess in a way I put my financial responsibilities ahead of my family responsibilities. On the other hand, my family had grown accustomed to a particular lifestyle. They couldn't continue to have the nice house and good car and also have me home all the time. Those elements just didn't jibe.

Toni traveled with me very rarely during our marriage, only to big events like the Kentucky Derby, Preakness, and Belmont Stakes—and to the championship Breeders' Cup races, of course. She made maybe four trips a year; having the children at home, it would have been difficult for her to make many more. My racing career eventually seemed of little interest to her, other than for the money it brought in. Carlie was barely a year old when Toni and I first parted. It was a trial separation designed to determine if we wanted to be together or not. As it was a legal separation (I was living in a different house), I stayed in constant touch with the family. Then after a few months, Toni and I decided we did want to be together; she insisted that I move back for the kids' sake. Early in 1994, I was home again. The months that followed were happy ones from my perspective. I think I was the best husband and father that I had ever been, but maybe that wasn't good enough.

That fall, Toni came with me to Churchill Downs for the Breeders' Cup races, a day I think I will never forget. I will certainly never forget the days that followed it. We flew to Louisville early in the week to settle in and relax. We had what I thought was a very enjoyable time. I was to ride One Dreamer in the Breeders' Cup Distaff. She was a big longshot, so it was a big surprise when she came in first. It really made the year for me to have won this race for Leonard Lavin, owner of Glen Hill Farms. He had tried to buy my contract when I was still an apprentice, but I hadn't wanted to ride in California then. So, winning on One Dreamer meant a lot to me.

We flew back to California immediately so I could ride a race at Hollywood Park on Sunday, the next day. I won that race and went off to play golf, as usual, on Monday, my day off. I returned home around four o'clock and found no one at home. That seemed very strange, considering that our household included four children and a live-in housekeeper. I walked through empty rooms on the way to the master bedroom and went into the master bath, where there was a telephone. I hadn't spoken to my parents all week and felt like talking to them. I was on the phone with my mother when I heard the front door open and footsteps in the hallway. Suddenly, Toni walked into the bathroom with a glare on her face. She didn't ask whom I was speaking to; she just said, "I need to talk to you." I told Mom I had to hang up, and Toni said, "I want you out of here."

"Excuse me," I said.

"I want you out of this house."

"You mean right now?" I asked. She shook her head yes. I was stunned, but I packed a couple of small duffel bags, climbed into my car, and drove off, thinking that this was probably just another one of our disputes. Toni was upset about something; I didn't know what but felt certain that, as usual, things would cool off in a day or so. Ron Anderson had been my agent for a couple of years by then, so I called him from my mobile phone in the car. "Toni and I have had an argument," I told him. "Could I come over to your house and spend the night?" He said that would be no problem. I stayed with Ron that night and spent most of the next day, Tuesday, just talking with him. He had already become a friend, familiar with the ups and downs of my marriage. I heard nothing from Toni, so I phoned her repeatedly and left messages. She wouldn't return my calls.

On Wednesday, I went to Hollywood Park to ride. After the races, I returned to Ron's house. When I walked in, he handed me an envelope. "You've been served," he said. "With what?" I asked. I was very confused. "They're divorce papers—I'm sure of it," he said. "Someone came to the house and asked me to deliver them to you." He was right. I had been served with divorce papers. What he didn't say was that my whole life was going to change. The divorce would alter me as a person. I had often been accused of being self-serving, of only looking out for number one, but from that time on, I became even more focused. And concerned. I started worrying more about myself, my future and my children's future. Other issues surfaced at the time those papers were served. One was that I was now solely responsible for keeping track of my finances, whereas Toni once handled all the bookkeeping. Another was that, although I thought I was very well off, I soon learned that I had been robbed of more than half a million dollars.

I had put a great deal of faith and trust in a business manager who had become a close friend. I paid very little attention to how he was dealing with my income, only to learn that much of it had vanished—through theft, not mismanagement. I never wanted to be involved in the financial aspect of my career. When I went from earning twenty-five hundred or three thousand dollars a week in Seattle to making six or seven times that much in Southern California, it really scared me. I mean, I was almost afraid to look at my paychecks. I remember some months would go by when I refused to see how much I made during a given week, because what I was earning didn't seem fair compared to the enjoyment I was having. All I wanted to do was go out and ride horses. Whenever I wanted to buy a car or go on a trip, I assumed there was money enough to do that. I also assumed I had put a lot of money away. But, as I was to learn, what funds I saved for the future had been wasted away by a thief who had died by then, so I was unable to get any of my money back.

Now, suddenly, it seemed clear that the only asset I had was my house. This proved to be another flawed assumption, for in reality that house had been a money pit. We'd had quite a bit of equity in it when the house was remodeled; then we took out a second mortgage. We basically overbuilt the house, and all of that equity vanished. There was very little for Toni and me to split. It was a shock for me to learn that when I finally moved out of the house Toni and I had shared, all I was able to take with me was a Dodge Viper sports car, a Ford truck, and the clothes in my closet. I had been riding racehorses for fifteen years and had earned millions of dollars in purses, but in 1994 I was virtually starting over.

When the initial divorce settlement came through and I learned what I would have to pay in spousal and child support each month, I was floored. To break even, I would have to continue earning an enormous amount of money, and that meant winning several races a week and several big-money stakes races every month. I had never been faced with that sort of pressure—of *having* to win. Until then, it had always been fun for me to go out and ride; it had never seemed like work. Now suddenly, I had to do it just so I could support my new financial responsibilities, all of which had been imposed on me by the court. The divorce itself would not be settled until 1998. During the interim, a lot of money would be drained off in attorneys' fees, mostly because of our mutual stubbornness. Also the lawyers, sensing that a lot of money was involved, tended to draw things out as long as they could. In the end, my children were the ones to lose, and the lawyers wound up with almost everything.

When I found out that I would have such a huge financial nut to crack every month, I panicked. I thought about just quitting the sport, because I had never ridden with a virtual noose around my neck and the nagging thought that, *God, I've gotta win this race.* For the first time, I worried about what my check was going to look like at the end of each week. Over the years, I had grown reconciled to the fact that there would be good weeks and bad weeks, but that it would all equal out in the end and I would do fine. Now, all of a sudden, I was being told I had to earn a specific amount.

I learned to be a disciplined person from my parents, but I have never liked being *told* to do anything. I like doing things on my own terms—not because I have to but because I want to. That's kind of the way I have lived my life—just like the horses I ride. They have to think that whatever they do is their idea or they don't do it.

Every six months, I can ask the court to review my earnings, with an eye to making some sort of adjustment. But in my business, six months is a long time to sustain a particular financial level. If I were hurt in a race tomorrow, my monthly level could not be recomputed until the next scheduled review date. When I retired, at the end of 1999, and ultimately became a salaried assistant trainer, for six months I had to maintain the spousal and child support commitments that had been placed on me when I was one of the top-earning jockeys in America.

At times, the pressure seemed almost unbearable. I had no money in the bank. I existed from paycheck to paycheck. I lived in digs far humbler than the mansion I had created for myself and my family. Saving very little, compared to what I was earning, I spent three years amassing enough for a down payment on the three-bedroom condominium I purchased about the time I remarried.

Although the day-to-day tensions of a failing marriage were gone, that period of separation was a difficult time for me. I was living by myself. I wasn't happy with anything in my life, particularly the legal system, which was making the divorce process so difficult. At first, after getting over the shock of being served papers, I thought, *Okay, this is gonna be fun.* Having quit school so young, I had missed out on high school parties, and I had never gone to college or experienced that kind of social life. I got married at eighteen and was a father when I was not quite twenty. I had never dated as an adult. *Now,* I thought, *I'm gonna have a good time. I'm gonna play the field.* Well, that idea lasted about a month. Things turned out to be very different from what I had expected after Toni and I separated.

What concerned me most was how I would restore my financial security. Yes, the horses were still there to be ridden, but my knees were beginning to trouble me. I didn't know how much longer I would be able to ride. What alternatives did I have? I had never actually held down a nine-to-five job. I had lived with the false assurance that I could quit riding any day I wished. Now, all of a sudden, came the twin realizations that I was not financially secure and that I was weighted down by a new burden I had created for myself.

Instead of dropping out, I hunkered down, working harder than I ever had at any time. My escape was the racetrack, and I came to depend on that to shut out everything else. It used to be that if things weren't good for me at home, they were really bad for me at the racetrack, and my performance suffered. If nothing else, going through a divorce has built a lot of character into me. As soon as I walk into the jocks' room, nothing else matters except riding horses and winning races. That's what is demanded of me. The owners who hire me always expect me to be 100 percent on my game, and I need to be. The expectations I lay on myself remain consistently high. It took me years to become comfortable with myself and the fact that I have been blessed with a special gift.

In late December 1994, just after the Santa Anita racing season opened, I got a phone call from a gentleman asking if I would be interested in going to Hong Kong. He offered me the chance to ride there, under contract, during the coming season, which would last approximately six months. What kind of money was involved? I asked. A lot, he assured me, all of it guaranteed. I didn't hesitate; I said yes, absolutely.

For the first time in my career, I would not be riding on a per-race basis, but would be contracted to ride racehorses for a set salary, along with the usual percentage of the winning purses. Now, instead of wondering what my paycheck would look like each month, I would know exactly how much my base earnings were going to be. It was like having a National Football League or major-league baseball contract. Of course, my contract also included some stipulations, fine print that allowed me to return to the States from time to time and also to terminate the contract legally. I would be allowed to fly back to the States on three separate occasions to ride in Grade I races. I would also be able to leave Hong Kong before the racing season ended if I were asked to ride a legitimate Triple Crown contender. I would take advantage of each of these escape clauses.

Life in Hong Kong proved different from anything I had experienced and so did riding races there. For one thing, the city itself is a melting pot of people of vastly different nationalities, a mixture that is reflected at the racetrack, where I found horses from various parts of the world and jockeys from England, France, Australia, and New Zealand. At any given time, there are only twenty-seven jockeys riding in Hong Kong, no more and no less, and it's extremely difficult to gain access to ride there professionally. You can't just hop a plane, fly there, and hope to be hired. You have to be *invited*, and once invited, you must be *accepted*. That was the first time I had ever been asked to present a résumé, but that's what the Hong Kong Jockey Club required before approving my contract.

Hong Kong has two racetracks: Happy Valley in downtown Hong Kong—which is like a racetrack in the middle of Manhattan—and Sha Tin, outside of town. I lived in Sha Tin in a house overlooking the track. It was peaceful, but getting there from the city—perhaps only a dozen miles as the crow flies—meant traveling traffic-choked highways and queuing up to pay tolls at tunnels bored through the mountains.

Racing in Hong Kong had a competitive edge, not only because top riders were involved but mainly because the purses were so big. The average purse earned for riding a winning horse was nearly four times what a winner might earn on an American track. Racing took place on dirt as well as on grass, but it was right-handed—the horses race clockwise—like so many tracks in England, unlike American tracks, which are uniformly left-handed, or counter clockwise. We raced Wednesday evenings at Happy Valley and Saturday afternoons at Sha Tin. Between racing days, there was plenty of golf, plenty of massages, and horse-training early in the day. Because of Hong Kong's extremely hot, humid climate, horses are trained at four o'clock in the morning and by seven o'clock, their training is finished. At first I thought I would never get used to the weather, but I did, finally. Everyone gets used to it.

My first trip home from Hong Kong was taken to ride in the Santa Anita Handicap in March 1995. My mount was Urgent Request, and on paper, at least, he had absolutely no chance of winning that race. I came back mainly because I was homesick for the States and really wanted to see my kids. I had gone to Hong Kong to find myself, and I did just that. I remembered an old saying, "The grass is always greener on the other side of the fence," and for me, the opposite was true. I got to the other side and immediately began to appreciate the life I had left behind.

Agreeing to ride Urgent Request gave me not only a free trip to the States—a weekend during which my children could visit me—but also a chance to ride a Grade I race. Urgent Request began as a big longshot then surprised everyone, myself included, by winning the race. While I was at Santa Anita, I was able to watch Kent Desormeaux ride a horse named Larry The Legend in a prep race for the upcoming Santa Anita Derby. Desormeaux was also scheduled to ride Afternoon Deelites in the Derby, which meant that at some point he would have to make a decision: one horse or the other. My agent, Ron Anderson, was staying with me in Hong Kong, but keeping track of everything going on elsewhere in the racing world and maintaining contact with the trainers of these two horses. I knew I was lined up to ride whichever mount Desormeaux declined. I believed I was in a good spot.

When Desormeaux chose to ride Afternoon Deelites, trained by Richard Mandella for owner Burt Bacharach, I flew back to California to ride Larry The Legend for trainer Craig Lewis, who was also the owner. My horse and Desormeaux's got into a thrilling stretch duel. About a sixteenth of a mile from the finish, Afternoon Deelites passed us, and there seemed no way we could possibly win. But the racing gods were looking after us that day, and my horse fought back. There was a photo finish that took a full five minutes for the stewards to study before announcing that we had won by a bob of the head. When my number flashed on the tote board, I was ecstatic—not only because I had won the Santa Anita Derby but also because I would be riding a legitimate contender in the Kentucky Derby three weeks later.

This was my way out, a chance to end my Hong Kong contract early, and I was ready to end it by then. I'd had enough of Hong Kong; it was a concrete jungle that had begun to close in on me. In that crowded city, with so many people viewing me all the time, I sensed what it would be like to be a monkey in a zoo. I felt no peace there, no privacy. Because of my success—I was winning 35 percent of my races, which was almost unheard of—I couldn't go anywhere without being recognized by local racing fans. I wasn't accustomed to dealing with that kind of celebrity.

As I flew back to Hong Kong, which I still had to do, of course, I felt wonderful. I had just won a million-dollar race; I would be riding the favorite in the Kentucky Derby; I would get to leave Hong Kong in less than a month. Ron Anderson met me when I got off the plane. He had a forlorn look on his face, and I wondered what was wrong. Why wasn't he excited? "Bad news, boss. Larry The Legend is done," he explained. The horse had fractured a bone; his career-ending injury had been discovered at some point during the seventeen hours I was in the air. I felt my world cave in around me.

A day or so later, the phone rang in our house and I heard Ron say, "Wayne, how ya doin'?" The two of them chatted for several minutes; then Ron came to me and said, "Wayne knows about Larry The Legend. He wants you to come home and ride Thunder Gulch in the Kentucky Derby." I knew Thunder Gulch. I had ridden him once in his second-to-last race as a two-year-old, the Remsen Stakes at New York's Aqueduct racetrack. I had flown there to ride Bertrando in a race that eventually became the Cigar Mile and found that I was also booked to ride Thunder Gulch that afternoon.

I didn't know the horse then, only that Wayne had just purchased him for a new client, Michael Tabor. He and I won the Remsen by a neck, but I thought he was just a big playboy. He lugged in with me constantly, clowned around, and didn't pay attention at all. Later, when I was living in Hong Kong, I watched videotaped races of all the Kentucky Derby contenders and felt that Thunder Gulch's antics were unchanged, even though he had turned three by then.

Mike Smith had been riding him, and though the horse had won a couple of big races in Florida, he had done so by small margins. When Mike switched to Talkin Man, Pat Day rode Thunder Gulch in the Bluegrass Stakes at the Keeneland racetrack in Lexington, Kentucky. He came in fourth, though he had been the heavy favorite, and Day chose not to ride him again. I watched his race in the Bluegrass and was unimpressed. Thunder Gulch seemed just as I remembered him: immature, still a cheater, not trying to run at all. I said, "Ron, you know what? I thought I was gonna be riding the winner of the Kentucky Derby, and now I won't be. I've made two trips home in the last month, and I don't want to make this one. I'd rather just stay here in Hong Kong for the rest of my contract."

Wayne called back the next day, and Ron said, "Look, Gary's not really interested." But Lukas insisted that I get on the phone. He and I had done very little business since 1991, but he obviously had been left without a rider for his horse. "Do me a favor," he asked. "Call Mike Smith and ask him about the horse." I agreed to make the call. I trusted Mike; we have been close friends and are always up-front and honest with each other. I would take his word on anything. When I got him on the phone, he leveled with me: "Gary, this horse *is* capable of winning the Kentucky Derby. From what I saw early in the year, he *has* got the talent. All he's gotta do is move forward a couple of lengths, and he's good enough to win this thing. I have no idea why he ran so poorly in the Bluegrass—I wasn't on him— but if you throw that race out, he fits with the rest of the Derby horses."

"All right, Mike," I said, "that's good enough for me." So I made another seventeen-hour flight to Los Angeles, then flew on to Louisville. I was expecting a difficult ride in the Kentucky Derby. I knew all of Thunder Gulch's tricks. I knew, for example, that he liked to get up next to a horse but not pass it, so I was expecting a battle, particularly in the stretch. But he surprised me. We came into the stretch about two lengths behind the pacesetters—Serena's Song and Talkin Man—and I asked him for his best run. In response, he gave me unbelievable acceleration. We won the race by two and a quarter lengths. Thunder Gulch didn't play around; he was like a boy who became a man that day.

That was the beginning of my relationship with the horse that would go on to sire Point Given, but if it hadn't been for Wayne Lukas encouraging me to ride him, who knows what would have happened? I might never have left Hong Kong!

Some years later, Mike Smith and I had dinner together at a restaurant right after he won a big race at Hollywood Park. When the waiter brought the bill, it was presented to Mike. "I ain't payin' that," he protested. "Stevens still owes me."

"What the hell do I owe you for?" I asked.

"Thunder Gulch, asshole. You still owe me." He was right, and I still do.

13 Judgment Calls

$\mathcal{T}$hunder Gulch was built like a bulldog: broad in the withers, shoulders, and hindquarters. He and Point Given had similar strides. Although he lacked the height of his most famous offspring, he wasn't small by any means. I stuck with him the rest of the year, most of the time successfully. In the 1995 Preakness Stakes, we finished third. There were no excuses. He had a good trip; he was just a little dull with me. Perhaps he had run too hard in the Kentucky Derby and was tired. Whatever the cause, he just didn't fire his best race at Pimlico that day. Had he peaked as the sportswriters were saying? Not quite.

He came back and won the Belmont Stakes very easily, then the Swaps Stakes at Hollywood Park and the Travers at Saratoga. I clearly remember the Travers, because my horse was very excitable that day. I didn't like the way he warmed up and was concerned about his cantankerousness going to the gate. Worse, the assistant trainer assigned to us had never handled him before.

Thunder Gulch was the kind of animal you didn't want to force. You had to just coax him, because if you tried to *make* him do something, he would become angry and rebellious. I guess we were not standing perfectly at the gate, so the assistant was determined to make the horse stand in what he considered the proper manner. I remember that the guy was pulling on the bridle and trying to push the horse forward; Thunder Gulch may have had one foot back and one foot ahead instead of being squared up.

After being pulled at and pushed two or three times, the horse got upset. When the gate opened, he went straight up in the air and I almost came off of him. He was, by far, the last horse out of the gate, left behind by about three lengths. But we won that race by about five lengths and it probably was the best race of his career, even though those few lost seconds, right at the start, could have cost us the victory. We went on to win the Kentucky Cup Classic at Turfway Park. Then we were back at Belmont Park in the fall for the Jockey Club Gold Cup, a major prep race for the Breeders' Cup. That's when he injured an ankle. It was not a life-threatening injury, but Thunder Gulch had become too valuable to risk racing as a four-year-old. He was immediately retired to stud.

In the days leading up to the Breeders' Cup races at Belmont Park in 1995, I was forced to make a decision—whether to ride Hennessey or Honour and Glory in the Juvenile. It was a very difficult decision to make, because both horses were very good, and both were trained by Wayne Lukas. Each had a different owner, however. This was a tough spot for me to be in, for though I sensed that Hennessey had a better chance of winning the Juvenile, for a variety of reasons I felt obligated to ride Honour and Glory. As it turned out, neither horse won, but that was one of the times when politics forced me into a decision I didn't think was necessarily the best one.

Although I didn't win any of the Breeders' Cup championship races that year, I did win the California Cup Classic at Santa Anita. Traditionally, that race occurs several days after the Breeders' Cup as the climax of a day of racing exclusively for California-bred horses—a sort of Breeders' Cup West. My mount was Luthier Fever, a horse I had won a couple of good races with, but his significance to me that day was reflected in what his win enabled me to do.

For a couple of weeks prior to the race, I had been admiring a bull-dog in a local pet store. His price tag was twenty-five hundred dollars, which I thought insane. It seemed unreasonable to consider paying that kind of money for a dog. Still, the animal appealed to me, even though I couldn't bring myself to open my wallet and shell out the money. Everyone around me knew I wanted to own that dog. What no one knew was the private pact I had made with myself: if I happened to get lucky and win the California Cup Classic, I would apply my share of the $250,000 purse money to purchasing the dog.

The Classic was the eighth race of the afternoon. At 4:30 I won the race; by 6:30 I had the little bulldog in my home. To honor the horse that had funded his purchase, I named the dog not Luthier, but Luther.

Soul Of The Matter was just one of many horses I have ridden that owed his success on the track not only to good breeding but also to masterful training. In pointing him to the first Dubai World Cup, then a $4 million race, Richard Mandella did something unique, by American standards, before shipping the horse to the United Arab Emirates. Knowing that the horse would have to carry 126 pounds in the World Cup, the trainer put lead pads under the saddle when he trained to get Soul Of The Matter used to pulling that much weight. Mandella basically trained his horse into the World Cup; there were no equivalent prep races leading up to it.

Exercise riders may weigh from 125 to 150 pounds, but Soul Of The Matter's regular exercise boy weighed only 105 pounds, and as a result his morning workouts were being clocked at much faster rates than most of the other horses'. By adding weight to the saddle, Mandella made sure the horse would be carrying as much of a load in training as he would be with me on him during the race.

I had ridden at Dubai once before, in 1993, when the racetrack first opened. A jockeys' championship was held there that year. Three years later, the first World Cup was held. I had never seen a place change so dramatically in such a short time. I remembered that the racetrack was situated in a remote area outside the city, but it was remote no longer. The city, with its new shopping malls and a great many more hotels, had grown right up to the edge of the racetrack. The facility itself, which was first class from the start, had many new amenities, including an expanded grandstand.

Dubai is like Hong Kong in that it attracts an enormous number of travelers and expatriates. People from Middle Eastern and Western European countries flock there for Thoroughbred racing each year. What is still amazing to me is that they all come for the sport. There is a religious prohibition against gambling.

Sending Soul Of The Matter to Dubai, even with Mandella's unique training program, was a huge gamble, because to the racing media and to European bookmakers alike, Cigar was the heavy favorite going into that race. No other horse was expected to present much of a challenge. We did, however. Coming into the stretch, which was about three-eighths of a mile from the finish line, we were running behind Cigar, ready to pounce whenever I felt the time was ripe. At the eighth pole, I did pounce and got us a neck in front of Cigar. For a brief moment, I thought we had put Cigar away, but he came back at us and won by half a length. I came away from that race with new respect for Cigar, eventually the top money-winning horse in the world, because Soul Of The Matter was such a good horse. It was disappointing to have made the lead yet not won the race. But Mandella and I both knew our horse had given us his best run. Being second to Cigar was nothing to be ashamed of; in that respect, the trip and the training that preceded it were both extremely successful.

It was usually judgment, my own and the trainer's, that convinced me to ride a particular horse, and in 1996 I shared Wayne Lukas's belief that Editor's Note was destined for big things. He was a big, strong horse with a mind of his own, and most of the time his mind was telling him to play around. He was a very difficult horse to ride. We entered the Kentucky Derby certain we were going to win, but didn't. We finished sixth. We were favored to win the Preakness, but didn't. Once again, the horse failed to fire.

For several months, I had been having problems with my left shoulder. It kept subluxing on me—dislocating and then popping back when I was whipping a horse left-handed. About two weeks before I was to ride Editor's Note in the Belmont Stakes, I was at Hollywood Park riding a filly that began lugging in badly in the stretch. A few strides before reaching the finish line, I raised my left arm to hit her left-handed, and my shoulder dislocated again. Only this time it didn't pop back into the joint.

After the race, it was obvious that I needed assistance. My filly was pulled up by the outriders. I dismounted and was put into an ambulance and taken to Centinela Hospital. Less than twenty-four hours later, I was in surgery having my rotator cuff repaired and screws put in my left shoulder to reattach the ligaments. Needless to say, healing from surgery and an incision that extended from my armpit to the top of my shoulder, I sat out the Belmont Stakes. Actually, I was there at the track, high up in the announcers' booth, doing the color commentary for ABC Sports. From that vantage point, I watched Editor's Note, with Rene Douglas aboard, win the race.

During a commercial break, sportscaster Al Michaels asked if I felt horrible because I wasn't riding. I told him truthfully that though disappointed, I didn't feel bad. People in racing had been saying that Lukas and I were too high on Editor's Note, that he wasn't nearly the horse we believed he was. We both had continued to have faith that Editor's Note would win big races, so I felt vindicated, even though I was not riding him in the Belmont. I did ride him again to win the Louisiana Super Derby later that year. That was further vindication of my judgment.

Meanwhile, I had to endure about six weeks of rehabilitation, which began the day after my operation. After all the surgical tightening came the task of getting 100 percent mobility back into the shoulder. It was extremely painful. I can say with authority that shoulder rehabilitation is the most agonizing rehabilitation there is —knees are easy by comparison. For weeks, a physical therapist worked with me daily, grabbing my arm and stretching it. At first, I couldn't lift my hand above my head, so there was a lot of work to be done.

With any injury, the unused muscles of the body part start to atrophy within twenty-four hours. In order to restore strength and flexibility to my shoulder, toning my muscles required an equal amount of attention. From day one, I worked with very light weights—they weighed ounces, not pounds—using a pulley system mounted on the wall. I pulled and pulled, and little by little, more and more weight was added until the muscles finally functioned as they once had. The screws remained. I have never felt them, which is just as well, because they can never be removed.

* * *

Sound judgment was the hallmark of another trainer I rode for in 1996, Michael Dickinson. He was highly eccentric, but I came to regard him as an absolute genius. Raised in England, Dickinson had earned his reputation in steeplechase racing, becoming a legend the year his horses came in first, second, third, and fourth in the Grand National, a race that as many as forty-four horses start but only ten usually finish, because so many horses fall. In search of new fields to conquer, Dickinson eventually switched to flat racing and moved to America.

I had never worked for him until being asked to ride Da Hoss at Belmont Park, in a prep race prior to the Breeders' Cup, which was to be held at Woodbine, just outside Toronto. After learning that I had the mount for Dickinson, other jockeys began making jokes about him: "Wait till this guy comes down and gives you a map of the race, with all your instructions written out."

"Come on, you guys are pullin' my leg," I insisted, but sure enough, two hours before the prep race, Michael Dickinson walked into the jockeys' quarters and asked for me. I met him in the waiting room, where trainers come to discuss strategy, and Dickinson introduced himself. We shook hands, and he whipped a sheet of paper out of the pocket of his sports jacket and showed me a list of all the positive and negative things about the horse he could think of. I don't remember exactly what was on that list, but I do recall him saying that Da Hoss's strongest suit was good tactical speed.

What Dickinson was telling me was exactly what his horse was going to be capable of doing that day, including how fast he thought the horse was going to run. Reminding me that he was pointing Da Hoss for the Breeders' Cup Mile, he insisted that we were one race away from Da Hoss's best race—and he told me precisely how fast he felt his horse would have to run to win it. I thought he was crazy.

In most of the races Da Hoss had won, the horse had run very close to the pace, which is just how he ran his race that day at Belmont Park. We were close to the pace, laying third and fourth the whole way, and then Da Hoss put in a fairly nice run down the stretch with me. He got a little tired at the end and finished second, but his time, to the second, was just what Dickinson had predicted. We hadn't won, but Dickinson was satisfied that everything had gone according to plan. He was pleased with the way the horse had run and with the way I had ridden him. We agreed that I should ride Da Hoss in the Breeders' Cup Mile.

Arriving in Canada for the big race, I checked the *Daily Racing Form* and noted that every horse entered in the Mile shared the same running style. There was a lot of speed among the fourteen contenders, and of course Da Hoss was known as a speed horse. Furthermore, we had drawn the six hole, right near the center of the pack. None of this was good news. The night before the race, I didn't believe Da Hoss had a good chance of winning because I thought Dickinson was going to tell me, once again, to stay close to the pace. I couldn't see myself being able to save any ground because there would be five horses between me and the inside rail, all trying to do the same thing. I had a vision of going into the first turn five wide, and I thought, *Oh, well, I'll just go out and ride the horse however he tells me to, and whatever we get, we'll get.* Talk about selling a man short!

The next day, Dickinson met me in the jocks' room at Woodbine and said, "I know you're going to think I'm mad, but I think the only chance for us to win the race is by taking this horse back." I looked up at him and just smiled. "What?" he asked. I said that I agreed, of course. Then *he* smiled and said, "Okay, listen. I just walked the turf course. There's been some heavy rain; the grass is on the soft side; and the horses haven't been using the turf course along the inside fence. Temporary rails were set up early in the week to protect the course, so the ground on the inside is fresh. Right on top of the rail down the backside is the best going, so what I want you to do is take this horse back immediately—after the first steps—and cut right to the inside rail. Just stay there till you get to the head of the stretch, then look for an opening. Down the stretch, the ground is pretty even all the way across, so I don't care where you're at. You get Da Hoss to the quarter pole and the race is yours."

Well, I loved this plan, of course, because I knew we would have no chance of winning if we ran close to the pace. However, as this horse had never come from far back, this would be something new for him—and a challenge for me as a rider, to get him to want to try a new tactic. When the race began, with his first stride out of the starting gate, I took a really strong hold of him and made a beeline for the inside rail. I had him dead last. To my surprise, everyone running in front of us was staying out three or four lengths off the rail. There would have been room for three horses to run up on the rail, but none of them did.

I was relaxed. I didn't move Da Hoss up; I let him take his time. Down the backside, it was as though the gates of heaven had opened up for me. Everywhere I wanted to be, there was room, so I started passing horses, one by one, as we approached the far turn. By the half-mile pole, I was laying third behind two pacesetters, but I was still on the rail—alone. From that point to the last eighth of a mile, I was virtually biding my time until I decided to ask him for his best run. If he responded the way I felt he would, I knew I was going to win the race.

Cash Asmussen was following right behind me on Spinning World, the horse that would win the Breeders' Cup Mile exactly one year later. Asmussen thought he had me any time he wanted, but at the eighth pole, Da Hoss just exploded, giving me the kind of acceleration that a truly great mile runner is capable of. The result: We went on to win by daylight, just as Dickinson had predicted.

Since I hadn't known Da Hoss very well, I would have been too intimidated to take matters into my own hands and ride him the way I did without Dickinson's specific instructions. If it had been up to me, riding for a new trainer, I would have resisted the urge to try changing the horse's style of running. Without Dickinson's advice, I would have ridden Da Hoss the way it looked liked I should on paper.

I am still astounded by how game that trainer was going into this race. Basically, what he was saying was, "Look, let's try this. If it works, it works; if it doesn't, it won't," an attitude that put me at ease. For my part, I thought, *Well, if I get stopped, I'll be stopped, and if I don't get a run, there's always another day.* The mutual respect that grew out of that race established a great friendship between Dickinson and me, one that would soon be tested.

Despite his easy-seeming win, Da Hoss suffered a tendon injury in the Breeders' Cup Mile and was out of competition for more than a year. I had the feeling he would never race again, but two months before the 1998 Breeders' Cup races, Dickinson called my agent, Ron Anderson, and announced, "I'm bringing Da Hoss back to the races. I'm going to win another Breeders' Cup with him." Obviously, he wanted me to ride him.

"The man really *is* crazy, completely mad," I told Ron. "There is *no* way this horse can win the Breeders' Cup. It's tough enough to win big races with one horse in back-to-back years, let alone to win on a horse that's had a year off recovering from an injury. To come back that way and win the most competitive one-mile race of the year? There's no way." I was already planning to ride another good miler that year, but I can't even remember the horse's name.

Ron actually laughed at Dickinson over the phone, but the trainer persisted: "Ron, I'll bet you twenty-five hundred dollars that I win the Breeders' Cup." Ron accepted the bet. My horse ran poorly; we finished eleventh, well back in the pack. I knew it had been a close finish, but I didn't know what horse had won. I was galloping out, after the race, weaving in and out of horses in an effort to see the winner. I knew Hawksley Hill had made a late run at the leaders, but it wasn't until I had galloped past the finish that I spotted the winner: Da Hoss. When he was interviewed in the winner's circle, Dickinson seemed more excited about winning twenty-five hundred dollars from Ron Anderson than about winning a million-dollar race. All I could do was smile.

Michael Stoute was another English trainer keenly in tune with his horses and supremely capable of explaining how he wanted them ridden. Because of him, I would have another important mount in the 1996 Breeders' Cup races at Woodbine that year. Like Michael Dickinson, Stoute had a handle on his horses' tendencies and a clear idea of how he wanted them ridden. More important, he was able to communicate his feelings precisely to me. If information is not communicated to me in the right way, then I probably won't pick up on it and it's not going to help at all.

The communication I had with Dickinson and Stoute was similar to what I had with Lukas and Barrera, though perhaps on a higher level. In a way, it was almost like telepathy. Very little may have been said, but a lot was communicated. Just as there are gifted riders, there are gifted trainers—people who are not only knowledgeable but skillful at sharing their knowledge. When they talk to me, a peaceful feeling comes over me, and I think to myself, *I know what you want. I understand what I have to do.*

I had never ridden for Michael Stoute before 1996, but through the representative of Sheikh Mohammed, I was asked to ride Singspiel, a Stoute-trained horse, in the Canadian International at Woodbine. When Stoute met with me, he explained that Singspiel was still learning: "When he gets to the front, he thinks his job is over and tends to want to ease up. So, ride him toward the front, but try and time your ride so you don't get in front any earlier than you have to. Otherwise, he'll pull up."

Stoute's instructions were clear, and I rode the horse exactly the way he asked me. I got in front with still a furlong left to go, but we won very easily. When we came back, the trainer asked what I thought about the race. I confessed that I had become a little excited and moved Singspiel a little bit early. "If I ride him more patiently than I did, with the closing kick he has, I think he can win the Breeders' Cup Turf." Stoute smiled. I think he appreciated that I admitted I hadn't ridden his horse perfectly. I think the relationship that evolved between me and Michael Stoute can be traced to that moment.

The Breeders' Cup races at Woodbine took place less than four weeks after the Canadian International. Stoute had two horses entered in the mile and a half Breeders' Cup Turf: Pilsudski and Singspiel. Perhaps because of this, his instructions to me that day contradicted what he had said before. Instead of urging me to ride more patiently, he told me to go ahead and let Singspiel show his speed. Coming into the stretch, I was laying second. I got in front at the same point when I had assumed the lead in the Canadian International, and Singspiel started playing around with me. Then Pilsudski came along and beat him by more than a length. What I did for Pilsudski is what I needed to have a horse do for me—lead me inside of the furlong pole so I would be in a position to pounce on him and win. Instead, Singspiel and I set up the race for the other horse.

The following year, I was asked to ride Singspiel in the Dubai World

Cup, but I refused. I told Ron Anderson I didn't think the horse could run successfully on dirt, so Jerry Bailey was asked to ride him. That year, the World Cup was delayed a full week because of rain. Due to his racing commitments in Florida, Bailey elected not to sit out the storm. He flew back to the States and announced he wouldn't be returning to Dubai to ride the race. I was asked once again if I would take the mount, and once again I refused.

I try to be diplomatic when refusing any offer to ride, but right or wrong, I often have only a gut instinct to rely on when deciding which horses to ride. With Singspiel in the World Cup, I was adamant. Bailey proved less so; he was persuaded to fly back to Dubai to ride him.

On race day, my dad joined me at Santa Anita at six thirty in the morning so we could watch the race together on closed-circuit TV. Three-eighths of a mile from the finish, Dad turned to me and asked, "What do you think?" I said, "I think I just made a four-million-dollar mistake." When Singspiel crossed the finish line first, all I could do was laugh. The mistake was definitely mine.

14 *Decisions, Decisions*

*I*t was near the end of the 1996 racing season that I first rode Gentlemen, a South American-bred colt trained by Richard Mandella, and the sensations I felt were memorable: goosebumps and chills running down my neck and spine. I knew in an instant that this was a great horse. Running at a really good pace but still just cruising, he could move faster than most other horses, and when I asked him for a little more, he would give it to me. When I asked for even more, he would accelerate again.

For me, riding Gentlemen was similar to what I felt aboard Point Given on a trip down the backstretch: no vulnerability at all, as though there was no other horse on the racetrack that could even compare with the one I was sitting on. Gentlemen personified great power and speed. He was a gorgeous animal, beautifully proportioned, but also an absolute handful. In the paddock, it took two handlers to keep him in check, but out on the racetrack, where there were no handlers, it was just me and the lead-pony rider, and nine times out of ten I was trying to keep his mind off the pony and strictly on us before a race began. Like Point Given, he reacted negatively to being disciplined. If I reacted harshly to something he did—and reached down to give him a slap with my whip—I knew I'd better be tied on securely because he would always retaliate. He might throw his head up, come to a dead stop, try to buck me off, or bite the lead pony. There was a mean streak in him. This was an animal you didn't want to annoy. I wanted to be his best friend when I was on his back.

Gentlemen was among the best of the best, one of the five top horses

I have ridden. I may never again have the opportunity to ride a horse of the quality of Gentlemen, In Excess, Thunder Gulch, Point Given, or Silver Charm. Horses like that are the kind that a trainer and a jockey might encounter only once in a lifetime, but I was fortunate to have ridden all five of them. I call them freaks, because each had an overabundance of talent plus an amazing ability to use that talent. Each also had a highly competitive spirit as well as an athletic body and an athletic stride.

Silver Charm was still a two-year-old when Bob Baffert first asked me to ride him in 1996, not long after I had recovered from shoulder reconstruction. I worked him one morning on the Santa Anita racetrack, and afterward Bob asked me what I thought. "He's a freak," I said. How else to describe the impression that horse had given me! But Bob was unsatisfied: "What the fuck does that mean?" he demanded. What it meant, I guess, was that Silver Charm impressed me with his energy and alertness, and as I worked him, it became clear that he could do things no other two-year-old could do at that stage. The colt had speed, but when I asked him, he would show even more speed—not all of his speed, maybe just half. I sensed that much more was there.

I worked Silver Charm several times in the months ahead and realized that he was extremely lazy. He never put a lot of work into his training. The first time I rode him in a race was in the Santa Anita Derby, a few weeks before the 1997 Kentucky Derby. Bob instructed me to make the colt show a lot of speed, to lay up close to the pace and not to let the front-runner loose on the lead. That would have been the filly Sharp Cat, one of the favorites, and Bob said, "Keep pressure on her all the way."

The trainer and I agreed that Silver Charm needed a good stiff race prior to the Kentucky Derby because he had been sluggish in his previous outings. Silver Charm didn't win the Santa Anita Derby, but he did finish second, a head behind his rival, Free House. It had seemed that we were going very slow, but after the race, when I saw the distance fractions posted on the tote board, I was very surprised. The time set by the front-runner in each segment of the race had been extremely fast, and Silver

Charm had run close to those fractions. That's when I knew for sure that he really was special, a truly great athlete. Because good horses like that fool you. They run much faster than they let you think.

I learned something important from Silver Charm that day—that he could be a very versatile horse. I didn't need to rush him; he didn't have to run near the lead. I could use his speed tactically to put him into a race but save his best for the final quarter of a mile. In the mile and one-eighth Santa Anita Derby, my colt put enormous pressure on Sharp Cat and still had enough left to put in a grueling last two furlongs.

That race gave Silver Charm the extra seasoning that Bob felt he needed to handle the mile and a quarter Kentucky Derby. We were confident as we flew off to Churchill Downs and equally confident two weeks later when Silver Charm ran in the Preakness Stakes in Baltimore. The horse won both races in much the same way: when he grabbed the lead, he wouldn't let any other horse run by him. We were then favored to win the Belmont Stakes and become the first Triple Crown winners in nineteen years. And an eighth of a mile from the finish, I was positive we *could* win. But at the sixteenth of a mile post, I saw a shadow coming up on the outside. Like most jockeys, I have good peripheral vision, so I can see things before they actually happen. At that stage of the race, Silver Charm was near the rail, and the shadow was in the middle of the track, outside of my horse's line of vision.

It was over in a flash: from well off the pace, Chris McCarron and Touch Gold swept by, snatching that victory from us. In a matter of about three seconds, I went from having the highest high I've ever had to the lowest low, an incredible mood swing. I was in a stupor for days—months, even—to have come that close to winning the Triple Crown and not to have had it happen. It was something I don't think I'll ever get over; the memory will never go away. After losing that race, I went into a deep, deep depression. No one knew that except the people closest to me.

It's wasn't just losing a big race that affected me that way, but losing the chance to put our sport back in the limelight by making news. Going into that final leg of the Triple Crown, I felt as if I had the whole country and the entire sport riding on my shoulders. To be beaten like that was like letting everyone down. I felt completely deflated.

Of course, there were naysayers who had been insisting that Silver Charm didn't deserve to win the Triple Crown because he wasn't a great horse. But I think he proved he *was* a great horse by what he did as a four-year-old, in 1998. After winning two major stakes races at Santa Anita, he was pointed to the four-million-dollar Dubai World Cup. But before shipping him to the United Arab Emirates, Bob entered him in the Grade I Santa Anita Handicap scheduled for early March.

I had a difficult choice to make because Gentlemen was also entered in the Big Cap. Which horse was I going to ride? I'd often had to choose between two good horses, but never between two *great* ones. Obviously, I didn't want to lose either mount, and I knew that whichever horse I chose not to ride, I would never be asked to ride again. Having won the Kentucky Derby on Silver Charm, I felt a strong loyalty to him. I also felt a certain loyalty to his owners, Bob and Beverly Lewis, who had been so good to me in the past. I had ridden and won on their filly Serena's Song many times. I let my heart guide my decision: I chose to ride Silver Charm.

But as luck would have it, Silver Charm wound up missing the Santa Anita Handicap because of an abscess in one hoof. He may have stepped on a stone or bruised the frog, the soft part of his foot, and an abscess had formed when blood beneath the damaged tissue became infected. The horse obviously couldn't run again, or even work, until the infection was gone. He missed the race and about ten days of training.

Actually, bypassing the Santa Anita Handicap may have been a blessing in disguise. I believed that if he ran hard in that race, he wouldn't be at his best in the Dubai World Cup three weeks later. When Silver Charm could work again, Bob trained him specifically for the Dubai World Cup, continuing to feel confident despite the pressure. *How fit was the horse?* people wondered. *Was his foot still bothering him?* He had been getting shots of Lasix, because he tended to bleed under stress. Lasix could be administered legally at every major American track by then, but it was prohibited in Dubai. How would the absence of Lasix affect him? Added to those concerns was the fact that Silver Charm would be the first Kentucky Derby winner in many years to race outside of the United States. Thus, he would carry the reputation of having won America's biggest and most glorious race halfway around the world. You don't want to go to another country and get your butt kicked if you're a Kentucky Derby winner.

To race in the World Cup, Silver Charm would have to endure a profound change not only of climate but of time zones as well. He had to be flown from California to Frankfurt and from there to Dubai. The trip was grueling because it took thirty-six hours, but the flight itself was probably less jarring than a lengthy road trip by van. For long flights by jumbo jet, each horse is loaded into a four-sided palette that's hoisted up through the belly of the plane. On some flights there are sixty to eighty horses plus the grooms who look after them and keep them hydrated. Of course, there are sedatives on board that can be administered if a horse suddenly goes nuts during its long confinement. After landing in Frankfurt, the horses are removed, watered and walked around before being returned to their palettes and loaded aboard another plane for the final leg of their journey. Upon arriving in Dubai, each horse is given several liters of electrolytes, by intravenous injection, to stave off the equine equivalent of jet lag.

Despite our concerns and the misgivings of many in the racing media, we won that four-million-dollar race by a short nose. At the finish, barely a sixteenth of an inch separated Silver Charm from his nearest rival, the Irish-bred Swain. It was one of the bravest performances made by any horse I have ever ridden. After he won that race, Bob backed off of him because he thought the horse needed a rest, and he did. He was very tired and deserved a layoff. The result, however, was that Silver Charm put on a lot of weight and got a little spoiled. Maybe he got used to the easy life. After a lengthy holiday, a lot of horses lose their incentive, their drive—that competitive edge. They are not likely to regain what they had. Historically, few horses have ever been the same after traveling to race in the Dubai World Cup. It's the rare horse that can bounce back to his best form after that experience.

Silver Charm did come back that fall to win two major stakes races, but then he was beaten in the Breeders' Cup Classic. He ran a gallant race but lost by less than a length, which was a switch. Usually he found a way to have his nose in front at the finish line. He was known for creating heart-stopping finishes, and he won a lot more photo finishes than he was ever beaten in. He was the epitome of a horse that would give you everything. In my own view, he was an overachiever. Maybe he wasn't meant to be as good as he was, but at his best he had an extraordinary will to win.

Months later, he bled badly during the 1999 Dubai World Cup, finishing sixth after running as the favorite, and was retired shortly thereafter. Gentlemen, too, was retired by that time—and for the same reason. He had come in fourth in the 1998 Santa Anita Handicap under Pat Day, who had accepted the mount when I chose to ride Silver Charm, and was retired by the end of that year. Cardiopulmonary bleeding is not rare among Thoroughbreds or athletes in any sport who perform great physical feats under stress. The problem is that when a horse bleeds repeatedly, scar tissue can form in the lungs and be so damaging to a horse's performance as to be career-ending. That's what happened to both Gentlemen and Silver Charm. They had become too valuable for their owners to risk their injury or fatality, so they were retired to stud.

There are very few racing pictures on the wall in my family room, but one of them is of Silver Charm crossing the finish line at the Kentucky Derby ahead of Captain Bodgit. I guess I'll always feel something for this horse that I never felt for any other horse I have ridden.

The year I rode Silver Charm to my third Kentucky Derby win, I began a three-year term as president of the Jockeys' Guild. It's an essential job, but in many ways a thankless one. There is no glory to be gained or money to be earned. Serving the guild means serving your fellow jockeys, and most of us riders learn very quickly to respect the well-being of our brethren. The Jockeys' Guild was formed in 1943 because of the need to improve the safety and well-being of professional riders. Membership is voluntary, but most professionals comprehend the value of membership and willingly pay annual dues and contribute a portion of their standard riding fees.

In the decades before the guild was established, all but the top riders were paid whatever trainers felt they were worth. There was no standard, no mandated pay scale, and the jockeys' quarters at even the best racetracks were substandard. It was not unusual for a jockey to sit in a closed car with the motor running and the heater on, trying to shed a few pounds. Today at most major tracks there is a steam room, a sauna, and exercise equipment—weights, treadmills, and stationary bikes. Some facilities even have swimming pools.

Much of what we do on the racetrack may seem effortless to the casual viewer, and many of us appear indestructible. But health issues and insurance coverage concern most of us as much as any other working person and nearly every head of family. The guild has paid attention to these issues and also focused a great deal of energy and time on safety. Today, there are safer racing surfaces, safety rails set up to protect us at most tracks, clothing requirements to lessen our injuries, and an ambulance follows behind us as we ride, ready to come to our immediate aid if there's an accident. As a body, we are concerned about the growing use of drugs on horses—not only because their well-being can be affected but also because, as riders, we are so vulnerable. On the whole, we are not advocates of medicating horses. We believe that no race-day medication should ever be allowed.

From the time I began riding professionally until the year I temporarily retired, the Jockeys' Guild had only four different presidents. One of them, Bill Shoemaker, held the post for many three-year terms, followed by Jerry Bailey. I assumed the presidency in 1997 and was reelected for a second term. But with my retirement came my resignation. Pat Day was eventually persuaded to take the assignment, and he did an outstanding job during the time he served.

There was a degree of honor involved in being selected by your racing colleagues and competitors to serve a greater cause, but the honor I felt during my three-year term was nothing compared to what I felt when I received an Eclipse Award in 1998. Eclipse Awards in various categories—similar to Hollywood's array of Oscars—are sponsored by the National Thoroughbred Racing Association, the National Turf Writers Association and the *Daily Racing Form*. The awards honor Eclipse, an eighteenth-century Thoroughbred that ran unbeaten in eighteen starts, then went on to sire winners of more than three hundred races. When I didn't win the jockey award in 1988 or 1995, I began to think I would never be recognized for anything I achieved. Induction into the Racing Hall of Fame in 1997 softened my distress, so I decided I would attend the Eclipse Award presentation again the following year. When my name was called, I felt elated.

It was a black-tie event in a crowded South Beach hotel ballroom, and when I accepted the award I was able to pay tribute to my parents, because of their constant support, and also to Ron Anderson, who had flown to Florida with me. I acknowledged him not only for the job he had done as my agent but also because of the personal loyalty he had shown me during the past seven years. He had gone to Hong Kong with me; he had lived through a divorce with me; he had been there for me as solidly in bad times as in good ones. I never considered myself his boss; I looked to him as *my* boss. Ron was my rock.

My personal life changed in 1998 because of another important decision I made. In March my divorce became final; in May I remarried. Nicola Woad and I had been acquaintances at the racetrack for some time; she exercised horses. That year, we began dating, drawn together because of our love of horseracing and also of antiques—we spent as many dates in antiques shops as we did in restaurants and movie houses. Neither of us was looking to get married, but it didn't take long for us to realize that we just couldn't be apart. We became engaged not long after our first date. Back in California, the Sunday after the 1998 Kentucky Derby, we started to review the many arrangements we would need to complete in order to be married in June. It all seemed too hectic. At that point, we were *ready* to be married. We wanted to be husband and wife, so why not just do it!

On Monday, I phoned Ron Anderson and my jockey friend Chris Antley around three o'clock in the afternoon and asked them both if they wanted to go to Las Vegas. "What for?" they asked. I told them Nikki and I had decided to get married. Three hours later, the four of us were boarding a plane. Chris was to be my best man; Ron, our witness.

Riding in Dubai is always an adventure. My dad and I enjoyed an eventful camel ride during the 1998 World Cup festivities in Dubai.

My first win at Royal Ascot in England came in 1997 aboard the Godolphin-owned Predappio.

The Thoroughbred Corporation's Royal Anthem, one of the world's best turf horses in 1999, winning at York (GB).

Winning for England's Queen Elizabeth II, at Ascot in 1999, aboard Blueprint.

Thunder Gulch's son Point Given (owned by The Thoroughbred Corporation and trained by Bob Baffert) captured two of the three legs of the 2001 Triple Crown. Here we are in the winner's circle after the Preakness.

©Shigeki Kikkawa

Showing some love to the trophy after Point Given's victory in the Preakness.

Point Given, winning by widening lengths, in the 2001 Belmont Stakes.

How's this for a who's who of racing? Trainers: Ron McAnally (far left) and
Charlie Wittingham (far right); bookend jockeys (from left to right): Eddie Delahoussaye, Laffit
Pincay Jr., Chris McCarron, and me at a Hall of Fame ceremony at Hollywood Park in 1998.

©Benoit Photo

Hoisting the trophy after Shoe led
us to victory in the international
jockeys' challenge at Santa Anita
in 1998.

In 1995, I guided Larry The
Legend to an upset victory over
Afternoon Deelites in the
Santa Anita Derby.

The courageous filly Serena's Song on her way to a second-place finish in the 1996 Breeders' Cup Distaff at Woodbine.

Da Hoss, trained by Michael Dickinson, cruises to victory in the 1996 Breeders' Cup Mile at Woodbine.

Sheikh Mohammed has won big races all over the world. Here I am in Dubai in 1998 with the Sheikh and his son.

In 1998, I thwarted Real Quiet's attempt at a Triple Crown by nosing him in a photo aboard Victory Gallop in the Belmont.

Neil Drysdale pulled off another one of his great training feats when he saddled War Chant (#11) to a Breeders' Cup Mile victory in 2000.

Burt Bacharach and I, striking a pose on a beautiful California day.

Posing with the Aga Khan, at The Curragh in Ireland.

©Healy Racing Phot

Queen Elizabeth II of England, giving me a few pre-race instructions at Ascot.

Once we had landed, Chris found an airport vending machine and bought a bouquet for Nikki. He hired a limousine and had the driver stop at a liquor store so he could gift us with a bottle of Dom Perignon. Then we drove off to the Little White Chapel, a place set up for instant weddings and where Elvis Presley was married. Nikki and I waited outside in the limousine while Chris and Ron went in to find out exactly what the procedure was. A half-hour later they came out, both laughing hysterically. "What's so funny?" I asked. They told me what questions they had asked the pastor, and the man said, "First of all, you guys need to go down and get a marriage license, but I gotta tell you: I've never married two men before!" Now we were all laughing as our driver made for the local courthouse.

This time Chris and Ron waited while Nikki and I went in to get the license. At nine o'clock we were ready to be married. After an overnight at the MGM Grand, we all flew back to Los Angeles. A month later, Nikki and I had a more formal ceremony—a renewal of the vows we had taken—at the Arboretum right across from Santa Anita Park. Only a handful of family members joined us in the rose garden for the actual ceremony, then we all proceeded to the site where a waterfall flowed into a creek. There, in that romantic setting, we celebrated our wedding with both of our families and a large circle of friends. The next day, Nikki and I flew to Maui for a weeklong Hawaiian honeymoon.

I was a happy newlywed and riding some of the best horses in training, but 1998 evolved into a painful year. The reason: my knees, which had been a growing problem for many years. Back in 1985, my right knee had been completely reconstructed after Irish Kristen hit the fence in a training gallop. Then, in 1995, while I was riding in Hong Kong, my horse shied to the right, and I felt a painful tearing in my left knee. Home from Hong Kong, I was determined to ignore the pain, focusing instead on riding stakes races leading up to the Triple Crown. Eventually, arthroscopic surgery was needed to clean out the damaged joint.

The left knee functioned well after that, but stress brought pain and discomfort to my right knee, nagging me like a toothache during the early part of 1997. I got through the Triple Crown season that year by getting cortisone shots, but the situation continued to worsen. Then, at the end of June, one day after I won the million-dollar Hollywood Gold Cup on Gentlemen, arthroscopic surgery was performed on my right knee.

Months later, the knee began to bother me again—I had obviously resumed riding too soon—but I seemed to have a high enough pain threshold to be able to ignore it. In August 1998, the worst happened: an accident involving my "good" left knee. I was warming up a two-year-old, Isitever, prior to a race at Del Mar, just standing up to start cantering when the colt shied. I knew he was about to shy—horses send signals—so I braced my left leg to keep from falling off when he ducked out to the right. I put all of my weight on my left leg and my knee twisted—that's what tore the cartilage. We were just cantering, but every time that horse's hoofs hit the ground, it was like somebody sticking a hot knife in my knee joint. Sweat was rolling down my face as we slowed down. I figured that if I sat down in the saddle, maybe the pain would subside. But I couldn't bend my knee without screaming. I kicked my foot out of the stirrup and let it dangle. The pain stopped when I straightened out my leg. I was afraid I had torn ligaments as well as cartilage. If so, I knew I faced six to eight months out of action.

My distress was evident to the track officials. An ambulance met me on the backstretch and hauled me off to the emergency room at Scripps Hospital in La Jolla. X-rays showed nothing, so I consulted an orthopedist. Dr. Kimball examined my knee and said he thought there was a significant tear in the outside meniscus. An MRI confirmed his diagnosis; I was relieved that no ligaments were involved. Dr. Kimball performed the thirty-five minute surgical procedure the next day, and I left the hospital as an outpatient. A week later, however, I was back. Because I faced close to a month of rehabilitation anyway, I decided to have my right knee worked on again. Dr. Kimball said that a piece of torn cartilage had been flipping back and forth, wearing away the top of my femur like sandpaper. In addition, he said, traces of arthritis were evident. I was understandably depressed, as I had hoped for something approaching a cure. Without that promise, I was fearful about my financial future: *My God, if I've gotta quit riding because of my knees, what am I gonna do for my kids?* That fear lingered well after my pain had subsided.

Three days after surgery, Dr. Kimball reexamined me and drew a considerable volume of fluid out of the damaged knee, at least sixty cubic centimeters. He explained that he had removed as much cartilage as he dared to and had repaired what little of it still remained. If he had removed all of it, I would have been left with bone on bone, which would have been impossible. He described a new procedure—a series of painful injections that were supposed to promote new cartilage growth—and also pointed to the possibility of doing a total knee replacement. He wasn't the first to suggest that possibility, but I couldn't imagine anyone riding competitively with a replaced knee. The prognosis wasn't too promising.

Physical therapy had begun, however. Three times a week, after having my legs stretched, I would use a stationary bike. There had been too little time for much muscle atrophy to have occurred, but I had to get my knees and legs working fully before I could subject them to the punishing stress of riding. This time, I wanted to be very careful. After my therapy, I would drive to the Del Mar racetrack—not to ride but to walk. I probably walked five or six miles a day.

Less than a month after surgery, I was riding again. The first morning that I got on horses, I felt as though I had a new lease on life. There was no pain in either knee, and I had full mobility. It was like having a new set of legs underneath me. The next morning, pain hit me again, not in my knees, but everywhere else: my arms, shoulders, back, hips, and thighs. It took a few days of riding before I felt really fit again. But I was realistic enough to understand that my injuries had been repaired, not eliminated. I was still very vulnerable. For perhaps the first time, I began thinking about how long I wanted to continue to ride, and since I didn't see myself doing anything else, I wondered how I could keep riding as long as I wished.

I had already begun thinking about riding in Europe. Earlier that year, when I was in Dubai to ride Silver Charm, I'd had the first of many conversations with Michael Stoute, by then Sir Michael Stoute, about the possibility of riding for him in England. Nothing was decided then, but a dialogue had begun, and the prospect was becoming more and more attractive to me.

15 Turning Points

*B*y March 1999, my arrangements with Sir Michael Stoute were confirmed, and a search was begun for a place for Nikki and me to live in England that summer. We had planned this as a permanent move, of course. So had Sir Michael. He felt that the two-year-olds he was training were going to turn into the best three-year-olds he'd ever had. By going to England in 1999, I would actually be preparing for the year 2000. I had hoped to be riding out my career there.

Of course, I would make periodic trips back to see my kids and also to ride. Because there was basically a six-month season of flat racing in England, beginning in early spring, I would be able to spend my winters riding at Santa Anita. It would be the best of all possible worlds: quality riding on two continents.

Very few people knew what I was planning, and in all honesty, I probably didn't give enough warning to the people I was riding for. Ron Anderson knew, of course. He was sad that I planned to leave, and very disappointed, but there were no hard feelings. I didn't have any guilt about leaving him at that time because he also was working as Chris Antley's agent, and the two of them were doing very well. Bob Baffert was another story. I think my relationship with Bob changed a little in the weeks leading up to my departure. I was his stable's principal rider then. I think his ego was damaged a little because after I had ridden for the strongest stable in North America—and probably the strongest stable since Wayne Lukas's heyday from the early eighties to the mid-nineties—I was suddenly leaving all that behind to go abroad.

I really wanted to keep the lid on my plans, though, in case things didn't work out. Also, I was worried that if it were widely known that I would be leaving the country, I might not get the mounts I hoped for because I would not be around to ride them later. I needn't have worried; just the opposite occurred. The months leading up to my departure were strong ones for me as a jockey.

I had ridden Manistique successfully the year before and then won two major stakes races on her in 1999. She turned out to be one of the strangest, most irritable mounts I have ever had, but I got along well with her. Her trainer, John Shirreffs, did an outstanding job with her. His sensitivity made a big difference. If she hadn't been treated with tender love and kindness, I don't think she would have been the filly she became.

Manistique was difficult and quirky. After a hard work or a hard race, she would refuse to eat—sometimes for days. She was a big, strong filly, but she could lose weight very quickly. I remember seeing John Shirreffs sitting in a lawn chair in front of her stall, holding up a dog's bowl. In it was a small amount of grain that Manistique would reach over and nibble on. Five or six times a day John would feed her from that dog's bowl; it was often the only way she would eat. If she got to a race in good shape, however, we knew she would run well. John wouldn't run her unless he was sure she was doing very well, and if she was, I had no trouble with her. I would get her out of the gate in good order and let her find her best stride.

Silverbulletday was another filly I favored. I rode her successfully at the same time that I was riding Manistique, though obviously in different races. I would rate her right up there with Winning Colors and Serena's Song—these were the three best fillies I have ever ridden. Each had brilliant speed plus the ability to carry that speed the distance of a mile and one-eighth. Mike Pegram owned Silverbulletday, a filly he named to honor his favorite beverage, Coors Light, the beer whose advertising slogan was "Grab a silver bullet." He likes to concoct composite names for many of his horses, and many of these names carry a not-so-subtle message.

Hookedonthefeelin was one of his favorites—I won the Landaluce Stakes on her at Hollywood Park. Another was Isitingood. To win acceptance, he said that he wanted to name that Thoroughbred Isn'titgood, but couldn't because apostrophes were discouraged in naming horses. People probably didn't comprehend the underlying sexual message, not even when he named another horse Isitever—which may have been an answer to the question the other horse's name seemed to pose.

Mike frequently gets refused when he proposes names for his Thoroughbreds, but he gets away with a lot, too. Recalling a tryst he had one night, pressed up against a fence at Gulfstream Park, he named a horse Loveontherail. Mike is a classic. Witty, likable, he is a self-made man who earned his fortune from McDonald's franchises, yet to meet him you wouldn't think he had two nickels to rub together. Mike had high hopes for Real Quiet, a colt that won the Kentucky Derby and Preakness Stakes in 1998. I rode Real Quiet for the first time a year later in the Texas Mile, coming in second. After we won the Pimlico Special, the horse was pointed toward the $600,000 Massachusetts Handicap at Boston's Suffolk Downs. It was to be my last race in North America.

Actually, I was scheduled to leave the country on the day of the Mass Cap, because I had to be in England by June 1. It had worked out that I could stop off in Boston on my way to London. Because the schedule had fallen in place so neatly, Nikki and I flew to Boston the day before the race and left right afterward. We had spent weeks organizing our clothing and gear, packing our trunks, and getting everything ready for shipment. By the time we left for Boston, I was ready. What I had really hoped, of course, was to be able to ride Silverbulletday in the upcoming Belmont Stakes, which was to be run about eight hours after the Epsom Derby, a race I was already committed to riding. I couldn't do it, of course. I had no choice; not even a round trip on the Concorde would have helped me.

I had actually fantasized about winning a double—victory in both the Kentucky Oaks and the Kentucky Derby—the same year but on two different horses. That would have been a milestone for me, but it didn't happen. I won the Oaks on Silverbulletday and pinned my hopes on winning the Kentucky Derby on General Challenge. I had won the Santa Anita Derby on that colt, and we were favored to win the Kentucky Derby. Although General Challenge was a very nervous horse, I went into the Derby with high expectations.

But just as he had done when he raced poorly before in the Louisiana

Derby, he basically ran his race before the starting gate opened. He was extremely anxious even before reaching the racetrack, behaving nervously in the paddock and in the pre-race warmup. The Kentucky Derby was won in storybook fashion by Chris Antley riding a longshot named Charismatic. John Mabee, who owned General Challenge, hadn't wanted to run him in the Derby, but Bob Baffert and I had convinced him to run the colt because we were both so confident. Mr. Mabee is essentially conservative, but he is also a very good horseman and an astute owner. He didn't care about the Kentucky Derby; he cared only about the future of his horse. He was disappointed in the horse's performance in the Derby. His announcement that General Challenge would definitely not run in the Preakness or Belmont Stakes would have freed me to ride Silverbulletday if I could have stayed in the United States a few days longer.

Instead of preparing to ride at Belmont Park in New York, I was flying to Boston to ride in the Massachusetts Handicap. It would be my first ride at Suffolk Downs and the first time Nikki and I visited Boston. I would have liked to have spent more time in that city and will definitely go back someday. It has a history I would have liked to explore. The weather was beautiful during our stay, the people were wonderful, but Real Quiet was beaten. We had been the heavy favorite; there had been a lot of fanfare associated with Real Quiet's coming to Boston. We had hoped to reward the huge crowd with a big, impressive victory, but that didn't happen. He was a tired third to Behrens and Running Stag. It's always embarrassing to lose a race you're totally expected to win.

There was no time to dwell on the loss, disappointing as it was, because I had to be at Logan Airport two hours before my London flight. I showered and dressed quickly and was running out of the jocks' room when my valet caught up to me. I had forgotten my body protector, the flak vest I always carried with me. Everything was so rushed that day. Nikki and I needed a police escort to get to the airport in time for our flight.

There were two reasons why I left the United States on a sad note: I felt I had let both Mike Pegram and Bob Baffert down, not only by failing to win the Mass Cap but also by being unable to ride Silverbulletday in the Belmont Stakes. I was sure she had a decent chance to win that race if given the proper trip. My sadness was compounded a week later when I watched the Belmont live, on satellite—not because Silverbulletday didn't win but because of what happened to Charismatic.

Six of us were gathered around the TV receiver at jockey Frank Dettori's house, cheering my friend Chris Antley on to what seemed a certainty—that he and Charismatic would win the Triple Crown. But Charismatic broke down in the final strides of the race. The sight of Chris, dismounted, supporting his horse's injured leg was unforgettable. We looked at each other and all six of us had tears running down our cheeks. I think that moment touched everyone who witnessed it.

Leaving the United States gave me the chance to look back on the changes I had observed and felt in my twenty years as a professional rider. What seemed clear was that the quality of horses in everyday racing had diminished and has diminished even more in the years since then. Year-round racing has made the difference. Horses that race more have shorter careers. Shorter racing careers, in turn, have caused a decline in the number of runners in each race and diminished the appeal of racing as well.

Greed has been a major factor. Prize money has gone up so much that few owners and trainers can resist running their horses year-round, instead of respecting the fact that their Thoroughbreds need rest at various points throughout the year. They are not machines. The stakes have become so high that horses travel much more than they used to. Travel is taxing; so is running on new tracks. At an earlier time, well before I began riding, the average horse would race six months of the year at most, and then be given the rest of the year to recover from injuries and stress. Today, from the time they first step on a racetrack as two-year-olds, a great many horses never go out of training—until they simply wear out. The result is that fewer horses are running on any given day, making it far less interesting for fans and horse players and more limiting for jockeys.

I am glad I'm not sixteen years old and just starting out, because I think it's more difficult now for a young up-and-coming rider to get the opportunity to ride quality horses than it was in the early eighties, for instance. If only five or six horses are competing in a race, it's the seasoned riders, the Hall of Famers, who will be tapped. A young jockey will find fewer and fewer opportunities when the fields are short. What's the solution? Only one seems logical—reduce the number of days a horse is raced each year. But that's totally unrealistic. It just isn't going to happen.

For the newest generation of owners and trainers, racing is much more of a business than a sport. There are young trainers who assemble as many as ten owners to buy one horse and then play the horseracing game like the stock market. Here's an example. They claim a horse after a twenty-five-thousand-dollar claiming race and then wait thirty days to run it again—not to rest the animal, but to allow that horse to be dropped in class. A claiming horse that runs again sooner than thirty days must be jumped up in class—run in a thirty-five-thousand-dollar claiming race, perhaps.

Thirty days after making their purchase, the new-owners' group runs their twenty-five-thousand-dollar horse in a sixteen-thousand-dollar claiming race. The winning purse is twenty thousand dollars. Knowing theirs may be the best horse in the race, they gamble additional money, certain he can beat the lesser runners. If their horse wins and is claimed for sixteen thousand dollars, they will have made 40 percent on their investment—more, if they have bet wisely—a pretty good return. The new owner might take another tack. He might run that horse again in two weeks in a twenty-five-thousand-dollar claiming race. If the horse is claimed, another set of owners might try the same stunt. So in six weeks, this horse might have had three different sets of owners and run at least three times—which can be taxing for the horse—for owners who don't care whether they own that horse for six days, six weeks, or six months.

There is nothing illegal about this practice, as far as the owners are concerned, but it's certainly unfair to the horse. And it illustrates the fact that where horses were once raced for their owners' enjoyment and the beauty of the sport, a great many horses are now raced just for money. Their owners want action. For them, horse ownership is a thirty-day investment, and horseracing is no longer the sport of kings.

* * *

When Nikki and I arrived in London, my new agent, Terry Norman, picked us up at Heathrow and drove us about ninety minutes due north to the town of Newmarket in Sussex. There, at Sir Michael Stoute's training yard, we had breakfast and an introductory chat. Nikki and I stayed just outside of town at the Bedford Lodge for a few days until we could move into the cottage we had leased in nearby Cheveley. It was more than a cottage, actually, despite its thatched roof and modest façade. It was a 450-year-old estate whose schoolteacher owner had gone on a six-month holiday. She had been running a bed-and-breakfast establishment there, but we took over the entire house. With six bedrooms, it had plenty of room when my children wanted to visit.

I had been to Newmarket before. Even so, the town was a revelation—another world, in fact. It's a horseracing town, the horseracing capital of the world. I would venture to say that if there were no horseracing, there would be no town. Everything revolves around that sport. At eight o'clock in the morning, when commuters are rushing to work, they have to stop their cars on the High Street to let horses cross in groups of forty on their way to train on the heath. Rush hour or not, in Newmarket, horses have the right of way.

My first days in Newmarket were hectic. The Epsom Derby was just a week off, and my own first race would take place within two days of my arrival. Still, I felt very comfortable. When I went to England, I was hoping to stay there, but I kept an open mind. Throughout my career, I have been a free bird, unafraid to take risks. I have seen the world through my racing and because of my racing I was willing to go anywhere. I have always been adventurous—and always realistic as well. I learned very early in my career to basically live day by day . . . and never try to predict the future.

16 *English Summer*

$\mathcal{T}$his was a first for me: I was standing in the walking ring at Ascot on a sunny afternoon in mid-June 1999. I was to ride the last race of the day, the Duke of Edinburgh Stakes, and I would be on the favorite, an English homebred named Blueprint. Before mounting my horse, I received last-minute instructions—not from the trainer but from the owner, a woman who knew the horse and also knew the course. She hadn't had a winner in this event in a dozen years, she said, so the race was important to her. It was equally important to me, a newcomer, having arrived in England less than three weeks before.

The owner told me how she thought the horse should be ridden and how the race probably would be run. She said her horse should lay up no worse than fourth, that I should keep him on the outside and wait till the last two furlongs before making my move. I listened to her carefully. She was warm and obviously very horse-savvy; she was also Queen Elizabeth II of England, and I was racing for the first time in her immaculate silks: royal purple with blood-red sleeves trimmed with gold embroidery. The Royal Ascot was her meeting. I recall that she was wearing a flowery pink dress and a bright pink hat. She was dressed the way my grandmother used to dress. To me she seemed friendly and extremely cordial.

I had been instructed to bow to her in the walking ring when we were introduced, but not to try and shake her hand. I did as I was told: I bowed to her, then out stretched a white-gloved hand for me to shake. Her trainer almost fell over.

As we left the walking ring together, he said, "I can't believe you did that." Then I said, "Wait till you see what happens when this horse wins." What does that mean? he wanted to know. "I'm gonna kiss her," I said, but he knew of course that I wouldn't.

The mile and a half Duke of Edinburgh Stakes went pretty much as the Queen had predicted. I was always close to the front, never worse than fourth, stalking the leaders from a great position on the outside. Two furlongs from the finish, I made my move. A horse I had passed early on pushed ahead of me at that point, but Blueprint came back beautifully, and we won by a length and a half. It was as exciting for me as the first win of my career, and the Queen was equally pleased.

The winners' ceremony in England is very different from what it is in the States. There is no blanket of flowers, no trophy presentation—although I did receive a trophy later. The jockey dismounts and unsaddles his horse. The owner and the racing manager step forward to pose with horse and rider for a couple of quick photos, and that's basically it. On to the next race.

Two years earlier, I had won the Hardwicke Stakes at the Royal Ascot meet on a horse named Predappio after flying to England from my home in California. Winning the Duke of Edinburgh Stakes was different. It validated the fact that I had become a truly international rider with the proven ability to handle track conditions and riding styles throughout the world.

Long before I married Nikki, who was born and brought up in England, I had wanted to ride there regularly. I had longed for the challenge, for the chance to meet new goals. Things can get a bit boring when you run out of goals. I think I also wanted to prove to myself and everyone else that I could be put into any environment and succeed: as an English rider or a French rider—whatever. I had never been one to rest on my laurels. In any professional sport, once you become successful you start second-guessing your abilities—in other words, being successful just *because* of your success. I thought maybe I was getting good horses all the time now because of the successes I'd had in the past. To be honest, there are certain horses I've ridden that I think could have won for any rider!

* * *

I had turned down the opportunity to ride abroad, in France, for Sheikh Mohammed, in 1987. I had been eager to have that experience, but was offered only a one-year contract and believed I needed at least two or three years to make a name for myself in Europe. At that time, I had been in Southern California just a few years and was starting to have some success. It seemed to me that if I went to France and was a failure—if things didn't go as I had hoped—it would be very difficult for me to regain my foothold at home when I came back.

So I held out. I needed something that would guarantee my riding career. It didn't seem wise to go to a foreign country unless I could do better financially than I had been doing at home. Being abroad for a two- or three-year period, with a firm commitment in my pocket, would have given me the financial security I needed at that time in my life. I was twenty-four years old, a husband and already a father.

Steve Cauthen, the young Kentucky rider who won the Triple Crown on Affirmed in 1978, wound up taking the job with Sheikh Mohammed in 1988, but I guess everything turned out pretty well for me because I won my first Kentucky Derby that year aboard Winning Colors. A year later, I was presented with basically the same contract that Sheikh Mohammed had offered before, but by then the price of poker had gone up a little. I turned down the offer again.

Perhaps if I had been single, with no family responsibilities, I would have been tempted. After 1994, when I was first separated from Toni and divorce proceedings had begun, I felt free to travel and do what I pleased. I was confident by then that my riding ability could take me almost anywhere I chose to go. I wanted my racing skills to travel. I wanted to smell the roses in other places.

The three months I spent riding in Hong Kong were a kind of mental rebuilding for me. Specifically, they signaled the beginning of a new type of education—the amazing part of racing around the world is that no two jurisdictions are alike. You cannot ride elsewhere with a strictly American train of thought. Each racing site has its own nuances. France is different from England; England is different from Hong Kong; Hong Kong is different from Japan. Wherever I went was all new to me, like starting over.

Arriving in Hong Kong for the first time in 1995, I was surprised to find that the flak jacket I was accustomed to wearing under my silks as a body protector was not being worn yet. Its use there would become mandatory a year later, just as it was at most racetracks in the United States and in most other countries that host Thoroughbred racing. This garment is a lightweight vest, like the bulletproof models worn by law enforcement agents. It's not particularly effective in cushioning a fall, but it does offer protection from a horse's hoofs if you happen to get stepped on or kicked. It's a potential lifesaver, reducing the number of internal injuries and broken ribs that may occur when you take a spill.

From my travels, I learned to adjust immediately to new conditions. I also became a quick study. That, fortunately, was what prepared me for the move to England. I knew what to expect; I knew it was going to be very different. No matter what I had accomplished in the United States, I knew I would have to prove myself all over again. The fact that I had done well at home didn't mean I was going to do well abroad. I was basically the new guy on the block.

It was when Sir Michael Stoute became one of the Queen's trainers after Lord Huntingdon's retirement in 1998 that I was offered the opportunity to become his stable's first jockey. I think he was impressed with my eagerness to travel but wondered why I was so willing to consider trading the successful career I had in the States for a move to England. After all, there could be no assured earnings base, as I would not be on salary. Although financial success was possible it would accrue only if I earned it. There were no guarantees; I understood that. We shook hands; that was our contract. I had come to trust Sir Michael, and I guess he trusted me.

Although I would be his principal rider, I would not be prevented from riding for other trainers as well, as long as Sir Michael always had first call on my services. Even so, I would be putting myself out on a limb, and that prospect was daunting, a real adrenaline rush. I felt determined not only to demonstrate my skills to the English, gaining the trust of their trainers and owners, but to myself as well.

I had butterflies before riding my first mount, Asef Alhind, at Sandown. It was what was called a selling race, the Addlestone Claiming Stakes, which was a mile and three-quarters long. That my horse was the heavy favorite didn't make the race any less challenging. I laid up near or on the lead for the entire trip. To me, it wasn't the prettiest win of any that I'd had, but it was a significant victory—a good way to start. You always dream of winning your first race anywhere you go—just as you always dream of winning your first race after recovering from an injury—although you know it's probably not going to happen. Obviously, winning the Addlestone took a lot of pressure off of me at the beginning.

The pressure was back the minute that race was over, however, as I went directly to Epsom for the Festival for the English Derby. That was another big hurdle, even though I didn't ride a winner. I had never ridden Epsom before, and the course turned out to be a little tricky. Ratcheting up the pressure was the fact that Pat Eddery had been riding my horse, Beat All, but was taken off so I could have the mount. The fans were stirred up—I found them much more savvy about horseracing than American fans. So was the British media. They took it as a slap in the face that an American rider had come over to replace a jockey who had been a ten-time English racing champion.

A few days before the big event, all the gypsies—tinkers, scrap-metal scavengers, horse traders, and other itinerants who live on the road in caravans and motor homes—moved into the infield according to custom. It's a carnival there each year, with boxing matches and heavy gambling going on. The group is loud, rude, and unruly, not one to walk among with your wife.

The Derby, second leg of the English Triple Crown, is probably the most prestigious race in England and one of the toughest, most punishing in the world for a three-year-old colt. On a course that is both uphill and downhill, it is a highly demanding mile and three-quarters contest. You have to have a totally committed mindset to ride it. Perhaps that was part of the mystique for me.

The race proved a grueling one: Beat All came in third and was never the same after that. He was eventually shipped to the United States, and I won a minor stakes race on him at Del Mar, but he never became the kind of horse we had expected. In fact, of the top four finishers in the 1999 English Derby, two never raced again, and the winner, Oath, would soon be retired. There were more than a dozen injuries to the twenty-odd runners.

Racecourses in England are deceptive; they may *look* flat, but they are not at all. There are enough ruts and undulations to make the ground extremely uneven. You have to be looking ahead constantly and, hopefully, have your horse prepared to be on the right stride in order to negotiate sudden dips. It's almost like setting a horse up for a jump. When you're heading into a dip, you hope that he doesn't take a misstep and lose his balance, because if he does, he'll lose momentum and you'll lose a length.

To ride on such courses you have to think ahead a bit more than you do in the States. After all, American tracks are relatively homogeneous. Belmont may be bigger than Santa Anita, but they're both flat, for one thing, and left-handed—you race counterclockwise. In England, no two courses are alike. Every day that you're preparing to ride a different course, you need to have a totally different mental approach.

I had never actually worked any of the courses I rode on. I walked them, or tried to, before I raced, but there were times when I would go to a new racecourse and arrive just in time to ride, with no chance even to walk the course. All I could do was study it on a map. I think it makes sense to physically walk a course the day you ride it. Even if you have ridden that course twenty times, it's important to try and walk it the day of the race. Just because the going was good on one particular day doesn't mean it will be good there a week or even a day later.

In England, racehorses seem to rely more on their riders than they do in the States, where they are likely to train on the same track every day and are all schooled to make left-hand turns. In England, you might take a horse that's never run a race in his life, load him into a van and ship him 150 miles on the day he'll be running. Then you lead him into surroundings he has never experienced and run him on a course that may have both right *and* left turns. Face it: this horse will have no idea where he's going, so he will have to rely on whoever is on his back, putting his trust in the rider to show him where to go. The animal is probably scared to death.

In England, there's not a great deal of emphasis on switching leads. Basically, horses on English courses switch leads only when they get tired. On certain courses, where there were sharp turns or a long straightaway, I made it a habit to try and get my horses to change leads *before* they got tired. That was new to the English, and I had good results.

Not every trainer would agree with this practice, particularly when horses are running well. Jack Van Berg, one of North America's great trainers, is always concerned about horses switching leads. He never likes to see one of his riders fussing with a horse. As long as your mount is running well and giving a good effort, he doesn't want you shaking the animal to make him switch leads.

Like Van Berg, I believe that there are right-legged horses and left-legged horses. Just as people are either left-arm dominant or right-arm dominant, I believe horses may have a more powerful lead, one side or the other. I also believe that when a horse shows signs of tiring, if you can get him to change leads, you can get an extra surge from him. It may not be much, but it may be enough to win your race.

On North American tracks, it's much easier to be in front in a race, because if a horse trains on the same track every day, he doesn't feel lost if he's leading. But when you're riding in England, particularly if you're racing on a new course, a horse on the lead may feel a bit lost. That's just my theory, of course; it's by no means law. I think that if a horse feels lost, he's uneasy. He doesn't know where he's going, and he really does want to be with the rest of the pack. Therefore, coming off the pace, if you can get a lead—by that I mean run with a horse in front of you—your mount will be much more comfortable: relaxed, traveling easy, not exerting a lot of energy, happy to be in the company of other horses. That's why the pace of English races tends to be relatively slow. They become sprint races in perhaps the last half mile. An English rider will put his horse into a drive a lot farther out in a race than riders in America do.

English jockeys are reluctant to be in front because they are afraid of being faulted for making a mistake. If they don't win, they fear their ride will be criticized. Therefore, most English jockeys are loath to go to the lead and set the pace. They feel that makes them very exposed, which, time after time, created great opportunities for me. Normally, during the first part of a race in England, no rider wants to be on the lead, but that was where *I* usually wanted to be. I wasn't afraid to go to the lead because of my conditioning; by that point in my career, I had developed a thorough understanding of pace. I wasn't afraid to lead because I usually had a good idea how fast I was going and how much horse I had underneath me. As a result, I won a lot of English races on the pace. The other jockeys caught on pretty fast, however, probably saying to themselves, *We're not going to turn Stevens loose on the lead;* we're *going to go to the lead.*

That was fine with me. I knew that if they were in front of me, they were probably going too fast, and I would pass them at the end anyway. I always tried to make my horse comfortable; it was a basic rule of thumb I tried to follow. I felt that if my horse was running easily in front, not using up a lot of energy, that was fine. If another horse chose to go in front of him early in the race, that was fine, too. The other horse was probably running too fast, doing too much too soon. I would back off of a too-fast pace and make my run late. I enjoyed doing that, too.

On every course I rode in England, I made certain adjustments, and I don't mean stirrup length. The undulations, which might have been six feet in length with a two-foot variation in height, were what made each course different. Because of these undulations—like giant speed bumps in reverse—I learned to sit on a horse differently from the way I do when I ride in the States.

There was no explanation for the undulations; they just happened. There might be a rise 100 yards past the dip you've just gone through, or a rise that could be up to three feet in length after you've ascended a hill. You could almost jump it rather than run over the top of it. In fact, you might have set yourself up for an undulation—the way a jump jockey would set a horse up for a hurdle—that is, if you could see it. Much of the time, you wouldn't know it was there until you were on top of it. Then, instantly, you would have to make sure the horse was on the right stride and not about to hit one of those dips or undulations with a stiff leg. You had to make sure he was comfortable and sufficiently balanced to go through it.

I believe this is the basis of racing successfully anywhere in the world: keeping your horse balanced and giving him confidence. If that balance is lost or the horse loses confidence in the rider, the race might as well be over.

I remember the York meeting during my summer in England. It was a four-day event, and there was steady rainfall on each of the meet's four consecutive days. The course was left-handed, very American in style, probably the most American of any English track. By the last event of the first day, we were racing about three lengths off the inner fence because everyone had been racing alongside that fence earlier—it was by far the shortest distance to the finish line—and the soft ground had become badly chewed up.

By the fourth day, when we came into the stretch, we would move like a herd across the width of the racecourse, which certainly went against racing mathematics as far as distance was concerned. Experienced jockeys knew it was better for their horses to find good ground to run on than attempt the precarious surface of the shortest course, so we literally hugged the right-hand rails on the stands' side. Unless you had ridden another race or walked the course that day, you wouldn't know where the best ground was. The idea was to try to find the fastest and safest surface to run on.

The Kempton racecourse has a switchback. You make a right-hand turn into the backstretch, then you turn left. At Goodwood, you do the same thing. You ride the course almost the way a Grand Prix driver would pilot a race car. You unbend the turns and make straight lines, riding as short a course as you can. Turning right and left, you try to shave the curves. I loved being on the lead and not being afraid to apply my own judgment, going places that other jockeys might not want to go.

Riding in England really sharpened my senses. I was a lot more alert when I went out to ride a race there than I'd had to be in all but the big classic races in North America—even when racing on straightaways. Straight English racecourses may be at least three times wider than most American tracks, and there were days when I found myself competing against more than thirty other riders. If the number I drew put me in the middle of the pack, I would do my handicapping with the trainer I was riding for, and we would try to figure out which horses would be on the faster side—toward the inner fence—and which would be on the slower side. And, yes, frequently two different races were being run.

Most horses are herd animals, preferring to race with a pack and running only as fast as their nearest competitors. The key to winning was to determine which pack to run with, inner or outer, because you could lead your pack of fifteen or more horses to the finish line and still be beaten by three or four lengths—by animals your horse was completely unaware of.

Not only did I have to adjust my riding style when racing in England; I also had to learn a whole new way of communicating—with both owners and trainers. We may speak the same language in our two countries, but the way we express ourselves is completely different. *What the jock said* was always an essential post-race report. But I wouldn't come back after a race I had just ridden and explain it the same way to Bob Baffert as I would to Sir Michael Stoute. I would use totally different terms to explain the same things to both men.

I might say to Bob, "Look, I had the horse up in the right spot. I was up close. He was taking nice hold of me, then he just folded underneath me. I don't know what happened." To Sir Michael, I would say, "Look, I had the horse handy. He was traveling well underneath me. He came off the bridle a furlong out, became unbalanced, and that was it."

Talking to owners, it would be the same thing: different terms to explain the same situations. In England, the owners are actually more involved in each race than they are in the States. They come down and greet you afterward, whether you've won or not, and you're expected to talk to them candidly. They want to know immediately what the jock felt and experienced. Reporting back was part of my job.

After Sir Michael, I was the first one to talk to an owner after a race. That shows how much a jockey's judgment is respected in England. For example, I had to call Lord Weinstock on a couple of occasions to talk to him about horses I had just ridden that were being pointed to certain races. I told him what I thought was the best plan for his horses, and I believe my opinion was valued.

I wouldn't say that English owners are necessarily more knowledgeable than Americans, but I would say that a lot more information is kept from an owner in the States than in England. Things are more open there; a lot more truth is exchanged between owner and jockey and trainer. Jockeys in England want the owners to know the truth; whereas in the States I wouldn't say that that has always been the case. Don't speak unless spoken to is pretty much law, or it was early in my career. Later, when owners or trainers asked my opinion, I was seldom afraid to give it. Anyone who didn't want to hear it would probably never have hired me again.

One reason I was attracted to riding in England was its grass racecourses, which I thought would be easier on my damaged knees than the constant pounding they had been getting on North America's hard dirt tracks. Unfortunately, that idea backfired on me. Those undulating courses, with both right- and left-hand turns, were as bruising to my knees as any tracks I had ridden anywhere. Within weeks of arriving in England, I knew that, though I hoped to ride abroad indefinitely, my body might not let me do what my mind and heart wanted so much.

In midsummer, when I received an offer from The Thoroughbred Corporation to ride for Prince Ahmed Salman and be groomed as the eventual assistant to the corporation's president, Richard Mulhall, I said yes. I knew that my riding days were limited and might soon be over. What I didn't know then was just how soon.

I ended my summer in England with forty-six wins, my last one at Sandown, where my first one had been. I was presented with a trophy, and twenty-five hundred people stayed on to cheer me. It was an amazing way to wind up an incredible season.

I went to England to cut back on my riding and spare my knees, but obviously didn't accomplish either. In fact, I worked harder than ever. When I left, however, I felt I had achieved a great deal of success in a much shorter time than most people thought possible. I was disappointed in myself, of course, because it seemed that by leaving before the season ended, I had let Sir Michael down. If things had worked out, I would have been happy to stay on.

I didn't ride every day, and I didn't ride every single race during the course of a day. Sir Michael never asked me to ride unless the race was significant or if he thought that a horse had a good chance to win. An apprentice rider was on hand to make the midweek roundtrips to distant racecourses. Sir Michael saved me mostly for the big weekend events that I could fly or drive to easily.

Things went well overall during my summer in England. I loved living there and was happy racing there. I was looking beyond my riding career when I decided to come back to the States. The contract I was offered guaranteed some security—not just for myself, but also for my children and my future. I left England certain I had not seen the last of it, but feeling I had left a part of myself there. I was sure I would be riding and living there again. If I'd had been without pain, I'd have returned there to race in a heartbeat.

17 Withdrawal and Return

'My first week back from England, I rode Anees, a two-year-old, in a maiden race at Del Mar. That was the second horse I would ride under my new contract with The Thoroughbred Corporation. His trainer, Alex Hassinger, was so certain he would win that the colt was already slated to be a Breeders' Cup contender. First came the Norfolk Stakes, however. He ran third, beaten by five lengths, but Alex still felt confident enough to enter him in the Breeders' Cup Juvenile at Florida's Gulfstream Park.

Was he overreaching? Most people thought so. Considering that, so far, all Anees had done was break his maiden, there was very little to instill much confidence. But about a month before the Breeders' Cup, Anees began training brilliantly. He was really progressing. His running times were not fast, however; his workouts were designed to build stamina so he could finish strongly. We would gallop slowly during the early part of a work, then run the last quarter very fast. This was a horse with a great finish.

Anees was shipped to Gulfstream three weeks before the 1999 Breeders' Cup; I arrived two weeks later in time to give the colt his final workout. The track was muddy the day we ran; there were not many horses working out on it. Anees went six furlongs in one minute, thirteen seconds, a very good workout. Alex and I phoned Mr. Mulhall to say how impressed we had been. But somehow the clockers managed to miss that performance; they recorded Anees's time as having been two seconds slower. The next day's *Racing Form* contained an article stating that the colt had been *unim-*

pressive in his workout and advising handicappers to toss him out of their betting—the colt had no chance.

Alex was aggravated. So was I; I had actually phoned a reporter to say how well Anees had worked. Right after the *Racing Form* article appeared, I received an anxious phone call from Mr. Mulhall questioning Anees's workout. I assured the boss that the colt had indeed worked very well and that I expected him to run well in the Breeders' Cup. I couldn't predict that we would win, but I guaranteed him that we would get a piece of the million-dollar purse. "We'll run one, two, or three," I said, adding, "We're gonna have to get lucky, you know. We're gonna have to get the right trip." This wasn't just idle talk; from every sign Anees was showing me, I felt that he would perform well in the Juvenile.

On Breeders' Cup day, the racetrack was biased heavily toward speed. Gulfstream has a sandy surface, but on that day the track felt deep and dry underneath us, a condition Anees wasn't used to. Worse, in the races that preceded ours, horses with speed were carrying their speed on that surface. I knew this was going to hurt our chances, as Anees was a stone-cold closer. As the day progressed, my hopes continued to deteriorate. As I left the paddock on the way to the racetrack, I remember thinking, *Okay, I'm not gonna change his running style. I'm just gonna ride him with a lot of patience, and what happens will happen.*

Anees didn't break alertly when the starting gate opened. He was a half-step slow, and for the first quarter mile, he wasn't getting hold of the racetrack. I took a very light hold of his mouth, letting him gain confidence underneath me and find his best stride. By the time he did, we had turned into the backstretch, six furlongs from home. We were about fifteen lengths off the lead, which seemed an insurmountable distance to make up. As we approached the half-mile pole, I gave Anees a little tap on the shoulder with my whip, encouraging him to lengthen his stride. Suddenly, we were passing horses one by one by one. As we approached the quarter-mile marker, we were probably seventh, at least eight lengths from the wire, but I had begun thinking, *My God, I'm gonna get a piece of this. I might run fourth here!* I still hadn't asked him for his best run yet.

Because of the powerful run he was making around the turn, I decided to wait until we straightened out in the stretch before asking him for his best. Then, as we entered the stretch, still no better than sixth, I reached down and hit him right-handed, and the colt just exploded underneath me. I was flying by other horses; by the eighth pole, I knew I was going to win. A sixteenth of a mile from the wire, I was in front. Suddenly, Anees's ears went straight up in the air, and he started looking up at the grandstands. To regain his attention, I hit him left-handed, and he ducked out, away from my whip. I thought to myself, *Don't blow this, Stevens. Don't do anything stupid. Right now, you've got the race in the bag.*

The challenge, in the final seconds of the race, was to keep Anees focused, which was difficult to do because he was relatively green. He didn't have a lot of racing experience; this was only the second time he was going to be in front, and he didn't know what to do with himself. Anees was not doing his best running when we hit the finish, but we were about three and a half lengths ahead. He won easily, but he had actually run hard in that race for only about fifty yards.

Prince Ahmed was ecstatic when we galloped back. He knew as I did that Anees would probably win the Eclipse Award as the year's two-year-old champion and be made the early favorite to win the next Kentucky Derby. I was particularly pleased because I felt that, with that victory, I had already returned The Thoroughbred Corporation's investment in me as their stable jockey.

I had left England in pain, and the pain didn't disappear when I was finally home. I knew I would have to make time to have my troubled right knee worked on again. Arthroscopic surgery was to take place right after the Breeders' Cup. I was not necessarily riding in pain, but the pre-race warm-ups had become very difficult for me, just sitting there with my knees folded up under me. With so much fluid accumulating, my right knee was no longer bending properly; I didn't have the flexion I needed to get from the paddock to the starting gate comfortably. But once a race began and I squatted down in riding position, with my seat off the saddle, I was in less pain. In the heat of battle, when I was going head to head with another horse, adrenaline would take over and I wouldn't feel a thing. But when a horse wasn't running well coming into the stretch, I could certainly feel my knee.

Cortisone shots to the knee joint had been injected twice while I was riding in England. Then by the time the Breeders' Cup races rolled around, I was getting shots about every four weeks, which was crazy and rarely recommended. Each time I had the shot, I also had fluid drained from my knee. The signs were unmistakable: I needed more surgery. I had also been troubled by a golf-ball-size cyst that was knotting up in my right knee. Twice before, when that knee had been operated on, the cyst had been removed, but each time, stubbornly, it had returned. It's back again, of course, but doesn't hurt. It's ugly looking, though. If I was a claiming horse, no one would ever claim me!

Dr. Tiboni had assured me I would get through the Breeders' Cup and scheduled surgery right after that, but unfortunately the surgery had to be delayed because there were a couple of important rides I would have to make. Richard Mulhall asked if I could hang on for two more weeks so I could ride Crafty Friend in the Cigar Mile at Belmont Park. I had won a stakes race on him at Saratoga that year, but he ran poorly at Belmont Park, despite my efforts. I flew back to California the day after the Cigar Mile and had surgery the following day.

The pain in my knee wasn't aggravated by any specific accident or injury; the problem stemmed from long-term wear and tear on my knees that had evolved into degenerative arthritis. I had damaged ligaments and torn cartilage repeatedly over the years, and with each repair, Dr. Tiboni would shake his head and wonder how long I could continue to endure such punishment. The worst problem for me was the bone damage I had inflicted. With almost no tissue left to cushion the joint, stress on my knees was translated into bone rubbing bone in a painful crunch, and that would be tough to correct. Time was a necessary healer, but I had never indulged that need. I was always impatient to get back to riding.

Before operating on me this time, Dr. Tiboni warned that, depending on how deeply ingrown the cyst was, I might be out of action as long as six weeks. On the other hand, he said, I might be back in only two. Obviously,

I wanted to be riding again sooner rather than later, even though I had promised my wife that I would take the proper time and not rush back.

In the first weeks after surgery, I wore a knee brace so I could walk without fear of injury and also play golf, which had become a passion. I set my sights on having a full card of mounts on the opening day of Santa Anita's winter season, December 26, 1999. That was a day that changed my life. After riding Desert Hero for The Thoroughbred Corporation in the Malibu Stakes and finishing sixth—praying the finish line would come soon so the pain would stop—I announced I was through. I said I couldn't compete in races if I was more focused on the pain I felt than the horses I was on. I was sure I would never ride again.

People around me refused to accept the fact that I had withdrawn from racing. Hardest hit was my mom. Having her youngest son retire was a big shock to her. Watching me ride—in telecasts and simulcasts that she and Dad would see, whether they were in Phoenix or Boise, wherever their horses took them—had been a big part of their lives. But Dad really supported my decision. He had become pretty laid back; he wasn't, when I was a kid. I guess I had given both of them a lot of thrills, which now would be gone. My folks were in Phoenix when I went to see them and explain my decision. They were stunned and disbelieving at first, but ultimately seemed content that I was happy and would not be in pain anymore.

One of the most difficult aspects of my decision to quit racing was concern about what my retirement would mean to Ron Anderson. I knew the impact of my withdrawal would be devastating, financially as well as personally, for here was a guy who would have to shift from having a six-figure income working for me to suddenly having no income and no jockey to represent. But I was certain Ron would land on his feet, that he wouldn't be without a rider very long. He bided his time and within a few months started working for Jerry Bailey, who became the top money-earning jockey in the United States in 2001.

My brother Scott, a top rider in the Southwest, had a particularly hard time accepting my retirement. He had started riding before I did and, as it seemed then, would finish well after I did. He called daily to report on people he knew who had received some sort of miracle knee cure. Other family members would call—and friends, too. Each of them pointed to some kind of herbal treatment, some drug, some form of surgery that they had heard could have miraculous results. I even got mail from strangers, all well-meaning, who suggested various cures and treatments.

I didn't want to insult anyone, but the concern had begun to wear on me. I wanted to say, *Leave me alone. This is the way it is. I appreciate your concern, but I have to move on now.* The truth is that I had already tried nearly everything that people proposed or suggested. I would occasionally get some relief, but it would be temporary. The stress of riding would put me right back where I had been. At age thirty-six, I had the knees of an octogenarian. If there was something that could have been done, something to undo the punishment and damage my knees had endured, I would have attempted it.

With the help of Prince Ahmed, who was adamant about my staying with The Thoroughbred Corporation, I got another medical opinion. I flew to New York to meet with a physician the prince recommended. The doctor took a series of X-rays, and when they were developed, came back into the examining room. "Stevens," he said, "you know that old saying, 'A picture is worth a thousand words'?" And I said, "Yes, sir, I do." Then he said, "Yours says only two words: 'you're screwed.' " He kept me there for forty- five minutes, basically counseling me on how to reorder my life. "I know what you're going through," he said, "but you need to drop it and get on with your new duties and the new opportunities you have. You're a famous person. You're not coming back as a rider and you won't come back. Forget about it."

Those were harsh words, but I needed to hear them. I needed to stop thinking about what might be or what could have been in terms of my riding career and think positively about the rest of my life. I needed my knees, of course. Everyone does. They support the weight of the body, whether you're climbing stairs, walking a golf course, or just getting out of a chair. I began resting them whenever I could, and I worked with a personal trainer to maintain a level of fitness I knew was important.

For twenty years, my days had been structured so I could get up at six o'clock in the morning, go to the track, work horses, then go directly to the jockeys' room and not get home until five thirty or six, exhausted. Suddenly, I had gone from being one of the top jockeys in the United States, and enjoying the competition, to doing nothing. I was used to the camaraderie of the jocks' room and seeing my colleagues there. It had been a life for me, and now that was gone. I didn't know what to do with myself. I was very confused about my future. I guess I had post-battle syndrome, the kind of depression that soldiers are hit with and all professional athletes are said to experience when they retire.

After years of carefully watching my weight, I was finally able to eat again. I was also able to see my body change as I looked in the mirror. It didn't take long for me to get depressed at my appearance. I wasn't fat, but my clothes no longer fit. I had gained fifteen pounds very quickly, and for the first time in my life, felt truly lost. I really struggled with not being able to ride. For about eight months, I felt like an offshore wind, changing directions constantly.

Essentially, I was trying to find myself again. First, I considered becoming a jockey's agent. Then I thought that Nikki and I should start training horses—she certainly had had that experience. And, of course, there was always sports TV. Over the years, I had been approached by various TV producers to provide racing commentary. During one three-week period, I wrestled with many options. Then Prince Ahmed settled the issue by offering me a chance to continue working for The Thoroughbred Corporation, but in a new role: as an assistant trainer being groomed for a job in management. It was an offer I couldn't refuse.

With Alex Hassinger the trainer then, my job was to do whatever he needed to have done, whether it was seeing to the horses' medications, helping him fill out the training charts, or simply helping him keep the employees happy. By cutting back on my food intake—eating very little breakfast, a light lunch, a decent dinner, and no snacks—I got my weight back to the 115 pounds that had become the norm for me, and I began taking a stiff mix of herbal medications that seemed to have a good effect. But mostly I concentrated on becoming an assistant trainer.

Alex's primary goal that winter was to lead Anees toward the 2000 Kentucky Derby, and he had developed a detailed training plan that got under way in January. Alex mapped out the days on which Anees would work. We looked at weather forecasts five days ahead of time to see exactly when we would be able to work—if bad weather was coming, we would have to move the workout up a day or set it back a day. Then Alex penciled in the races he wanted Anees to run in leading up to the Derby—and if we had to miss a race because of injury or illness, what races could be slotted in instead.

These are some of the issues a trainer needs to consider. It's almost like a football team gearing up for the Super Bowl, except that in football there are usually a couple of players at each position, so if there's a problem, you just fill in with another guy. In Thoroughbred racing, each horse is an individual. And it takes an exceptional animal to accept the training that's needed to win a Kentucky Derby. The horse must be made of steel. A trainer, too, must be very special, treading a fine line between training a horse too hard or not hard enough, at the same time keeping the horse sound and fit.

It seemed to me that Anees, a very young three-year-old, was still growing, still developing. There were strained muscles and other setbacks to deal with that spring. Everyone in The Thoroughbred Corporation was hoping that we would have the horse ready for the Derby, and we would have, I think, if the Derby had been run in September instead of when it traditionally occurred, on the first Saturday in May. We were able to run him in only two prep races leading up to the big race at Churchill Downs. We were trying to do something that proved impossible.

Once I stopped riding, I was physically comfortable again and relatively pain-free. I was taking care of myself properly, perhaps for the first time in my career, eager to have my life back on an even keel. I was used to caring for horses—I had been around barns since my brother Scott and I worked for our dad's training operation back in Boise—so I knew the drill: feed, clean, medicate, care. But as the weeks passed, I found working behind the scenes less than gratifying. More and more, I longed to be the man who got the leg up in the saddle rather than the man on the ground doing the hoisting.

Not surprisingly, I experienced the same gnawing fear of failure I had known when I first began riding because I knew everyone was expecting great things of me as a horse trainer. That's what was driving me, giving me an edge, that determination to succeed. Occasionally, I would test myself while down at the barns and try working a horse. I felt like the dog you put a shock collar on—every once in a while, he needs a jolt to remind him. When I got back on a horse, for a few minutes, it would feel so good. Then I would begin working the animal and get a stabbing pain that I knew I didn't want to have to endure again. I was put right back where I had been, knowing that I was better off staying on the ground. Of course, by continually testing the knee, I was impeding the healing process.

Eventually, I stopped testing myself and, instead, directed my energies toward my new job: dealing with some forty two- and three-year-olds, plus a few older horses in training. There also were the breeders' sales to prepare for and attend. That spring, after a routine examination, my physician, Dr. Tiboni, the man who had always played devil's advocate where my knees were concerned, stunned me with good news: he said I could make plans to start working horses again.

He had no reason to be leading me on. He could see that, for the first time in maybe two years, there were no signs of swelling in either knee joint. I had 100 percent flexion with minimal discomfort, whereas four or five months earlier, I'd had only 65 percent flexion with massive discomfort. He couldn't pinpoint the cause of my improvement—perhaps it was a combination of the surgery and the vitamin and herbal supplements I had been taking—but radical improvement was evident.

Dr. Tiboni measured my quadriceps. He said he wouldn't release me to ride again until I had another three-quarter-inch growth on my right quad—my right knee was the one he had just operated on. Obviously, I had let the muscle atrophy because I was favoring that leg. I met with my personal trainer and told him how important it was to make sure the quads continued to develop and didn't start to atrophy again. "If I get even a little bit of pain," I said, "we've got to jump right in and continue the rehabilitation." He just smiled and said, "That's what I've been trying to tell you for the last two months." So we understood each other.

Frankly, I was in shock. I had finally become resigned to the idea of not riding anymore, but now, suddenly, getting back in the saddle had become a possibility again. I decided to proceed slowly and not tell anyone. I would work horses and try to stay consistent, and see how that felt. If I could ride without pain, and perform at the level I had been used to, I would do it. Otherwise, I wouldn't even try.

Until I knew for certain what I would do, I tried to fill my life with activities to keep me occupied, to keep my mind off the riding question. But I couldn't. This was, in many ways, the most difficult time of my life. We were in Del Mar that summer, and I was spending time with my wife, taking my kids to the beach, playing golf. But I was also very bored. The better I felt, the more I missed what I had once been doing.

A number of possibilities were still spinning in my head when I decided to withdraw from The Thoroughbred Corporation. The summer was not yet over, but I was now completely on my own. The gleam in my eyes was apparent, however. Everyone who knew me was aware that I hoped to start back riding soon but couldn't even think of doing that until my insurance claims were settled. When the settlement finally did come through, it was clear that I would never qualify for the kind of personal liability coverage I had maintained over the years. So if I chose to ride again, I would have to do so at my own risk. I had to prepare myself for that—and also for the possibility that my knees might not hold up under the stress of riding races.

Okay, now what? I wondered. By then, I had learned that I could never force myself to be something I wasn't, or pursue something that I didn't have my heart in, 100 percent. I am the kind of person who wants things to happen tomorrow. Now I knew I would have to be patient; I assured myself that whatever was out there would jump out at me at the right time.

"How are your knees coming?" It was Sir Michael Stoute's voice on the long-distance wire. He called often that summer to check up on me. I confided in him that I had been thinking about a comeback. "What if you could ride for Neil Drysdale?" he asked. Neil was also English—and a good friend. "I could put in a word for you." I said I thought that would be great. Then, *boom*, it happened.

I had known Neil before, having ridden for him periodically, but I had not known him well. In our first serious conversation following Sir Michael's phone call, he asked if I really planned to ride again, and I said yes. "When?" he wanted to know. "Can you be ready for the Breeders' Cup? Because I'm gonna run War Chant in the Mile and win it." Now, this discussion took place at least two months before Breeders' Cup Day. I hadn't worked, let alone ridden a horse yet, and War Chant hadn't raced since the Kentucky Derby. Also, the horse had never run on turf. Was this all wishful thinking on Neil's part, or genius? I would soon find out.

At the beginning of the year, War Chant had been touted as one of the Derby favorites, along with Fusaichi Pegasus, another Drysdale-trained colt. Fusaichi Pegasus went on to win the Derby; War Chant ran ninth. Still, when I finally worked him on the turf, I found him exceptional. I was impressed with his athletic ability and, frankly, with the way he handled the grass.

Neil entered him in a prep race at Santa Anita on October 14. He won by a length and a quarter, but I sensed that I had moved him in front a bit too early. I felt that I should ride him more patiently, the way I had ridden Singspiel, and not produce him until the critical moment. That had been only his sixth race, so he was still pretty naïve about the whole racing scene. Daring him to race in and win the Breeders' Cup Mile—against the best milers in competition, many of them more mature—was a reflection of just how good Neil knew him to be.

It seemed to me that the only way to win the Mile was to take War Chant back, much the same way I had ridden Da Hoss at Woodbine, and make one solid run with him in the last quarter mile. I knew he had one good run in him, and obviously that should occur at the end. The horse had been headstrong in his morning works. To avoid setting him off, I knew I would have to be very peaceful on his back. I didn't want to rush him into doing anything.

War Chant was one of the favorites in the Mile, but when we drew post eleven, the extreme outside position, a few of the handicappers backed off. They said, in effect, "No way can he win from an outside post going a mile. With the turn coming up so quickly, he'll be forced wide and lose too much ground." But I felt confident. I knew War Chant to be an exceptional miler; I knew how fast he could accelerate.

When the race began, he came away from the gate more relaxed than I had expected, and I found myself farther off the pace than I wanted to be. But *I* stayed relaxed and, without any encouragement from me, War Chant started picking off horses going into the far turn. I was at least seven lengths off the lead at that point, with one horse on the outside of me. I had to swing to the outside to avoid being penned in as we entered the stretch. Then, when he saw daylight ahead of him, my horse delivered a great burst of speed and went on to win by a neck.

It was a thrilling victory for me, after having been out of action for the better part of a year, perhaps the greatest accomplishment of my career. I owed this opportunity to the bonds of friendship I shared with Sir Michael Stoute, with Neil Drysdale, and with War Chant's owners, Marjorie and Irving Cowan. As I pulled up after the race and headed for the winner's ceremony, I was swept up in the emotion of the moment.

I had truly, and absolutely, come back.

18 Racing Rivals

*A*s a child, I fought hard with my brothers, although I loved them both, and also fought a lot at school. I really upset my mom once when I got sent home from school for fighting. Later, I promised her I would never fight again—not because I was afraid to but mainly because the aftermath was always so painful. But I think fighting made me stronger mentally. Early in my riding career, I fought continually in the jockeys' quarters and was fined a lot for doing so. At one point, I was actually on probation in Oregon for fighting in the jocks' room. If anyone crowded me on the racetrack or did anything I felt was wrong, I would just come back and beat him up. I felt I had to establish the fact that I would not be messed with when I rode.

When Winning Colors failed to win the Preakness in 1988, I blamed the loss on the way Pat Day rode Forty Niner, packing me so far from the rail. I was really angry when I came back to the weigh-in room, and I was determined to beat the hell out of Pat. I was in the shower alone when he came in, but before I could raise a fist, he looked me straight in the eye and said, "Gary, I'm sorry. It wasn't me. I was riding to instructions." I remained upset with him, but we didn't fight.

Sometimes peace is impossible in the jocks' room, particularly among young riders. Feuds start, and often the only way they can end is with jockeys exchanging fists. Angel Cordero, Jr., used to keep a set of boxing gloves in the sauna. If there was going to be an altercation, the fighters were locked in the hot box, told to put on the gloves, and punch the anger out of their systems.

Pat Valenzuela and I were fierce competitors. Our differences turned into fistfights too many times to count. These were really brawls, and many of them turned nasty. I remember the last fight we were ever involved in. It was at Santa Anita, sometime around 1990. We'd had a heated exchange on the racetrack, and the argument accelerated as we came back. We were mouthing off loudly at one another, as we had been at least ten times during the previous five years. Inside the jocks' room, Valenzuela took a swing at me. I ducked, and he hit me on top of my head with his fist. I wasn't hurt, but he shattered his wrist. He was out of action for six weeks because of a stupid fight. That was a good lesson for me; I don't fight anymore.

I have had very few close friends among the riders I compete with on the racetrack. The jockeys I have been closest to are Mike Smith and the late Chris Antley, along with my brother Scott, who has also been my mentor. Mike, Chris, and I shared a special bond. We always rooted for each other and respected each other on and off the racetrack. I have always loved beating Mike Smith, and I know how much Mike loves to beat me. And Chris and I got no bigger thrill than beating each other. We each knew we had a gift that made us special, and what we had in common was something almost spiritual. The three of us were never afraid to talk about religion and about our beliefs.

Mike is very religious. I was raised in the Baptist church, but because my best childhood friend, Jeff Hebert, came from a family of devout Catholics, I spent about as much time in his church as I did in mine. The result is that I've always been very open about religion and my belief in a Higher Being. Chris and I shared the conviction that, whether we truly believed in God, as I do, or some other Higher Being, all of us were put on Earth to live life to its fullest, really enjoy living, and make people happy. Chris was one of the most sensitive and compassionate people I have ever met, the kind of man who would buy food for the homeless or stop at the side of a road to rescue an injured bird, then try to nurture it back to health.

That's the Chris Antley I knew and miss very much. What drew us together is that we liked to do many of the same things, such as shooting pool, riding motorcycles, and watching sports on TV. We always enjoyed making each other laugh, and one of the things we laughed a lot about was that people were paying us so much to do what we loved: *ride*. He was very easy to be around. It was no accident that I asked him to act as best man when I married Nikki.

Early in our relationship, I became Chris's confidant. He was a lonely person, but he was able to talk to me about the things that were bothering him—in his personal life and in his professional life. Like me, he had been on his own, alone, since he was in his teens, but unlike me, he remained troubled by the loneliness he felt. Since I was blessed with a big brother I could always call on for riding advice or criticism, or just to talk, I assumed that role for Chris.

When Chris was going through a slump, he would come to me and ask for advice. What I always told him is what my brother would have told me: "You're doing nothing wrong. Your stables have gone into a bit of a cold spell, but they're going to come out of it. Keep doing what you've done all your career. Don't try to change anything; just go back to the basics of what you learned as a kid. Forget about changing your whipping style or the length of your stirrups. Do what feels natural to you—and right."

Chris and I first met in New York in the late eighties. We were both in our twenties, though he was three years younger. Both of us were pretty cocky. I considered myself the young hot gun on the West Coast, and he was the even younger hot gun on the East Coast. Because we had so much in common, we immediately became close friends. We shared the same mental approach to riding and the same will to win—to be second best to no one. Our real closeness developed when Chris moved to California in 1994, and we started spending a lot of time together. His career had come to a standstill in the East; I think he moved West to get a fresh start. His work ethic had not been what it probably should have been, and he had lost the confidence of a lot of the trainers. Chris was an addictive person. It was no secret that he had started to have problems with alcohol and drugs. Still, he was a brilliant rider. Ron Anderson, who would act as his agent for about four years during the same time he was also mine, respected Chris as much as I did. "He's scary good," said Ron, who recalled when Chris won five races at Hollywood Park in a single afternoon. A year or two earlier, he had hopped by helicopter from Aqueduct in New York to the Meadowlands in New Jersey—and won nine races the same day. Chris had family, but they were back in South Carolina where he was born. He didn't talk about his childhood very much, and I never asked. In many ways, I became a surrogate brother for Chris, just as Ron became a father figure for Chris.

There were occasional arrests, but I don't think Chris ever spent a night in jail. He went willingly into rehab, however. That was in 1997, and he was supposed to remain for thirty days. He stayed longer, maybe ninety days or more. He had grown to feel comfortable, he was taking care of everyone around him and the house they lived in, using his own money to make repairs. He was handy, as it happened. He could fix a toilet or rehang a door. And he was generous. At Thanksgiving he bought turkeys, so everyone in his halfway house could have a holiday dinner. I think he needed to create a family for himself, which is why it took him so long to get out of rehab, and when he did, he had no place to go.

Nikki and I were recently married and living in a three-bedroom condominium in Pasadena, so we offered him a room. "Stay with us until you can get yourself sorted out," I told him, "Make yourself at home." I was thinking that he would be with us for maybe two or three weeks, until he found a place to buy or rent. Instead, he became a fixture. He stayed because he was so comfortable in these surroundings with Nikki and me. It wasn't as though he was hurting financially. He had money; he was also very intelligent about the way he invested it. As a matter of fact, he was such a shrewd Wall Street trader that he starting sharing his stock picks in an e-mail newsletter he called *The Ant Man Report*.

The weeks he lived with us stretched into months, and since Nikki and I were newlyweds, there came a point when we felt we needed some time alone. Finally, I appealed to Ron. "We've gotta get Chris out of here," I told him, "He has to be on his own again; he's gotta get stabilized; he's gotta begin riding again. It's time for him to get on with his life."

With Ron's help and a little encouragement from Nikki and me,

Chris moved out—and immediately became part of Ron's household. He stayed there a long time. He also started a rigorous training program to lose weight and get himself fit to ride again. He was up to 135 or 140 pounds, but he wasn't fat. He had always been a workout fanatic; when he wasn't riding, he was training. He looked like a miniature bodybuilder. With so much muscle, it was hard for him to get the weight off, so he rode his bike. It was nothing for him to ride it forty or fifty miles a day. There were no halfway measures with Chris. Whatever he did, he was obsessed.

Both Ron and I had urged him to start riding races again, so every morning he would come out to the track and work horses as earnestly as a young apprentice. He had won the Kentucky Derby on Strike the Gold in 1991 and proved that he had great ability, but he was having to prove himself all over again to try and get back some business. He was giving 100 percent of his effort, and every trainer knew it. They also knew that he'd had serious problems.

I was traveling a lot then, so when I was out of town, he always covered for me, riding the mounts that would have been mine. Most were one-shot arrangements and he knew it, but he didn't care. He loved the sport. He loved horses. He would take anything he could climb aboard as long as he could ride. Chris's talent was such that it didn't matter if he was away from the track six months or a year; the first day that he was back was as though he had never missed a day. He had once been known by everyone in racing as a world-class rider, but a lot of people thought he was washed up.

Until the 1999 Kentucky Derby, Chris had ridden infrequently for Wayne Lukas, but Wayne was desperate that year. He had a colt named Charismatic that he thought might have a chance to win the Derby but couldn't get anybody to ride him. So with encouragement from Charismatic's very supportive owners, Bob and Beverly Lewis, Wayne took a chance on Chris Antley.

Chris won the Kentucky Derby in spectacular fashion; then he went on to win the Preakness and was favored to win the Belmont Stakes—and probably would have, if Charismatic hadn't broken down. Because Chris was such an emotional man, that loss may have been the beginning of the end for him. He had actually saved the colt's life by pulling him up, dismounting, and supporting the injured leg until a splint could be put on the fractured bone. But not winning the Triple Crown when he had expected to really hit him hard.

It was during this time that he met Natalie Jowett, who was a producer with ABC Sports. They got married, and in the final months of his life, she was carrying his child. Chris hadn't started riding again after Charismatic's breakdown, and I sensed he was on a downward spiral. At the time he and Natalie were married, Chris was planning to make another comeback, but he never did.

He bought a beautiful home in Pasadena and was having some renovation work done on it. I hadn't seen him for several months, but two days after Breeders' Cup 2000, which happened to be the last day of that year's Oak Tree meet, Nikki and I drove over to his home. The front door was open, so we walked in. "Is Chris around?" I asked a workman. "Yeah, he's here somewhere," the man said. I could hear the shower running in one of the spare bathrooms, so I pounded on the door and hollered: "Are you in there, Ant Man? Open the door." I heard the shower door creak, then the bathroom door opened and Chris stuck his head around the corner. He had soap in his hair and wore a big smile. "Hey, asshole," he said, "I wondered when you'd be showing up." I told him we would wait for him out back.

It was nine thirty in the morning, but he seemed totally out of it. I suspected that he was under the influence, but I didn't know of what. We talked—he talked, mostly—for more than two hours until I had to leave for the track to ride. He seemed depressed and paranoid. He insisted he was in danger. He said he felt threatened—by whom, we never knew— and insisted he had driven his wife off, to protect her and the baby they were expecting. Much of what he said didn't make sense to me, but it certainly made sense to him. He seemed to think everything was caving in around him. He felt doomed, I think, and nothing Nikki or I could say to him would have an impact.

We had to leave, though he didn't want us to. I was aware that he had been in rehab again, that drug intervention had been tried and had failed. Sadly, I knew it was not in my power to make him change the course of his life. "I didn't come over here to pay you to stop whatever you're doing," I said, "but you know you've got a friend you can talk to. Call me if you need me." He said he would but never did. As we drove off, I told Nikki, "I think that's the last time we'll ever see Chris alive." We were both in tears. Later that month, I tried to reach him by phone as I was driving to Hollywood Park one morning, but he wouldn't pick up.

On December 2, I got a call at 5:45 A.M. It was Chris's wife, phoning from her home in Connecticut. "Gary, it's Nat," she said. "He's gone."

He had been found dead in his home from what Pasadena police described as "severe trauma to the head." Was it murder? Various drugs were discovered in his house and later in his body. Had he been whacked by some big-time dealers because the police were closing in on him? Or was it suicide? Had he died of self-inflicted wounds? I had come to think he was going to take his own life. And maybe he did. None of us will ever know. The only way I have been able to achieve closure is by accepting what the police concluded weeks later: accidental overdose.

I read a eulogy at a memorial service in California but did not fly to South Carolina for the funeral. I just felt that Chris would have wanted me to go on with what I was doing. Ron Anderson went, though. Six months later, after riding Point Given across the finish line in the Belmont Stakes, I gestured heavenward with my whip in silent tribute to my friend and colleague. Then, the day after Breeders' Cup 2001, which took place in New York, Nikki and I drove to Connecticut with Ron for the christening of Chris and Natalie's baby, Violet Grace. She is my goddaughter. Her godmother is Natalie's sister, who read aloud a biblical passage. I didn't do that; I spoke extemporaneously of my feelings about Chris Antley and said how privileged I felt to have been asked to become a special person for a child who would be raised without a father.

"The role I am taking on will be difficult," I said. "Though I'll be thousands of miles away, I will always be very close to Violet Grace Antley. She will be on my mind all the time. And throughout her life, I'll do whatever it's possible for me to do, the way Violet's father would have wanted me to do it—everything from the heart."

19 *Endless Quest*

here is no such thing as the perfect ride. Although I am certain of that, it is something I strive for: I approach each ride with the idea that I have to improve on my last one. The one thought I have every day when I go out to race is that if I don't better myself in some way, it will have been a wasted effort. I feel I have to learn something with every ride. Each time, I am reaching for something greater than before, and I guess that if I am always reaching for it, I probably have never attained it. I think of perfection as a kind of impossible ideal, a symbol of the unattainable in any sport or action.

As far as I am concerned, the perfect ride would be one with no flaws, no mistakes at all. Even though there are a lot of things that a rider really can't control, I would like to think that I do have control over nearly everything when I am on a horse's back—from affecting the animal's temperament and keeping him from stumbling, to the way he expresses that temperament and how he warms up before a race. Everything. Perfection would mean I am in control of all that, plus the way the horse actually runs his race.

For me, as a rider, a race begins in the saddling paddock the moment I get on a horse's back, and it doesn't end until after I dismount. My job is still not over when the race itself ends, because as we cross the finish line most of the time I am already thinking about that horse's next race and what I might do to improve his performance. I am sure people are not aware of this; there are trainers who aren't aware of it either.

I continue to believe that the most important part of a race and the horse's performance in it is the pre-race warmup. If a horse warms up well and is content and happy moving to the starting gate, he is likely to perform much better than an animal that is unsettled and upset, or unhappy with the situation around him. Much of the time, I have control over that, but much of the time I don't. For example, often Mother Nature intervenes and it rains, and some horses don't like running on a muddy track. If I have ridden a horse before, I can tell from warming him up if he is in a bad way.

For example, I thought that Distorted Humor, a horse Elliot Walden trained, was the best short-distance sprinter I was riding in 1998. He ran two powerful races in Kentucky, and I flew to New York to ride him the week of the Belmont Stakes. But on race day the track came up muddy and his race was a disaster. He ran just horribly, but I knew that he would— from the way he was acting in the warmup. He was totally different from the animal I was used to.

I am convinced that horses have a sixth sense, and I know from experience that communication *can* take place between horse and rider in a language without words. When I am really in tune with a horse, I feel I know what he is thinking, and—this may seem a little "out there"—he seems to know what I am thinking, too, before I even make a move. Because I can sense the moves *he* is going to make before he actually makes them, I try to be constantly prepared and stay a step ahead. It's like a quarterback seeing a play develop in his head—having a visual image of something happening before it actually occurs. Finally, what has to exist between rider and horse is trust built on mutual respect.

At a young age, I had some real fearful moments on horses. I was often cowed by their strength and by what I knew they could do, and fearful that *they* might be in control instead of the two of us working together as a team. I realized ultimately that as soon as a horse senses that he, not the rider, is in control, that rider is in trouble. The horse really wants to know that someone is taking charge.

It's like being caught in an undertow at the beach: anyone who doesn't respect or fear the ocean is foolish, but that doesn't mean you don't go near the water. Similarly, you have to respect the power a horse has, yet you have to be comfortable with that power. I have never been bitten or kicked by a horse, and that's because I was brought up to respect how quick horses can be. Like most creatures, they need their space, and that need must be respected.

I never expect a horse to adjust to me; I know I have to adjust to every horse I get on. I have to come to grips with their mindset and be aware that I will not be able to change it. I didn't know this as a young rider, however; I think such knowledge is part of the maturing process, something acquired from years of riding. Most important, I think that once an animal senses that I respect his power, I can become one with him.

Some Thoroughbreds weigh 1,100 or 1,200 pounds; as a rider, I have rarely weighed more than 115. No way can I force them to do anything they don't want to do. So my job is to coax them into working *for* me—as part of a team. You have to function this way or nothing can be accomplished; the horse is going to rebel, and with his size and strength, he will win every battle. And every race is, in its way, a battle to be won or lost.

I take every race seriously. I do my homework, working out the strategy of a race, and I never lock myself into any set game plan. Certainly I try to visualize what may happen, but things tend to unfold a little differently from the way I imagined. The people with whom I have the best relationships show their confidence in me by turning me loose to make my own decisions.

I never allow myself to be governed by too-specific instructions. Although it might seem appropriate for a trainer to say, "We want you laying third, off the lead," what would happen if the pace is slow? Then where would he want me? I would have no choice but to rush to the front, right? I couldn't just let my horse dawdle. No, a trainer cannot tie a jockey's hands; he has to release a rider to his own judgment and his own instincts. I think a great rider, in addition to having good ears and great vision, must also have good instincts and very quick reactions.

For example, when I am behind a wall of horses—say, I am laying sixth behind a five-horse spread—I know I can't simply go around all five of them and still win. I will have to get through somewhere, somehow, so I will be sitting back, trying to judge which horse is traveling the most easily. Obviously, I don't want to get behind the horse that's going to slow down first because that will take me out of the race. So as the race unfolds, from the time the starting gate opens, I am always trying to judge which horse I think will be my main competition.

I always handicap a race beforehand, looking at the past race performances of every horse I am up against, and my handicapping is totally different from any gambler's or horseplayer's. Whenever I am riding, no matter what caliber of race it is and regardless of what the oddsmakers say about my horse's chances, while reading the *Daily Racing Form,* I try to figure out what's going to make mine the best horse in the pack—that is, what I can do to make my horse win.

I don't necessarily win by being on the best horse. Sometimes I win races by making somebody else have a bad trip or putting the favorite in a kind of predicament so I can beat him. There is nothing illegal about doing that as long as I can maintain a straight course and not bump or interfere with him as I push to get ahead. I am paid to win.

A gambler handicapping a race he wants to bet on has absolutely no impact on the outcome of that race; whereas I feel that I *can* affect the race according to the way I ride and the strategy I devise. I may alter my strategy two or three times while the race is being run, depending on how fast the pace is or if the horse I thought was going to be in front stumbles at the start—all of a sudden, he is nowhere in sight, and having the second-fastest speed in the race, I'll find myself setting the pace, instead of tracking it, and everything will be different.

The other good jockeys I ride with are certainly doing the same thing, trying to figure out how to get me beat. When I am winning races, it's as though I go out on the track with a bounty on my head, but that only makes me a better rider. I feel fortunate to be competing with truly great riders, day in and day out, because I always know what they are thinking. I love beating one of them because I know I have beat somebody good. They're all gentlemen, athletes who handle themselves with integrity. I admire that a lot.

I have raced many times against my brother Scott, starting at a young age. He is one of the best horsemen I have ever ridden with and the best teacher I have ever known. I always enjoy watching him ride; I appreciate his horsemanship. When Scott is in a race with me, I want to make sure I beat him. But if I am running seventh or eighth and not going to have any impact on the finish of the race, you can bet I will root for him, hoping he will win.

That same feeling sometimes translates into a regard for some of the other jockeys I ride with. In the 1998 Kentucky Derby, when I knew my horse, Indian Charlie, had no chance of winning, I cheered Kent Desormeaux when he passed me, hoping Real Quiet could grab and hold the lead. I was rooting for Bob Baffert's team.

I am always pleased when a new rider with talent comes into the jockeys' room. It makes my job more challenging; it also brings out the best in me. If I were riding with second-rate jockeys every day of the year, I would probably not be motivated so strongly toward self-improvement. If I had gone back home to ride in Boise, Idaho, and stayed there, I am certain I would not have earned the kind of satisfaction I get riding with the jockeys I compete with all the time. Racing against the best riders in the world, men and women, too, who can make split-second decisions and are aware of everything going on around them in a race, I have no choice but to sharpen my skills and improve on what I do. Physical strength and athletic ability are only part of the picture; 50 percent of winning races is mental.

I think the closest I have ever come to achieving a perfect ride was in the 1998 Belmont Stakes aboard Victory Gallop. I had been on that horse only once before, in the Preakness. Alex Solis had ridden him in the Kentucky Derby, but the Prestons, who owned the horse—Art, Jack, and J. R.— took Solis off, which was a big step for them, and they received a lot of criticism for taking it. Alex had made no mistakes in the Derby, but they apparently felt that if I had ridden that race, I would have made different decisions, ones that could have put them in the winner's circle. In truth, however, they couldn't really fault Alex's ride.

The Prestons have been very good to me over the years. They have been as confident of me as I have been of them. And I have never felt pressure. Any time you are in an environment where someone trusts you 100 percent, you are going to perform a little bit better than when you work with people who question the way you do your job. You are more likely to succeed at what you do if the environment is right; I think most people can relate to that.

So when asked, I felt obliged to ride Victory Gallop in the Preakness. My instructions from Elliot Walden, who trained the horse, were to keep him closer to the pace than he had been in the Derby—within a few lengths of the front-runners. I agreed, believing that, if we were up near the Derby winner, Real Quiet, entering the homestretch, we would have a better chance to run him down. But the plan backfired and we finished second. We took away Victory Gallop's closing punch by trying to keep him so close to the front.

By the end of that summer, having ridden both horses, I knew that Real Quiet was the better athlete. I also knew that Victory Gallop had more heart. Real Quiet had a lot of coyote in him; he wouldn't give you everything he had unless you forced him to. He didn't have the killer instinct. But Victory Gallop would give you his life and his soul with little urging.

Elliot is one of those trainers with whom I share excellent communication. What I describe as the communion between horses and riders should also exist between riders and trainers. Say, if I was talking to Bill Shoemaker, he can relate certain situations to me that are easy for me to understand because he spent decades riding races before he began training horses; whereas most trainers have never been on a racetrack themselves. Often, it is difficult for them to communicate with me fully before a race or to absorb communication from me afterward when I try to tell what happened. But some trainers are special; I can look into their eyes as we talk, and it is almost as if I am dealing with another jockey, someone who *has* ridden races.

Elliot has been good for me to work for. We can say a few words to each other and, between us, the message is clear. The night before the Belmont, for example, we spoke for maybe three minutes. I quickly realized that each of us had exactly the same racing strategy in mind.

"What do you think?" he asked, and I said, "Well, I believe we've got to let this horse go back to his old style, and his best asset is his closing kick." Elliot put his hand up, smiled, and replied, "Enough said. I'll see you tomorrow. Sleep good." That was it; those were my only instructions for the Belmont, my almost perfect ride.

I have had the same kind of communication with trainers such as D. Wayne Lukas, Richard Mandella, Bob Baffert, and Neil Drysdale—people with talent plus the ability to recognize talent—and also with the late Laz Barrera, who used to say to me, in broken English, when I went out to the paddock, "Look, you got any brain, use it." And that was it, the only instruction I ever received from Laz for I can't count how many big races I won for him. Such trainers have had confidence in my abilities, just as I have had confidence in their training skills. If they have done their job, they will allow me to do what I am being paid to do—which is try not to make any mistakes.

Nobody knows what a rider's strategy will be except the rider himself, and the way the 1998 Belmont Stakes unfolded was an absolute match with the strategy I had in mind. I felt certain the race was going to be won or lost with my show of patience. Regardless of what I wanted to do aboard Victory Gallop, deep down inside I knew I would have to *wait* to do it.

To win at a mile and a half distance on that horse, I knew I would have to take my time. Throughout the race, I kept telling myself not to make my big move too early and to be stronger in the last eighth of a mile than I had been in any race I had ever ridden. My mission was to keep Victory Gallop relaxed and alert but unrushed; I couldn't let him make his run until the critical moment.

That's the tack I had agreed to take. But as we rounded the far turn and approached the homestretch, I was hit with a little panic, afraid that I'd blown it—that I'd waited too long. Real Quiet had established a huge lead, and it looked as though there was no way any horse could catch him. Although I could feel that I had an abundance of energy underneath me going into the stretch, in no classic race like that had I ever made up so much ground in the last quarter of a mile. And in none of the races I had seen—as far back as I could remember—had a winning horse turned in such an incredible run in the last leg. But Victory Gallop did it, and we won by a nose, ending Real Quiet's bid to become the first horse in twenty years to win all three Triple Crown races.

The truth is, if I *hadn't* waited, my move would have been premature. If we had pushed ahead in front of Real Quiet at any other point in the stretch except where we did—in that final jump—we would have been second. Why? Because barely one jump beyond the finish line, when Real Quiet finally saw us, he shot forward, a neck in front. One of the ironies of Thoroughbred racing is that, less than a year later, I would ride Real Quiet in the Pimlico Special—and win.

What ultimately won the Belmont Stakes for us, in addition to Victory Gallop's miraculous late-race speed and power, was that Real Quiet was slowing down a bit. It wasn't so much that he was tiring but that he had a tendency to get lazy. Riding against him in the Preakness, I had seen that if he got in front too early, with no other horses at his flanks, he would start to play and not focus on running anymore. I could tell that was happening from the shifting around he did and the way his ears twitched as he moved when Victory Gallop and I were running second, behind him. I felt that our best chance of beating him in the Belmont was to launch a kind of sneak attack, the same thing McCarron and Touch Gold had done to Silver Charm and me the year before. At the finish line, Victory Gallop was in front for only one stride, but it was the *right* stride at the *right* moment. I felt that it was the best ride I'd ever put on a horse, though it might not have been an absolutely perfect ride.

I would have to say that I was at least eleven lengths off the lead when I made my move, and it wasn't as though there was a clear field ahead of me. I had to thread my way forward, and doing so was one deciding factor in my favor. I successfully split two horses, running between them, and then just before entering the stretch I had a choice to make—either go around two more horses or split them, too. By then, I felt that Real Quiet's lead was so large that if I went around those two horses, I would lose ground and never catch up.

There was just a narrow gap between the two horses, but I pointed Victory Gallop at it. Horses need options, just as riders do. You can point a horse at a gap that's very narrow, but if he is so unwilling that you would have to really urge him to get him through it, it's better to go around.

Victory Gallop was the kind of horse that would run at a brick wall if you moved him toward it. So when I pointed him at that narrow opening, he just dropped his head and went for it. I didn't have to urge him. That was another deciding factor. Then actually entering the stretch, I had to split two more horses because going around them would have cost us the race.

I was wearing seven pairs of goggles that day—enough, I thought, to last for a mile and a half. Normally, I wore only two pairs—not just to protect against dirt clods and mud but as a shield against a flying loose shoe. If a metal shoe comes off of a horse, which *can* happen during a race, it flies back at about forty miles an hour. If I was traveling at, say, thirty miles an hour, that horseshoe could make impact at seventy miles an hour. And if it should somehow strike my goggles and I was wearing only one pair, it could shatter the lenses and cause serious eye damage.

I couldn't see too well through seven pairs of goggles, though well enough for what I had to do, but being on a come-from-behind horse and riding on a track that was dense with moisture, I knew they were necessary. As each pair became splattered with mud, I'd pull it down under my chin and expose a clean pair—that took a split second. When I realized I had only two clean pairs left and a lot of ground still to cover, I was afraid I was going to run short. So I pulled the dirty goggles down halfway and lowered the next clean pair halfway, right above them. My eyes were fully protected and I managed to look out of only the bottom portion of the fresh set. In a sense, I got double use out of what protection I had left.

Besides having a very good horse on Belmont Stakes day, I was certain I really did contribute to our astonishing win. That was truly a jockey's race, which is often the case when comparable horses are running. You come back to the jocks' room and shake the winning jockey's hand and say, "Man, you got me. That was a great ride. I was on the best horse, but you rode a great race—you got me, today." It's mutual respect. I guess it would have been like John Elway going up to Joe Montana after a Super Bowl game if Montana had thrown a touchdown pass in the final five seconds and won the game. If this had ever happened, I would have expected Elway to go up to Montana and say, "Man, what a game you played. That was awesome!"

Awesome, and then some, was the ride I had on Silver Charm in the

1998 Kentucky Cup Classic at Turfway Park. Despite a few humbling losses he had endured that year, Silver Charm was the 1–2 favorite in the race. Second choice on the tote board was Wild Rush, at 2–1, and in the end it looked like a match race. Silver Charm was like his old self, gaining ground at the far turn and finally coming up on Wild Rush and his rider, Pat Day, at the finish. Did we make it? I couldn't tell.

Galloping out after crossing the wire, Pat's first words were, "What a horserace! Do you know who got it?" I said I hadn't any idea. "Neither do I," he shouted, "but it was a great horserace!" That's what we live for—it's not just winning, it's the competition and knowing that you've tested yourself and been tested by the best. That is what's fun.

When the photos were in, the stewards proclaimed the race a dead-heat tie for first. So both of us had won. Two trainers and two sets of owners crowded into the winner's circle, and Pat and I exchanged handshakes for the photographers. Later, as we were walking back to the jocks' room when there were no media around—a kind of private moment—Pat asked how many races I had ridden since having both knees operated on that summer. "Three," I said. "And you rode like that?" he exclaimed. "You're an incredible human being."

To me, that was the supreme compliment. Pat Day and I had not always been friends. We'd had that angry exchange after the bumping incident in the Preakness. But time had passed, and I guess I had matured a bit. I think I had become less volatile and more contained in the middle years of my racing career.

It's great that I'm paid the kind of money I earn to ride in the big events, but there is more to it than money. Competing in and winning the Dubai World Cup on Silver Charm in 1998—I would ride that race a million times to get the thrill I had. And those Kentucky Derbys? I would pay any amount to experience the adrenaline rush I received from winning those races. They were the ultimate thrill rides.

When I won my first Kentucky Derby aboard Winning Colors, people said to me, "Now that you've won the Derby, where do you go from here?" Well, anyone who has ever won the Kentucky Derby knows that the feeling you get only increases each time you do it. I guess it's like being addicted to a drug: once you have experienced it, you want it even more.

It's better the second time, and the third time is even better than the earlier one.

I felt a kind of inner peace after my ride on Winning Colors. Flying home to California the next morning, I could almost hear myself say, "Man, I did it. This is what I wanted—to win a Kentucky Derby—and nobody can ever take this feeling away from me." You think the feeling is going to last the rest of your life, but after about a week's worth of riding and being beaten in at least one photo finish, the feeling fades. You can't relive it until you win the Derby again. You try to simulate it, but it doesn't stay with you and it doesn't come back. You have to enjoy it while the feelings are there and then press to enjoy it again. I guess I became addicted to that feeling.

Certainly there is a downside. After winning the first two Triple Crown races aboard Silver Charm, I thought I had a good chance of winning the third one and earning a place in the history books. It didn't happen. The next year's Belmont was a virtual replay, except that I was on Victory Gallop and *I* was the one to end a horse and rider's bid to win the Triple Crown. I empathized with Kent Desormeaux; I knew, as few others did, the shattering disappointment he had experienced. There haven't been too many of us who have come that close to a win as big as that only to have it taken away.

Where Victory Gallop was concerned, I do think that had I ridden him in the Kentucky Derby that year, I might have made a difference. If I had been on him then and had won that race, I might have been familiar enough with him to win the Preakness, too. But those events are part of a history I had no control over. There is no point dwelling on what-ifs. You have to go on to the next race and another chance to attempt a perfect ride.

So, when all is said and done, what does the perfect ride really mean? I guess that's open to interpretation. Certainly, it has a number of connotations for me. But even with the ups and downs I have experienced—the wins, the losses, the triumphs, the injuries, the terrible disappointments—I have no reason to be anything but positive. I have always been my own worst critic, but the thrills I have enjoyed are what has made my racing career so special.

For me, the concept of the perfect ride is something very personal. I wouldn't say that my life has been perfect, far from it, but the idea of the perfect ride—the hope of achieving it—has been an overriding lure, a dream that has motivated and sustained me from the first moment I mounted a horse.

Gary's Greatest Rides

◇

"*Comparing horses is difficult for me to do,*" *says Gary Stevens,* "*but their performance records show how good they really are. I have one favorite mount: Silver Charm. He and the others listed here represent the best horses I have ever ridden.*"

ANEES. Career Earnings: $699,200

DATE	TRACK	RACE	DIST.	TYPE	TIME	FINISH	FIRST THREE FINISHERS
6/6/00	Churchill	8	1¼	Ky. Derby	2:01	13	Fusaichi Pegasus, Aptitude, Impeachment
4/8/00	Santa Anita	5	1⅛	S. Anita Derby	1:49	4	The Deputy, War Chant, Captain Steve
3/19/00	Santa Anita	7	1¹⁄₁₆	San Felipe	1:42.3	3	Fusaichi Pegasus, The Deputy, Anees
11/6/99	Gulfstream	8	1¹⁄₁₆	B.C. Juvenile	1:42.1	1	Anees, Chief Seattle, High Yield
10/10/99	Santa Anita	7	1 mi.	Norfolk	1:35.3	3	Dixie Union, Forest Camp, Anees
9/3/99	Del Mar	3	1 mi.	Md. Sp. Wt.	1:37.3	1	Anees, Silver Axe, Guilty Moment
8/21/99	Del Mar	5	5 ½ f.	Md. Sp.Wt.	1:04.2	6	Tavasco, Brave Stew, Valiant Vision

BERTRANDO. Career Earnings: $3,185,610

DATE	TRACK	RACE	DIST.	TYPE	TIME	FINISH	FIRST THREE FINISHERS
1/14/95	Santa Anita	5	7 f.	San Carlos	1:21.2	6	Softshoe Sure Shot, Ferrara, Subtle Trouble
1/2/95	Santa Anita	8	1⅛	San Gabriel	1:49.1	6	Romarin, Inner City, Ianomami
11/26/94	Aqueduct	8	1 mi.	NYRA Mile	1:36	10	Cigar, Devil His Due, Punch Line
11/5/94	Churchill	10	1¼	B.C. Classic	2:02.2	6	Concern, Tabasco Cat, Dramatic Gold
10/15/94	Santa Anita	5	1⅛	Goodwood	1:46.4	1	Bertrando, Dramatic Gold, Tossofthecoin
9/17/94	Belmont	8	1⅛	Woodward	1:46.3	5	Holy Bull, Devil His Due, Colonial Affair
8/13/94	Del Mar	4	1¼	Pacific Classic	1:59.2	8	Tinners Way, Best Pal, Dramatic Gold
7/28/94	Del Mar	8	1 mi.	Wickerr	1:36.1	1	Bertrando, Bon Point, Daros
11/6/93	Santa Anita	8	1¼	B.C. Classic	2:00.4	2	Arcangues, Bertrando, Kissin Kris
9/18/93	Belmont	8	1⅛	Woodward	1:47	1	Bertrando, Devil His Due, Valley Crossing
8/21/93	Del Mar	3	1¼	Pacific Classic	1:59.2	1	Bertrando, Missionary Ridge, Best Pal
7/24/93	Monmouth	11	1⅛	Iselin Hand.	1:49.1	3	Valley Crossing, Devil His Due, Bertrando
7/3/93	Hollywood	3	1¼	Hyd. Gold C.	2:00	2	Best Pal, Bertrando, Major Impact
5/3/93	Belmont	9	1 mi.	Metropolitan	1:34.1	2	Ibero, Bertrando, Alydeed
3/6/93	Santa Anita	5	1¼	S. Anita Hand.	2:00.2	9	Sir Buford, Star Recruit, Major Impact
2/8/93	Santa Anita	8	1¼	C.H. Strub	2:00.3	2	Siberian Summer, Bertrando, Major Impact
1/16/93	Santa Anita	8	1⅛	San Fernando	1:51.1	1	Bertrando, Star Recruit, The Wicked North
12/26/92	Santa Anita	8	7 f.	Malibu	1:20.3	3	StaroftheCrop, The Wicked North, Bertrando

BERTRANDO *continued*

DATE	TRACK	RACE	DIST.	TYPE	TIME	FINISH	FIRST THREE FINISHERS
4/4/92	Santa Anita	5	1⅛	S. Anita Derby	1:49.1	2	A.P. Indy, Bertrando, Casual Lies
3/15/92	Santa Anita	8	1 1/16	San Felipe	1:42.3	1	Bertrando, Arp, Hickman Creek
11/2/91	Churchill	6	1 1/16	B.C. Juvenile	1:44.3	2	Arazi, Bertrando, Snappy Landing
10/13/81	Santa Anita	8	1 1/16	Norfolk	1:42.4	1	Bertrando, Zurich, Bag
9/11/91	Del Mar	8	1 mi.	D.M. Futurity	1:36.2	1	Bertrando, Zurich, Star Recruit
8/25/91	Del Mar	9	6 f.	Md. Sp. Wt.	1:10.1	1	Bertrando, Ebonair, Simple King

CRIMINAL TYPE. Career Earnings: $2,351,817

DATE	TRACK	RACE	DIST.	TYPE	TIME	FINISH	FIRST THREE FINISHERS
9/15/90	Belmont	8	1⅛	Woodward	1:45.4	6	Dispersal, Quiet American, Rhythm
8/4/90	Saratoga	7	1⅛	Whitney H.	1:48.3	1	Criminal Type, Dancing Spree, Mi Selecto
6/24/90	Hollywood	8	1¼	Hyd. Gold C.	1:59.4	1	Criminal Type, Sunday Silence, Opening Verse
5/28/90	Belmont	8	1 mi.	Metropolitan	1:34.2	1	Criminal Type, Housebuster, Easy Goer
5/12/90	Pimlico	10	1 3/16	Pimlico Sp.	1:53	1	Criminal Type, Ruhlman, De Roche
4/14/90	Oaklawn	8	1⅛	Oaklawn H.	1:47.1	4	Opening Verse, De Roche, Silver Survivor
4/1/90	Santa Anita	8	1⅛	San Bernardino	1:47.1	2	Ruhlman, Criminal Type, Stylish Winner
3/4/90	Santa Anita	8	1¼	S. Anita Hand.	2:01.1	2	Ruhlman, Criminal Type, Flying Continental
2/1/90	Santa Anita	8	1⅛	San Antonio	1:49	1	Criminal Type, Stylish Winner, Ruhlman
1/28/90	Santa Anita	8	1 1/16	San Pasqual	1:42.2	1	Criminal Type, Lively One, Present Value
1/12/90	Santa Anita	8	1 mi.	allowance	1:36	1	Criminal Type, Script, Lowell
12/17/89	Hollywood	7	1 mi.	allowance	1:34.3	1	Criminal Type, Good Deliverance, Charlton
11/18/89	Hollywood	6	1 mi.	allowance	1:34.2	3	King Taufan, Good Deliverance, Criminal Type
11/2/89	Santa Anita	7	1 mi.	allowance	1:35.3	2	Splurge, Criminal Type, Mr. Dandy Dancer
10/22/89	Santa Anita	5	1⅛	allowance	1:47.3	2	Sepoy, Criminal Type, Charlatan
5/13/89	Hollywood	7	1 1/16	allowance	1:43.3	3	Remar, Pure Expense, Criminal Type
4/24/89	Santa Anita	9	1⅛	allowance	1:49.3	4	Northern Drama, Ornery Guest, Elite Regent
4/12/89	Santa Anita	7	1 1/16	allowance	1:42.2	3	Awesome Bud, Elite Regent, Criminal Type
11/5/88	Saint-Cloud (Fr)		1½	Prix Le Fabuleux	2:36.4	8	Robore, Valuable, Plaza Gizon
9/25/88	Saint-Cloud (Fr)		1½	Prix Secambre	2:34.3	5	Hello Calder, Andaroun, Opposite Abstract
9/27/87	Longchamp (Fr)		1 mi.	Prix des Chenes	1:44.2	6	Harmless, Albatross, Titus Groan
8/24/87	Deauville (Fr)		1 mi.	Prix de Caen	1:46.4	1	Criminal Type, Pintoriccio, Antiqua
8/3/87	Clairefontaine (Fr)		1 mi.	Prix des Tritons	1:41.3	2	Hymen, Criminal Type, Le Play

DA HOSS. Career Earnings: $1,931,558

DATE	TRACK	RACE	DIST.	TYPE	TIME	FINISH	FIRST THREE FINISHERS
11/7/98	Churchill	7	1 mi.	B.C. Mile	1:35.1	1	Da Hoss, Hawksley Hill, Labeeb
10/11/98	Colonial	8	1⅛	allowance	1:49.1	1	Da Hoss, John's Call, Mercedes Son
10/26/96	Woodbine	7	1 mi.	B.C. Mile	1:35.4	1	Da Hoss, Spinning World, Same Old Wish
8/11/96	Penn Nat'l	9	1 1/16	Penn Gov's C.	1:41.1	1	Da Hoss, Grand Continental, Joke
7/29/96	Saratoga	8	1 1/16	Fourstardave	1:40.2	1	Da Hoss, Green Means Go, Rare Reason
7/4/96	Belmont	8	1 mi.	Poker Hand.	1:33.3	3	Smooth Runner, Mighty Forum, Da Hoss
11/26/95	Hollywood	7	1⅛	Hyd. Derby	1:46.2	3	Labeeb, Helmsman, Da Hoss
10/28/95	Belmont	3	6 f.	B.C. Sprint	1:09	13	Desert Stormer, Mr. Greeley, Lit De Justice
9/22/95	Meadowlands	9	1 1/16	Pegasus H.	1:40.4	2	Flying Chevron, Da Hoss, Ghostly Moves
9/4/95	Del Mar	8	1⅛	Del Mar D.	1:48	1	Da Hoss, Lake George, Tabor
7/23/95	Hollywood	8	1⅛	Swaps	1:49	2	Thunder Gulch, Da Hoss, Petionville
5/27/95	Gulfstream	9	1 1/16	Jersey Derby	1:43	1	Da Hoss, Claudius, Crimson Guard
5/13/95	Illinois D.	9	1⅛	Illinois Derby	1:48.4	2	Peaks And Valleys, Da Hoss, Western Echo
4/29/95	Gulfstream	5	1 mi.	allowance	1:36.3	1	Da Hoss, Sham Francisco, How Chief
3/25/95	Aqueduct	8	1 mi.	Gotham	1:36.4	2	Talkin Man, Da Hoss, Devious Course
3/4/95	Aqueduct	8	6 f.	Best Turn	1:11.1	1	Da Hoss, Pat N Jac, Candy Cone
10/30/94	Turfway	12	6 f.	ATBA Sales	1:07.1	1	Da Hoss, Mo Crystal, Kid Myers
10/18/94	Turfway	4	6 f.	Trial	1:09.4	1	Da Hoss, Mo Crystal, Booker
9/24/94	Turfway	3	5½ f.	Md. Sp.Wt.	1:03.2	1	Da Hoss, Socializedmed.., Water Dog Willie

GENTLEMEN. Career Earnings: $3,608,598

DATE	TRACK	RACE	DIST.	TYPE	TIME	FINISH	FIRST THREE FINISHERS
11/7/98	Churchill	10	1 ¼	B.C. Classic	2:02	DNF	Awesome Again, Silver Charm, Swain
10/10/98	Belmont	10	1 ¼	J.C. Gold C.	2:00	2	Wagon Limit, Gentlemen, Skip Away
9/19/98	Belmont	9	1 ⅛	Woodward	1:47.4	2	Skip Away, Gentlemen, Running Stag
8/15/98	Del Mar	7	1 ¼	Pacific Classic	2:00	2	Free House, Gentlemen, Pacificbounty
6/28/98	Hollywood	7	1 ¼	Hyd. Gold C.	2:00	3	Skip Away, Puerto Modero, Gentlemen
3/7/98	Santa Anita	8	1 ¼	S. Anita Hand.	2:02.1	4	Malek, Bagshot, Don't Blame Rio
2/7/98	Santa Anita	6	1 ⅛	San Antonio	1:47.3	1	Gentlemen, Da Bull, Refinado Tom
9/20/97	Woodbine	6	1 mi.	Woodbine Mile	1:36.1	5	Geri, Helmsman, Crown Attorney
7/9/97	Del Mar	5	1 ¼	Pacific Classsic	2:00.2	1	Gentlemen, Siphon, Crafty Friend
6/29/97	Hollywood	6	1 ¼	Hyd. Gold C.	1:59.1	1	Gentlemen, Siphon, Sandpit
5/10/97	Pimlico	9	1 ⅜	Pimlico Sp.	1:53	1	Gentlemen, Skip Away, Tejano Run
3/2/97	Santa Anita	7	1 ¼	S. Anita Hand.	2:00.1	3	Siphon, Sandpit, Gentlemen
2/2/97	Santa Anita	7	1 ⅛	San Antonio	1:47.1	1	Gentlemen, Alphabet Soup, Kingdom Found
12/22/96	Hollywood	9	1 ⅛	Native Diver	1:45.1	1	Gentlemen, Dramatic Gold, Don't Blame Rio
11/30/96	Hollywood	9	1 ⅛	Citation Hand.	1:45.2	1	Gentlemen, Smooth Runner, Via Lombardia
9/28/96	Bay Meadows	8	1 ⅛	Bay M. Hand.	1:45.4	1	Gentlemen, Party Season, Petit Poucet
7/27/96	Del Mar	3	1 1/16	allowance	1:42.1	1	Gentlemen, Dernier Empereur, Pinfloron
6/19/96	Hollywood	8	1 1/16	allowance	1:41.4	6	Dramatic Gold, Cleante, Flying Marfa
11/4/95	Hipodromo (Arg.)		1 9/16	Arg. Derby	2:36	1	Gentlemen, Flirteando, Passion Lead
10/17/95	San Isidro (Arg.)		1 ¼	Gran Premio J.C.	1:58.3	4	Espiro, Bat Atico, Munecote
9/9/95	Hipodromo (Arg.)		1 mi.	Polla de Potrillos	1:34.2	1	Gentlemen, Munecote, Zagaleojo
8/5/95	San Isidro (Arg.)		1 mi.	Gran P. 2000 Guineas	1:32.2	1	Gentlemen, Espiro, Munecote
6/26/95	San Isidro (Arg.)		1 mi.	Premio Prohibida Oca	1:35	1	Gentlemen, Potritio, Diddler
6/10/95	San Isidro (Arg.)		1 mi.	Premio Don Juan Tag	1:35.3	2	Tusayan, Gentlemen, Che Lazy

POINT GIVEN. Career Earnings: $3,968,500

DATE	TRACK	RACE	DIST.	TYPE	TIME	FINISH	FIRST THREE FINISHERS
8/20/01	Saratoga	10	1 ¼	Travers	2:01.2	1	Point Given, E Dubai, Dollar Bill
8/5/01	Monmouth	11	1 ⅛	Haskell	1:49.3	1	Point Given, Touch Tone, Burning Rome
6/9/01	Belmont	10	1 ½	Belmont	2:26.2	1	Point Given, AP Valentine, Monarchos
5/19/01	Pimlico	11	1 ³⁄₁₆	Preakness	1:55.2	1	Point Given, AP Valentine, Congaree
5/5/01	Churchill	8	1 ¼	Ky. Derby	1:59.4	5	Monarchos, Invisible Ink, Congaree
4/7/01	Santa Anita	5	1 ⅛	S. Anita Derby	1:47.3	1	Point Given, Crafty C.T., I Love Silver
3/17/01	Santa Anita	7	1 ¹⁄₁₆	San Felipe	1:41.4	1	Point Given, I Love Silver, Jamaican Rum
12/16/00	Hollywood	4	1 ¹⁄₁₆	Hyd. Futurity	1:42.1	1	Point Given, Millennium Wind, Golden Ticket
11/4/00	Churchill	8	1 ¹⁄₁₆	B.C. Juvenile	1:42	2	Macho Uno, Point Given, Street Cry
10/14/00	Belmont	9	1 ¹⁄₁₆	Champagne	1:41.2	1	Point Given, AP Valentine, Yonaguska
9/16/00	Turfway	12	1 ¹⁄₁₆	Ky. C. Juvenile	1:47	1	Point Given, Holiday Thunder, The Goo
8/26/00	Del Mar	7	7 f.	Md. Sp. Wt.	2:23.2	1	Point Given, High And Low Vixen, Qawaqeb
8/12/00	Del Mar	6	5 ½ f.	Md. Sp. Wt.	1:04	2	High Cascade, Point Given, Westward Angel

ROYAL ANTHEM. Career Earnings: $1,888,180

DATE	TRACK	RACE	DIST.	TYPE	TIME	FINISH	FIRST THREE FINISHERS
2/12/00	Gulfstream	10	1⅜	Gulfstream B.C.H.	2:11.1	1	Royal Arthem, Thesaurus, Band Is Passing
11/6/99	Gulfstream	9	1½	B.C. Turf	2:24.3	2	Daylami, Royal Anthem, Buck's Boy
9/11/99	Leopardstown (Ire.)		1¼	Irish Champion	2:08.3	5	Daylami, Dazzling Park, Dream Well
8/17/99	York (Eng.)		1⅜	Juddmonte Int'l	2:07	1	Royal Anthem, Greek Dance, Chester House
6/18/99	Ascot (Eng.)		1½	Hardwicke St.	2:28.3	2	Fruits of Love, Royal Anthem, Sea Wave
6/4/99	Epsom (Eng.)		1½	Coronation Cup	2:40.1	2	Daylami, Royal Anthem, Dream Well
11/7/98	Churchill	9	1½	B.C. Turf	2:38.3	7	Buck's Boy, Yagli, Dushyantor
10/18/98	Woodbine	6	1½	Canadian Int'l	2:29.3	1	Royal Anthem, Chief Bearhart, Parade Ground
7/25/98	Ascot (Eng.)		1½	K.Geo & Q. Eliz	2:29	3	Swain, High-Rise, Royal Anthem
6/19/98	Ascot (Eng.)		1½	K. Edward VII	2:34.3	1	Royal Anthem, Kilimanjaro, Scorned
6/6/98	Newmarket (Eng.)		1¼	Fairway Stakes	2:02.1	1	Royal Anthem, Kilimanjaro, Sensory
5/16/98	Newbury (Eng.)		1¼	Hatherden Maiden	2:08	1	Royal Anthem, Generous Rosi, Cyber World

SERENA'S SONG. Career Earnings: $3,283,388

DATE	TRACK	RACE	DIST.	TYPE	TIME	FINISH	FIRST THREE FINISHERS
11/9/96	Churchill	8	1 mi.	C.D. Distaff	1:36.1	2	Fast Catch, Serena's Song, Bedroom Blues
10/26/96	Woodbine	6	1⅛	B.C. Distaff	1:48.2	2	Jewel Princess, Serena's Song, Different
10/6/96	Belmont	9	1⅛	Beldame	1:47	2	Yanks Music, Serena's Song, Clear Mandate
9/14/96	Belmont	9	1 1/16	Ruffian Hand.	1:41.4	2	Yanks Music, Serena's Song, Head East
8/25/96	Monmouth	9	1 1/16	Iselin Hand.	1:41.2	3	Smart Strike, Eltish, Serena's Song
8/3/96	Saratoga	8	1⅛	Whitney Hand.	1:48.3	2	Mahogany Hall, Serena's Song, Peaks and Valleys
7/21/96	Hollywood	9	1⅛	Vanity Hand.	1:47	2	Jewel Princess, Serena's Song, Top Rung
6/29/96	Belmont	9	1⅛	Hempstead H.	1:41.3	1	Serena's Song, Shoop, Restored Hope
6/1/96	Churchill	10	1⅛	Fleur de Lis H.	1:50.1	1	Serena's Song, Halo America, Alcovy
5/18/96	Pimlico	4	1⅛	Pim. Distaff	1:49.3	1	Serena's Song, Shoop, Churchbell Chimes
5/3/96	Churchill	7	1 1/16	Louisville B.C.	1:42.2	2	Jewel Princess, Serena's Song, Naskra Colors
4/12/96	Oaklawn	9	1 1/16	Apple Blossom	1:41.3	3	Twice the Vice, Halo America, Serena's Song
3/2/96	Santa Anita	7	1¼	S. Anita Hand.	2:02	7	Mr.Purple, Luthier Fever, Just Java
2/17/96	Santa Anita	6	1 1/16	Santa Maria H.	1:42.1	1	Serena's Song, Twice the Vice, Real Connection
1/27/96	Santa Anita	8	7 f.	S. Monica H.	1:21.2	1	Serena's Song, Exotic Wood, Klassy Kim
10/28/95	Belmont	4	1⅛	B.C. Distaff	1:46	5	Inside Information, Heavenly Prize, Lakeway
10/7/95	Belmont	7	1⅛	Beldame	1:48.3	1	Serena's Song, Heavenly Prize, Lakeway
9/23/95	Turfway	9	1 1/16	T.P. Bud B.C.	1:41.3	2	Mariah's Storm, Serena's Song, Alcovy
9/3/95	Belmont	8	1⅛	Gazelle H.	1:47.1	1	Serena's Song, Miss Golden Circle, Golden Bri

SERENA'S SONG *continued*

DATE	TRACK	RACE	DIST.	TYPE	TIME	FINISH	FIRST THREE FINISHERS
7/30/95	Monmouth	11	1⅛	Haskell	1:48.4	1	Serena's Song, Pyramid Peak, Citadeed
7/8/95	Belmont	9	1¼	CCA Oaks	2:03.4	2	Golden Bri, Serena's Song, Change For a Dollar
6/9/95	Belmont	8	1⅛	Mother Goose	1:50.1	1	Serena's Song, Golden Bri, Forested
5/19/95	Pimlico	10	1⅛	Black-Eyed Susan	1:48.2	1	Serena's Song, Conquiestadoress, Rare Opportunity
5/6/95	Churchill	8	1¼	Ky. Derby	2:01.1	16	Thunder Gulch, Tejano Run, Timber Country
4/1/95	Turfway	11	1⅛	Jim Beam	1:49.3	1	Serena's Song, Tejano Run, Mecke
3/12/95	Santa Anita	8	1¹⁄₁₆	S. Anita Oaks	1:42.3	1	Serena's Song, Urgan, Mr's Shb
2/19/95	Santa Anita	8	1 mi.	Las Virgenes	1:35.2	1	Serena's Song, Cat's Cradle, Urbane
1/29/95	Santa Anita	8	7 f.	Santa Ynez B.C.	1:21.2	1	Serena's Song, Cat's Cradle, Call Now
12/17/94	Hollywood	9	1¹⁄₁₆	Hyd. Starlet	1:41.1	1	Serena's Song, Urbane, Ski Dancer
11/5/94	Churchill	5	1¹⁄₁₆	B.C. Juv. Fillies	1:45.1	2	Flanders, Serena's Song, Stormy Blues
10/8/94	Santa Anita	8	1¹⁄₁₆	Oak Leaf	1:41.4	1	Serena's Song, Call Now, Mama Mucci
9/3/94	Del Mar	8	7 f.	DM Debutante	1:21.2	4	Call Now, How So Oiseau, Ski Dancer
8/12/94	Del Mar	8	6½ f.	Sorrento	1:15.4	3	How So Oiseau, Ski Dancer, Serena's Song
7/25/94	Hollywood	8	6 f.	Hyd. Juvenile	1:10	2	Mr. Purple, Serena's Song, Cyrano
7/9/94	Hollywood	4	6 f.	Landaluce	1:10	1	Serena's Song, Embroidered, Cat's Cradle
6/25/94	Hollywood	3	5 f.	Md. Sp. Wt.	:57.2	1	Serena's Song, Valid Attraction, Guise
5/28/94	Churchill	1	5 f.	Md. Sp. Wt.	:59	5	Phone Bird, Me My, BJ Shiny Gold

SILVER CHARM. Career Earnings: $6,944,369

DATE	TRACK	RACE	DIST.	TYPE	TIME	FINISH	FIRST THREE FINISHERS
6/12/99	Churchill	9	1⅛	S. Foster Hand.	1:47.1	4	Victory Gallop, Nite Dreamer, Littlebitlively
3/26/99	Nad A Sheba (UAE)		1¼	Dubai World C.	2:00.3	6	Almutawakel, Malek, Victory Gallop
3/6/99	Santa Anita	5	1¼	S. Anita Hand.	2:00.3	3	Free House, Event of the Year, Silver Charm
1/30/99	Gulfstream	10	1⅛	Donn Hand.	1:48.1	3	Puerto Madero, Behrens, Silver Charm
1/10/99	Santa Anita	8	1¹⁄₁₆	San Pasqual	1:10.4	1	Silver Charm, Malek, Crafty Friend
11/27/98	Churchill	11	1⅛	Clark Hand.	1:49	1	Silver Charm, Littlebitlively, Wild Rush
11/7/98	Churchill	10	1¼	B.C. Classic	2:02	2	Awesome Again, Silver Charm, Swain
10/17/98	Santa Anita	8	1⅛	Goodwood B.C.	1:47.1	1	Silver Charm, Free House, Score Quick
9/26/98	Turfway	10	1⅛	Ky. C. Classic	1:47.2	1	Silver Charm, Wild Rush, Acceptible
7/25/98	Del Mar	8	1¹⁄₁₆	San Diego Hand.	1:41	5	Mud Route, Hal's Pal, Benchmark
6/13/98	Churchill	9	1⅛	S. Foster Hand.	1:48.3	2	Awesome Again, Silver Charm, Semoran
3/28/98	Nad Al Sheba (UAE)		1¼	Dubai World C.	2:04.1	1	Silver Charm, Swain, Loup Sauvage
2/7/98	Santa Anita	8	1⅛	C.H. Strub	1:47.1	1	Silver Charm, Mud Route, Bagshot
1/17/98	Santa Anita	8	1¹⁄₁₆	San Fernando B.C.	1:41.4	1	Silver Charm, Mud Route, Lord Grillo
12/26/97	Santa Anita	8	7 f.	Malibu	1:21.2	2	Lord Grillo, Silver Charm, Swiss Yodeler
6/7/97	Belmont	9	1½	Belmont	2:28.4	2	Touch Gold, Silver Charm, Free House
5/17/97	Pimlico	10	1³⁄₁₆	Preakness	1:54.4	1	Silver Charm, Free House, Captain Bodgit
5/3/97	Churchill	8	1¼	Ky. Derby	2:02.2	1	Silver Charm, Captain Bodgit, Free House
4/5/97	Santa Anita	6	1⅛	S. Anita Derby	1:47.3	2	Free House, Silver Charm, Hello

SILVER CHARM *continued*

DATE	TRACK	RACE	DIST.	TYPE	TIME	FINISH	FIRST THREE
3/16/97	Santa Anita	7	1 1/16	San Felipe	1:42.2	2	Free House, Silver Charm, King Crimson
2/8/97	Santa Anita	6	7 f.	San Vicente	1:21	1	Silver Charm, Free House, Funontherun
9/11/96	Del Mar	8	7 f.	D.M. Futurity	1:22.4	1	Silver Charm, Gold Tribute, Swiss Yodeler
8/24/96	Del Mar	6	5 1/2 f.	Md. Sp. Wt.	1:03.1	1	Silver Charm, Gold Tribute, So Easy
8/10/96	Del Mar	3	6 f.	Md. Sp. Wt.	1:10	2	Deeds Not Words, Silver Charm, Constant Demand

SILVERBULLETDAY. Career Earnings: $2,821,750

DATE	TRACK	RACE	DIST.	TYPE	TIME	FINISH	FIRST THREE FINISHERS
7/23/00	Delaware	8	1 ¼	Delaware Hand	2:02.1	3	Lu Ravi, To Music, Silverbulletday
7/4/00	Monmouth	9	1 ⅙	Molly Pitcher	1:43	2	Lu Ravi, Silverbulletday, Bella Chiara
6/3/00	Churchill	9	1 ⅛	Fleur de Lis	1:48.1	2	Heritage Of Gold, Silverbulletday, Roza Robata
5/5/00	Churchill	7	1 ⅛	Louisville B.C.	1:42.4	4	Heritage Of Gold, Roza Robata, Bella Chiara
4/19/00	Keeneland	8	1 1/16	Doubledogdare	1:43.3	1	Silverbulletday, Roza Robata, Pepita Ramoja
11/6/99	Gulfstream	3	1 ⅛	B.C. Distaff	1:47.2	6	Beautiful Pleasure, Banshee Breeze, Heritage Of Gold
10/10/99	Belmont	5	1 ⅛	Beldame	1:47.3	2	Beautiful Pleasure, Silverbulletday, Catinca
9/11/99	Belmont	9	1 ⅛	Gazelle	1:47.3	1	Silverbulletday, Queen's Word, Awful Smart
8/21/99	Saratoga	8	1 ¼	Alabama	2:02.3	1	Silverbulletday, Strolling Belle, Gandria
7/10/99	Monmouth	9	1 1/16	M.B.C. Oaks	1:43.1	1	Silverbulletday, Boom Town Girl, Bag Lady Jane
6/5/99	Belmont	9	1 ½	Belmont	2:27.4	7	Lemon Drop Kid, Vision and Verse, Charismatic
5/14/99	Pimlico	11	1 ⅛	Black-Eyed Susan	1:47.4	1	Silverbulletday, Dreams Gallore, Velvet Star
4/30/99	Churchill	9	1 ⅛	Ky. Oaks	1:49.4	1	Silverbulletday, Dreams Gallore, Sweeping Story
4/3/99	Keeneland	8	1 ⅛	Ashland	1:41.3	1	Silverbulletday, Marley Vale, Gold From the West
3/13/99	Fair Grounds	9	1 1/16	F.G. Oaks	1:44.4	1	Silverbulletday, Runwy Vnus, Brushed Halory
2/20/99	Fair Grounds	9	1 1/16	Davona Dale	1:44.1	1	Silverbulletday, Brushed Halory, On a Soapbox
11/28/98	Churchill	9	1 1/16	Golden Rod	1:43.4	1	Silverbulletday, Here I Go, Lefty's Dollbaby
11/7/98	Churchill	5	1 1/16	B.C. Juvenile	1:43.3	1	Silverbulletday, Excellent Meeting, Three Rings
10/10/98	Keeneland	8	1 1/16	Alcibiades	1:42.1	1	Silverbulletday, Extended Applause, Grand Deed
8/29/98	Del Mar	8	7 f.	D.M. Debutante	1:22.1	4	Excellent Meeting, Antahkarana, Colorado Song
8/8/98	Del Mar	8	6 ½ f.	Sorrento	1:17.2	1	Silverbulletday, Excellent Meeting, Colorado Song
6/27/98	Churchill	7	5 ½ f.	Debutante	1:04.3	1	Silverbulletday, The Happy Hopper, Mancari's Rose
6/13/98	Churchill	3	5 ½ f.	Md. Sp. Wt.	1:04.3	1	Silverbulletday, Forever Misi, Drive Thru Blues

THUNDER GULCH. Career Earnings: $2,915,086

DATE	TRACK	RACE	DIST.	TYPE	TIME	FINISH	FIRST THREE FINISHERS
10/7/95	Belmont	10	1 ¼	J. C. Gold Cup	2:00.1	5	Cigar, Unaccounted For, Star Standard
9/3/95	Turfway	10	1 ⅛	Ky. C. Classic	1:49.2	1	Thunder Gulch, Judge TC, Bound by Honor
8/19/95	Saratoga	8	1 ¼	Travers	2:03.3	1	Thunder Gulch, Pyramid Peak, Malthus
7/23/95	Hollywood	8	1 ⅛	Swaps	1:49	1	Thunder Gulch, Da Hoss, Petionville
6/10/95	Belmont	8	1 ½	Belmont	2:32.1	1	Thunder Gulch, Star Standard, Citadeed
5/20/95	Pimlico	10	1 3⁄16	Preakness	1:54.2	3	Timber Country, Oliver's Twist, Thunder Gulch
5/6/95	Churchill	8	1 ¼	Ky. Derby	2:01.1	1	Thunder Gulch, Tejano Run, Timber Country
4/15/95	Keeneland	7	1 ⅛	Bluegrass	1:49.1	4	Wild Syn, Suave Prospect, Tejano Run
3/1/95	Gulfstream	10	1 ⅛	Fla. Derby	1:49.3	1	Thunder Gulch, Suave Prospect, Mecke
2/18/95	Gulfstream	9	1 1⁄16	Fountain of Yth	1:43.1	1	Thunder Gulch, Suave Prospect, Jambalaya Jazz
12/18/94	Hollywood	8	1 1⁄16	Hyd. Futurity	1:40.3	2	Afternoon Deelites, Thunder Gulch, A.J. Jett
11/26/94	Aqueduct	7	1 ⅛	Remsen	1:53.4	1	Thunder Gulch, Western Echo, Mighty Magee
11/1/94	Aqueduct	8	1 mi.	Nashua	1:37.2	4	Devious Course, Mighty Magee, Old Tascosa
10/23/94	Aqueduct	7	7 f.	Cowdin	1:24.3	2	Old Tascosa, Thunder Gulch, Adams Trail
10/4/94	Belmont	3	6 f.	Md. Sp. Wt.	1:11	1	Thunder Gulch, Porphyry, Last Effort
9/16/94	Belmont	3	6 f.	Md. Sp. Wt.	1:11.1	3	Crusader's Story, Porphyry, Thunder Gulch

213

VICTORY GALLOP. Career Earnings: $3,505,895

DATE	TRACK	RACE	DIST.	TYPE	TIME	FINISH	FIRST THREE FINISHERS
8/1/99	Saratoga	9	$1\frac{1}{8}$	Whitney Hand.	1:48.3	1	Victory Gallop, Behrens, Catienus
6/12/99	Churchill	9	$1\frac{1}{8}$	S. Foster Hand.	1:47.1	1	Victory Gallop, Nite Dreamer, Littlebitlively
3/28/99	NadAlSheba (UAE)		$1\frac{1}{2}$	Dubai World C.	2:00.3	3	Almutawakel, Malek, Victory Gallop
3/3/99	Gulfstream	3	$1\frac{1}{16}$	allowance	1:43.3	1	Victory Gallop, Delay of Game, Dancing Guy
11/7/98	Churchill	10	$1\frac{1}{4}$	B.C. Classic	2:02	3	Awesome Again, Silver Charm, Swain
8/28/98	Saratoga	9	$1\frac{1}{4}$	Travers	2:03.2	2	Coronado's Quest, Victory Gallop, Raffie's Majesty
8/9/98	Monmouth	11	$1\frac{1}{8}$	Haskell	1:48.3	2	Coronado's Quest, Victory Gallop, Grand Slam
6/6/98	Belmont	9	$1\frac{1}{2}$	Belmont	2:29	1	Victory Gallop, Real Quiet, Thomas Jo
5/16/98	Pimlico	10	$1\frac{3}{16}$	Preakness	1:54.3	2	Real Quiet, Victory Gallop, Classic Cat
5/2/98	Churchill	8	$1\frac{1}{4}$	Ky. Derby	2:02.1	2	Real Quiet, Victory Gallop, Indian Charlie
4/11/98	Oaklawn	9	$1\frac{1}{8}$	Ark. Derby	1:49.4	1	Victory Gallop, Hanuman Highway, Favorite Trick
3/2/98	Oaklawn	9	$1\frac{1}{16}$	Rebel	1:44.3	1	Victory Gallop, Robinwould, Whataflashyactor
11/1/97	Laurel	10	$1\frac{1}{8}$	Laurel Fut.	1:53.3	2	Fight for M'Lady, Victory Gallop, Essential
10/11/97	Colonial D.	9	1 mi.	Chenery	1:36.4	1	Victory Gallop, Fight for M'Lady, Personal Favor
9/1/97	Colonial D.	9	7 f.	New Kent	1:22.3	1	Victory Gallop, Unreal Madness, Lusita's Choice
8/2/97	Laurel	1	7 f.	Md. Sp. Wt.	1:26.4	1	Victory Gallop, Essential, DoIEver
7/20/97	Delaware	1	5 f.	Md. Sp. Wt.	:59.3	5	Carreras, He's A Charm, Duck Grayson

WAR CHANT. Career Earnings: $1,130,600

DATE	TRACK	RACE	DIST.	TYPE	TIME	FINISH	FIRST THREE FINISHERS
11/4/00	Churchill	5	1 mi.	B.C. Mile	1:34.3	1	War Chant, North East Bound, Dansili
10/14/00	Santa Anita	9	1 mi.	Oak Tree B.C.M.	1:33.3	1	War Chant, Road To Slew, Sharan
5/6/00	Churchill	8	1¼	Ky. Derby	2:01	9	Fusaichi Pegasus, Aptitude, Impeachment
4/8/00	Santa Anita	5	1⅛	S.A. Derby	1:49	2	The Deputy, War Chant, Captain Steve
3/4/00	Santa Anita	9	1 mi.	San Rafael	1:36.2	1	War Chant, Archer City Slew, Cocky
1/16/00	Santa Anita	2	1¹⁄₁₆	allowance	1:42	1	War Chant, Reba's Gold, Smooth
11/28/99	Hollywood	8	6 f.	Md. Sp. Wt.	1:10.3	1	War Chant, Ladir, Strollin

WINNING COLORS. Career Earnings: $1,526,837

DATE	TRACK	RACE	DIST.	TYPE	TIME	FINISH	FIRST THREE FINISHERS
11/4/89	Gulfstream	6	1⅛	B.C. Distaff	1:47.2	9	Bayakoa, Gorgeous, Open Mind
10/21/89	Aqueduct	7	1 mi.	Bud. B.C.	1:33.4	4	Wakonda, Foresta, Toll Fee
9/30/89	Turfway	9	1¹⁄₁₆	Bud B.C.	1:44.3	1	Winning Colors, Grecian Flight, Lawyer Talk
9/9/89	Belmont	8	1 mi.	Maskette	1:35.3	4	Miss Brio, Proper Evidence, Apostar
5/13/89	Shuvee	9	1¹⁄₁₆	Shuvee H.	1:40.4	7	Banker's Lady, Rose's Cantina, Grecian Flight
4/23/89	Hollywood	8	7 f.	A Gleam H.	1:21.3	4	Daloma, Survive, Behind the Scenes
11/5/88	Churchill	6	1⅛	B.C. Distaff	1:52	2	Personal Ensign, Winning Colors, Goodbye Halo
10/15/88	Keeneland	8	1⅛	Spinster	1:51	4	Haila Cab, WillaontheMove, Integra
9/10/88	Belmont	8	1 mi.	Maskette	1:34.1	2	Personal Ensign, Winning Colors, Sham Sy
6/11/88	Belmont	8	1½	Belmont	2:26.2	6	Risen Star, Kingpost, Brian's Time
5/21/88	Pimlico	9	1³⁄₁₆	Preakness	1:56.1	3	Risen Star, Brian's Time, Winning Colors
5/7/88	Churchill	8	1¼	Ky. Derby	2:02.1	1	Winning Colors, Forty Niner, Risen Star
4/9/88	Santa Anita	5	1⅛	S. Anita Derby	1:47.4	1	Winning Colors, Lively One, Mi Preferido
3/13/88	Santa Anita	8	1¹⁄₁₆	S. Anita Oaks	1:42	1	Winning Colors, Jeanne Jones, Goodbye Halo
2/20/88	Santa Anita	8	1 mi.	Las Virgenes	1:36.4	2	Goodbye Halo, Winning Colors, Sad But Fast
1/20/88	Santa Anita	8	1 mi.	La Centinela	1:36.3	1	Winning Colors, Little Password, Forewarning
12/27/87	Santa Anita	3	6 f.	allowance	1:09.4	1	Winning Colors, Floral Magic, Constantly Right
8/13/87	Saratoga	3	7 f.	Md. Sp. Wt.	1:24.1	1	Winning Colors, Epitome, Bippus

Glossary

———◇———

allowance race   A horse race that is below a stakes race in class, in which the horses are not for sale, as in claiming races. These races are often run under restricted conditions. For example, an allowance race may be limited to horses that have won only one race.

bush tracks   Small racetracks; the minor leagues of racing.

claiming race   A horse race in which each horse in the race is for sale for an established price. Most races held in the United States are claiming races.

clerk of scales   A racetrack official whose job it is to make sure that the jockeys (and their tack) weigh what they're supposed to before and after a race.

coming over   When a horse isn't holding a steady path and is veering to the left or right.

coming off of (a horse's) heels   When a jockey moves his mount to prevent clipping heels with the horse in front of him. Clipping heels can cause a serious accident.

cracked heels   An equine injury where the area of skin/hair just above and behind a horse's hoof develops cracks.

daylight (to win by daylight)   When a horse wins a race by a length or more.

fire (the horse didn't fire)   A horse that, on a given day for whatever reason, doesn't run to his ability.

float (a horse) out   When a jockey deliberately takes a path that makes another rider take his mount wider.

four-bagger   When a horse wins four races in a single day.

furlong   One eighth of a mile.

futurity trials   Important races for two-year-old horses.

get the mount   To get the assignment to ride a certain horse.

going wide   When a jockey or horse races in an outside path.

graded-stakes winners   Horses that have won one of the most important races, as graded by committee. Races can be graded either I, II, or III. The Kentucky Derby is a Grade I race.

high canter   A horse's gait that is faster than a trot but still not a full gallop.

hook (hook a horse)   When a rider or horse does not let another horse go by during a race.

hot box   The sauna, where riders go to lose weight.

journeyman rider   After an apprentice rider wins a certain amount of races, and then a certain amount of time passes he becomes a journeyman and is no longer given a weight allowance, (i.e., allowed to carry less weight).

laying (laying second, for example)   To keep a horse in a certain position during the running of a race.

leads   A horse's lead refers to which foreleg he's putting down first during a gallop.

lug in/lug out   When a horse does not hold a straight path, but instead moves either in or out, sideways.

outrider   A racetrack employee, on horseback, whose job it is to run and gather loose horses.

pace (off the pace)   The pace is the speed at which a race is run. To come from off the pace to win a race is to fail to be on the lead during the early running.

percent (my 10 percent)   Jockeys typically receive 10 percent of the purse money that their mounts win. If a horse wins sixty thousand dollars, a jockey will get six thousand dollars.

pickup mount   To get the assignment to ride a horse that another rider originally committed to ride.

pole (the three-eighth pole)   Poles are placed around the racetrack to mark their distance from the finish. The three-eighth pole is located three furlongs from the finish line.

post (the outside post)   A horse's position in the starting gate is called his post. An outside post refers to one of the outermost stalls in the gate.

purse   The prize money in a given race.

race meet   A race meet is a select amount of days on which racing will occur. These can vary greatly in length from one day to several months. For example, Saratoga's race meet is six weeks long.

rate (to rate a horse)   For a jockey to deliberately keep a horse off the pace.

run-off   For a horse to drop his rider and run free.

scratch   To keep a horse out of a race. Trainers often scratch horses for health reasons or to run in a different race. Stewards, or the track veterinarian may also scratch a horse if he is deemed unruly or unsound.

sound (the horse was sound)   When a horse is in good physical condition.

starter   An official who watches the whole field and opens the gates when the horses are ready to go. The assistant starter is a racetrack employee whose job it is to make sure all the horses are standing calmly facing forward when the gates open.

stone-cold loser   A horse that never wins.

take him back ("I took him back")   When a jockey deliberately rates a horse.

take off (take off a)   When a jockey chooses not to ride a mount he originally accepted, usually because of injury.

tote board   A display board that lists the changing odds of all the horses in a race.

turf-miler   A horse that is well suited to running a mile on the turf.

turn of foot   A horse with a good turn of foot can accelerate quickly during a race.

way of going   The way a horse moves when he gallops.

weight allowance   Apprentice jockeys, because of their lack of experience, are usually allowed to carry less weight than journeyman riders. This is called their weight allowance.

wire (the wire)   The finish line.

Index

— ◇ —